Microsoft® Windows® XP
Step by Step, Second Edition

Online Training Solutions, Inc.

PUBLISHED BY
Microsoft Press
A Division of Microsoft Corporation
One Microsoft Way
Redmond, Washington 98052-6399

Library of Congress Cataloging-in-Publication Data pending.

Printed and bound in the United States of America.

2 3 4 5 6 7 8 9   QWT   9 8 7 6 5 4

Distributed in Canada by H.B. Fenn and Company Ltd.

A CIP catalogue record for this book is available from the British Library.

Microsoft Press books are available through booksellers and distributors worldwide. For further information about international editions, contact your local Microsoft Corporation office or contact Microsoft Press International directly at fax (425) 936-7329. Visit our Web site at www.microsoft.com/learning/. Send comments to *mspinput@microsoft.com*.

Microsoft, ActiveX, ClearType, Hotmail, Microsoft Press, MSN, NetMeeting, Outlook, PowerPoint, Verdana, Windows, the Windows logo, Windows Media, and Windows NT are either registered trademarks or trademarks of Microsoft Corporation in the United States and/or other countries. Other product and company names mentioned herein may be the trademarks of their respective owners.

The example companies, organizations, products, domain names, e-mail addresses, logos, people, places, and events depicted herein are fictitious. No association with any real company, organization, product, domain name, e-mail address, logo, person, place, or event is intended or should be inferred.

This book expresses the author's views and opinions. The information contained in this book is provided without any express, statutory, or implied warranties. Neither the authors, Microsoft Corporation, nor its resellers or distributors will be held liable for any damages caused or alleged to be caused either directly or indirectly by this book.

Acquisitions Editor: Alex Blanton
Project Editor: Laura Sackerman

Body Part No. X10-81702

Contents

Contents

What's New in Microsoft Windows XP

You'll notice some changes as soon as you start Microsoft Windows XP. The desktop background, *Start menu*, and taskbar have a new look. But the features that are new or greatly improved in this version of Windows go beyond just changes in appearance. Some changes won't be apparent to you until you start using the program.

Windows XP comes in several editions:

- *Windows XP Professional* is designed for businesses of all sizes, and in some cases might be appropriate for home use, if you have a networked environment within your home. You can upgrade to Windows XP Professional from Microsoft Windows NT Workstation or Microsoft Windows 2000 Professional.

- *Windows XP Home Edition* is designed for home computers that are not operating within a network domain. (Windows XP Home Edition computers can be included in a network, but not under a domain controller.) Windows XP Home Edition is designed as the upgrade from Microsoft Windows 98 or Microsoft Windows Millennium Edition (Windows Me). Windows XP Home Edition includes great new features that make it easy to work (and play) with the multimedia and Internet capabilities of your computer.

- *Windows XP Media Center Edition* is specially designed to provide a rich multimedia home entertainment experience through your computer. Media Center PCs have upgraded hardware that you can use to watch and record television shows, play DVDs, and manage your music collection. Media Center PCs are generally built with higher-end hardware configurations that you can use to store and work with large media files. This book does not specifically cover Windows XP Media Center Edition.

- *Windows XP Tablet PC Edition* enables handwriting recognition and other pen and ink technologies that are specific to tablet-style personal computers. This book does not specifically cover Windows XP Tablet PC Edition.

- *Windows XP 64-Bit Edition* runs only on specific types of computers that support 64-bit computing. These computers are designed for specialized work that requires a lot of memory, such as high-level graphic and multi-media design. This book does not specifically cover Windows XP 64-Bit Edition.

The exercises in this book cover the features of Windows XP that you are most likely to need and assume that you have *administrative privileges* on your computer. Unless an exercise is specifically for Windows XP Home Edition, screenshots depict the Windows XP Professional user interface.

About Windows XP Service Packs

A service pack is a periodic, planned, product update that includes a number of feature and performance improvements, some planned by the company, some requested by customers, and others necessitated by bugs or other issues discovered after a product ships. Windows XP Service Packs are available as free updates to your installed Windows XP Professional or Windows XP Home Edition operating system. If you purchased your computer after the release of a service pack, the service pack might be pre-installed on your computer by the manufacturer. The Windows XP Service Packs apply only to Windows XP Professional and Windows XP Home Edition.

Windows XP Service Pack 1 (SP1), released in September 2002, contains updates that address the following areas of Windows XP functionality:

- Security fixes, operating system reliability, and application compatibility. SP1 includes all the security patches created since Windows XP was first released in 2001, critical updates created during Microsoft's 2002 Trustworthy Computing initiative, and Windows Messenger version 4.7, an updated instant messaging program with added security features (also available as a free-standing Internet download).

- New features. SP1 includes support for USB 2.0, Microsoft .NET Framework, and upcoming new computer hardware including Tablet PCs.

- New middleware options. SP1 includes functionality with which you can easily specify the programs you want to use for browsing the Web, playing media clips, reading e-mail, and sending instant messages. You use a simple interface to choose all the standard Microsoft applications or any other applications that are installed on your computer.

Windows XP Service Pack 2 (SP2), released in July 2004, contains all the elements of SP1 plus additional updates, including:

- Security technologies that improve the ability of Windows XP–based computers to withstand malicious attacks from viruses and worms. These technologies include network protection, memory protection, safer e-mail handling, more secure Internet browsing, and improved computer maintenance.

- Bug fixes. SP2 includes over 300 code fixes made since the release of SP1. A full list of these fixes including links to the problem descriptions is available at *go.microsoft.com/fwlink/?linkId=20403*.

■ Software updates. SP2 includes Microsoft Windows Media Player 9 Series.

SP2 is not a required upgrade, but it might improve the way your programs run with Windows XP Professional or Windows XP Home Edition. The SP2 upgrade is recommended to ensure that your Windows XP installation is as secure as possible.

For more information about service packs, see "Why Service Packs are Better Than Patches" at *www.microsoft.com/technet/archive/community/columns/security/essays /srvpatch.mspx.*

How New Features Are Identified

new for
WindowsXP

New in
Windows XP
Icon

To help you quickly identify features that are new or greatly enhanced with this version of Windows, this book uses the **New for Windows XP** icon in the margin whenever those features are discussed or shown. If you want to learn about only the new features of the program, you can skim through the book, reading the topics that show the **New for Windows XP** icon.

The following table lists the new features that we think you'll be interested in, as well as the chapters in which those features are discussed.

To learn about this new feature	See
Album view thumbnail images and photo management	Chapter 1, page 3
Automatic Updates	Chapter 1, page 4
CD Burning	Chapter 4, page 101
Compressed (zipped) Folders	Chapter 5, page 135
Desktop Cleanup Wizard	Chapter 2, page 40
Fast User Switching for Multiple Users of a Computer	Chapter 1, page 3 Chapter 3, page 61
Help and Support Center	Chapter 1, page 4
Improved Consumer/Professional "Look and Feel"	Chapter 1, page 3
International Options	Chapter 6, page 163
Internet Connection Sharing	Chapter 7, page 185
Media Folders (My Music, My Pictures)	Chapter 5, page 118
MSN Explorer	Chapter 9, page 246
My Pictures Screen Saver	Chapter 6, page 155
New Connection Wizard	Chapter 7, page 180
Online Print Ordering Wizard	Chapter 9, page 277

To learn about this new feature	See
Photo Printing Wizard	Chapter 9, page 277
Pinning Programs	Chapter 2, page 25
Redesigned Start menu	Chapter 1, page 3
Remote Assistance	Chapter 1, page 4 Chapter 10, page 307
Scanner and Camera Wizard	Chapter 4, page 98
Search Companion Integration	Chapter 1, page 3 Chapter 5, page 144
Setting Default Middleware Programs	Chapter 4, page 112
Speech Recognition	Chapter 6, page 170 Chapter 6, page 175
Theme Improvements	Chapter 6, page 150
Updated user interface	Chapter 1, page 2
Welcome Screen	Chapter 1, page 3
Windows Firewall	Chapter 7, page 185
Windows Media Player	Chapter 9, page 255
Windows Movie Maker	Chapter 9, page 266

For additional information about these and other new features, consult the Windows XP Help and Support Center.

For more information about Windows XP, see *www.microsoft.com/windowsxp/*.

What's New in This Second Edition

Microsoft Windows XP Step by Step, Second Edition is an expanded version of the best seller *Microsoft Windows XP Step by Step Limited Edition* (Microsoft Press, 2001). Released in conjunction with Microsoft Windows XP Service Pack 2 (SP2), this edition includes information about the SP2 operating-system update and offers new and expanded coverage of topics such as security, middleware, and communications.

In addition to the content changes listed in the following table, the layout of this book has been updated to make the content more accessible to readers.

See Also For a guide to the reader aids used in this book, refer to "Using the Practice Files" on page xvii and "Conventions and Features" on page xix.

Every topic in this book has been reviewed and updated. The following topics are new in this Second Edition or have significant changes from the Limited Edition.

Chapter	Topic
Chapter 1: Getting Started with Windows XP	Updating and Safeguarding Your Computer System
Chapter 3: Managing Computer Security	Analyzing Your Computer's Security
	Configuring Security Zones
	Ensuring Effective Virus-Checking
	Configuring Windows Firewall
Chapter 4: Working with Hardware, Software, and Middleware	Installing a New Software Program
	Installing Windows Components
	Using Multiple Monitors
	Expanding Your Laptop with Peripheral Devices
	Changing Your Default Middleware Applications

Chapter	Topic
Chapter 8: Communicating with Other People	Creating a Passport Account
	Getting to Know Windows Messenger
	Setting Up Windows Messenger
	Adding Contacts to Windows Messenger
	Sorting Contacts into Groups
	Sending and Receiving Instant Messages
	Expressing Emotions Online
	Changing Your Windows Messenger Status
Chapter 9: Having Fun with Windows XP	Using MSN Explorer
	Maintaining Your Privacy
	Allowing and Restricting Objectionable Content
	Setting Your Windows Media Player Options
	Using Windows Media Player
	Watching DVD Movies
Chapter 10: Solving Problems	Contacting Product Support

In addition, the book's CD-ROM also contains new resources and other materials, including the following:

- Microsoft Windows XP Step by Step, Second Edition, in electronic format (eBook)
- Microsoft Computer Dictionary, Fifth Edition eBook
- Plus! Photo Story 2 LE software
- Microsoft Windows Movie Maker 2 software
- Links to Windows XP–related downloads
- Links to sources of additional information about Windows XP

Getting Help

Every effort has been made to ensure the accuracy of this book and the contents of its CD-ROM. If you run into problems, please contact the appropriate source for help and assistance.

Getting Help with This Book and Its CD-ROM

If your question or issue concerns the content of this book or its companion CD-ROM, please first search the online Microsoft Knowledge Base, which provides support information for known errors in or corrections to this book, at the following Web site:

www.microsoft.com/learning/support/search.asp

If you do not find your answer in the online Knowledge Base, send your comments or questions to Microsoft Press Technical Support at:

mspinput@microsoft.com

Getting Help with Microsoft Windows XP

If your question is about Microsoft Windows XP, and not about the content of this Microsoft Press book, first consult the resources listed in Chapter 10, "Solving Problems." If you do not find your answer in the Microsoft Windows XP Help and Support Center or through the other resources listed, please search the Windows XP Product Support Center or the Microsoft Knowledge Base at:

support.microsoft.com

In the United States, Microsoft software product support issues not covered by the Microsoft Knowledge Base are addressed by Microsoft Product Support Services. The Microsoft software support options available from Microsoft Product Support Services are listed at:

support.microsoft.com

Outside the United States, for support information specific to your location, please refer to the Worldwide Support menu on the Microsoft Product Support Services Web site for the site specific to your country:

support.microsoft.com

Using the Book's CD-ROM

The CD-ROM inside the back cover of this book contains all the practice files you'll use as you work through the exercises in this book. By using practice files, you won't waste time creating samples files and folders—instead, you can jump right in and concentrate on learning how to use Microsoft Windows XP.

Important The CD-ROM for this book does not contain the Windows XP operating system. You should purchase and install that operating system before using this book.

Minimum System Requirements

To use this book, your computer should meet the following requirements:

Computer/Processor

Computer with a Pentium 133-megahertz (MHz) or higher processor

Memory

64 MB of RAM

Hard Disk

Hard disk space requirements will vary depending on configuration; custom installation choices might require more or less hard disk space.

245 MB of available hard disk space with 115 MB on the hard disk where the operating system is installed. The practice files needed to work through the exercises in this book require 15 MB of available space.

Important This book includes instructions for installing Microsoft Windows XP Service Pack 2. The Service Pack 2 installation process requires up to 1700 MB of available hard disk space.

Operating System

Microsoft Windows XP Professional or Microsoft Windows XP Home Edition

Drive

CD-ROM drive

Floppy disk drive

Display

Super VGA (800×600) or higher-resolution monitor with 256 colors

Required Peripheral Devices

Microsoft Mouse, Microsoft IntelliMouse, or compatible pointing device

Optional Peripheral Devices

Scanner	Printer	Speakers
Camera	External storage device	Microphone

Optional Applications

Microsoft Office XP, Microsoft Office System 2003, or later

Installing the Practice Files

You must install the practice files on your hard disk before you can use them in the chapters' exercises. Follow these steps to prepare the CD's files for your use:

1 Insert the CD-ROM into the CD-ROM drive of your computer.

An End User License Agreement appears. Follow the on-screen directions. It is necessary to accept the terms of the license agreement to use the practice files. After you accept the license agreement, a menu screen appears.

Important   If the menu screen does not appear, start Windows Explorer. In the left pane, locate the icon for your CD-ROM drive, and click this icon. In the right pane, double-click the StartCD executable file.

2 Click **Install Practice Files**.

3 Click **Next** on the first screen, select **I accept the terms in the license agreement**, and then click **Next**.

4 Click **Next** and then click **Install**.

5 After the practice files have been installed, click **Finish**.

Within the installation folder are subfolders for each chapter in the book, as indicated in "Using the Practice Files."

6 Close the CD window, remove the CD-ROM from the CD-ROM drive, and return it to the envelope at the back of the book.

Copying Practice Files

If an exercise instructs you to copy files from the practice folders to your desktop, follow these steps:

1 Click the **Start** button, and then click **My Documents**.

2 In the My Documents window, browse to the folder that contains the practice files for that exercise.

3 Hold down the **CTRL** key, click each of the specified files until you've selected them all, and release the **CTRL** key.

4 Press **CTRL+C** to copy the files to the clipboard.

5 Right-click a blank spot on the taskbar, and click **Show the Desktop**.

6 Press **CTRL+V** to paste the files to the desktop.

Using the Practice Files

Each exercise is preceded by a paragraph or paragraphs that list the files needed for that exercise and explain any preparation you need to take care of before you start working through the exercise, as shown here:

BE SURE TO log on to Windows and have an active Internet connection available before beginning this exercise.
OPEN Control Panel, and then display the User Accounts window.

The following table lists the folders that contain each chapter's practice files.

Chapter	Folder	Subfolder
Chapter 1: Getting Started with Windows XP	No practice files	
Chapter 2: Working Efficiently in Windows XP	Working	Shortcuts
		Arranging
		Cleaning
Chapter 3: Managing Computer Security	Computer	UserAcct
Chapter 4: Working with Hardware, Software, and Middleware	Software	Programs

Chapter	Folder	Subfolder
Chapter 5: Working with Files and Folders	Structure	Views
		Information
		Creating
		Organizing
		Searching
Chapter 6: Personalizing Windows XP	Personalizing	ScreenSaver
		SpeechToText
Chapter 7: Making Connections	Connecting	Sharing
Chapter 8: Communicating with Other People	No practice files	
Chapter 9: Having Fun with Windows XP	Playing	Playlist
		Photos
Chapter 10: Solving Problems	Solving	Backup

Uninstalling the Practice Files

After you finish working through this book, you should uninstall the practice files to free up hard disk space.

Tip If you saved any files outside the *My Documents\Microsoft Press\Microsoft Windows XP SBS* folder, they will not be deleted by the following uninstall process; you will have to manually delete them.

Follow these steps:

1 On the Windows taskbar, click the **Start** button, and then click **Control Panel**.

2 In Control Panel, click **Add or Remove Programs**, and then if necessary click **Remove a Program**.

3 In the list of installed programs, click **Microsoft Windows XP Step by Step Second Edition** and then click the **Remove** button.

4 Click **Yes** when the confirmation dialog box appears.

5 After the files are uninstalled, close the **Add or Remove Programs** dialog box and Control Panel.

Important If you need additional help installing or uninstalling the practice files, please see "Getting Help" earlier in this book. Microsoft Product Support Services does not provide support for this book or its CD-ROM.

Conventions and Features

You can save time when you use this book by understanding how the *Step by Step* series shows special instructions, keys to press, buttons to click, and so on.

Convention	Meaning
1 **2**	Numbered steps guide you through hands-on exercises in each topic.
●	A round bullet indicates an exercise that has only one step.
(CD icon)	This icon at the beginning of a chapter reminds you to install the files used in the exercises.
new for **Windows**XP	This icon indicates a new or greatly improved feature in this version of Microsoft Windows.
Tip	This section provides a helpful hint or shortcut that makes working through a task easier.
Important	This section points out information that you need to complete the procedure.
Troubleshooting	This section shows you how to fix a common problem.
start	When a button is referenced in a topic, a picture of the button appears in the margin area.
ALT+TAB	A plus sign (+) between two key names means that you must press those keys at the same time. For example, "Press **ALT+TAB**" means that you hold down the **ALT** key while you press **TAB**.
Boldface type	Program features that you click or press are shown in black boldface type.
Blue italic type	Terms explained in the glossary are shown in blue italic type.
Red boldface type	Text that you are supposed to type appears in red boldface type in the procedures.
Italic type	Folder paths, URLs, and emphasized words appear in italic type.

Quick Reference

4 Browse to the file or folder, and then click **OK**.

5 Click **Next**.

6 Enter the name of the shortcut, and then click **Finish** to close the wizard.

35 **To change the icon for a shortcut**

1 Right-click the shortcut, and click **Properties** on the shortcut menu.

2 Click the **Shortcut** tab, and click **Change Icon**.

3 Select a new icon, and then click **OK**.

35 **To create a shortcut for a Web site**

1 Right-click an open area of the desktop, point to **New** on the shortcut menu, and click **Shortcut**.

2 Type the URL of the Web site in the **Type the location of the item** box, and click **Next**.

3 Enter a name for the shortcut, and click **Finish** to close the dialog box.

35 **To copy or move a shortcut from the desktop to the Quick Launch toolbar**

1 Right-click the desktop shortcut, and drag it to the Quick Launch toolbar.

2 Click **Copy Here** or **Move Here** on the shortcut menu.

35 **To lock or unlock the taskbar**

● Right-click the taskbar, and click **Lock the Taskbar** on the shortcut menu.

35 **To delete a shortcut from the Quick Launch toolbar**

● Right-click the shortcut, and click **Delete** on the shortcut menu.

39 **To have Windows XP arrange your desktop shortcuts**

● Right-click an open area of the desktop, point to **Arrange Icons By** on the shortcut menu, and then click **Auto Arrange**.

40 **To have Windows XP remove unused desktop shortcuts**

1 Right-click an open area of the desktop, point to **Arrange Icons By** on the shortcut menu, click **Run Desktop Cleanup Wizard**, and click **Next**.

2 Select the desktop shortcuts you want to delete, click **Next**, and click **Finish**.

40 **To delete a shortcut, program, file, or folder from the desktop**

1 Right-click the item you want to delete, and click **Delete** on the shortcut menu.

2 In the confirmation box, click **Yes** to delete the item.

Chapter 3 Managing Computer Security

Page 46 **To change your computer's name**

1   On the **Start** menu, click **Control Panel**.

2   Click the **Performance and Maintenance** icon.

3   Click the **See basic information about your computer** task.

4   Click the **Computer Name** tab, and then click **Change**.

5   Type your new computer name in the **Computer name** box, and click **OK**.

6   If prompted, enter your user account name and password, and then click **OK**.

7   Restart your computer.

50 **To create a user account on a Windows XP domain-connected computer**

1   On the **Start** menu, click **Control Panel**, and then click **User Accounts**.

2   On the **Advanced** tab, click **Advanced**.

3   In the left pane of the Local Users and Groups window, click the **Users** folder.

4   On the **Action** menu, click **New User**.

5   Enter the user information, click **Create**, and then click **Close**.

6   Click the **Close** button to close the Local Users and Groups window, click **OK** to close the **User Accounts** dialog box, and then click the **Close** button to close the Control Panel window.

50 **To change the group to which a Windows XP domain-connected computer user account is assigned**

1   On the **Start** menu, click **Control Panel**, and then click **User Accounts**.

2   In the **Users for this computer** list, click the user name, and click **Properties**.

3   On the **Group Membership** tab, click **Other**, and click the group name in the drop-down list.

4   Click **OK** to close the **Properties** dialog box, and then click **OK** to close the **User Accounts** dialog box.

5   Click the **Close** button to close the Control Panel window.

50 **To delete a user account on a Windows XP domain-connected computer**

1   On the **Start** menu, click **Control Panel**, and then click **User Accounts**.

2   In the **Users for this computer** list, click the user name, and click **Remove**.

3   When prompted to confirm the removal, click **Yes**.

4   Click **OK** to close the **User Accounts** dialog box.

5   Click the **Close** button to close the Control Panel window.

57 **To create a user account on a Windows XP workgroup-connected computer**

1 On the **Start** menu, click **Control Panel**, and then click **User Accounts**.

2 Click **Create a new account**.

3 Enter a name for the new account, and then click **Next**.

4 Specify the account type, and then click **Create Account**.

5 Click the **Close** button to close the User Accounts window, and then close the Control Panel window.

57 **To change a user account type on a Windows XP workgroup-connected computer**

1 On the **Start** menu, click **Control Panel**, and then click **User Accounts**.

2 Click the account that you want to change, and then click **Change the account type**.

3 On the **Pick a new account type** screen, click the new account type, and then click **Change Account Type**.

4 Click the **Close** button to close the User Accounts window, and then close the Control Panel window.

57 **To create a user account password on a Windows XP workgroup-connected computer**

1 On the **Start** menu, click **Control Panel**, and then click **User Accounts**.

2 Click the account you want to change, and then click **Create a password**.

3 Enter a password in the **Type a new password** box, and re-enter the password in the **Type the new password again to confirm** box.

4 Enter a password hint in the **Type a word or phrase to use as a password hint** box, and then click **Create Password**.

5 Click the **Close** button to close the User Accounts window, and then close the Control Panel window.

57 **To delete a user account from a Windows XP workgroup-connected computer**

1 On the **Start** menu, click **Control Panel**, and then click **User Accounts**.

2 Click the account that you want to change, and then click **Delete the account**.

3 Specify whether you want to keep or delete any files the user has created, and then click **Delete Account**.

4 Click the **Close** button to close the User Accounts window, and then close the Control Panel window.

61 **To switch quickly among computer users**

1 On the **Start** menu, click **Control Panel**, and then **User Accounts**.

2 Click **Change the way users log on or off**.

3 Select the **User Fast User Switching** check box, and click **Apply Options**.

64 **To analyze your computer's security**

1 Log on to the Internet. In the Address box, type http://www.microsoft.com/technet/security/tools/mbsahome.mspx, and then press **ENTER**.

2 Click the **download the English version of this program** link.

3 Click **Run**, and click **Next** three times to move through the wizard.

4 On the **Start Installation** page, click **Install**.

5 When the installation is complete, click **OK**, and then **Close**.

6 Double-click the **Microsoft Baseline Security Analyzer** desktop shortcut, and click **Scan a computer**, and then **Start scan**.

7 Click **Close** when finished scanning.

68 **To configure security zones**

1 Log on to the Internet.

2 On the **Tools** menu, click **Internet Options**.

3 Click the **Security** tab.

4 Click the **Custom Level** button to display the **Security Settings** dialog box.

5 Make your customizations, and then click **OK**.

68 **To block access to specific Web sites**

1 Log on to the Internet.

2 On the **Tools** menu, click **Internet Options**.

3 Click the **Restricted sites** icon, and then click the **Sites** button.

4 In the **Add this Web site to the zone** box, type the name of the Web site you want to block, and then click the **Add** button.

75 **To examine your Windows Firewall settings**

1 In the Control Panel window, click **Security Center**.

2 Click **Windows Firewall**.

1   Remove the speakers from their packaging, if you have not already done so.

2   Link the two speakers using the connector cable.

3   Position the speakers to the left and right of your monitor to provide stereo sound quality.

4   Plug the speakers into a nearby power outlet using the AC adapter cord.

5   Plug the speakers into the speaker jack on the sound card at the back of the computer using the connector cable.

1   Remove the microphone from its packaging, if you have not already done so.

2   Plug the microphone connector cable into the audio input jack on the sound card on the back of your computer.

1   Click the **Start** button, and then on the **Start** menu, click **Control Panel**.

2   Click **Sounds, Speech, and Audio Devices**, and then click the **Sounds and Audio Devices** icon.

3   On the **Voice** tab, click **Test hardware** and then click **Next**.

4   Conduct the speaker text, adjust the **Playback**.

5   Click **Next**, and then **Finish** to end the test.

●   Connect the printer to the appropriate port.

1   Connect the printer to the appropriate port.

2   On the **Start** menu, click **Printers and Faxes**.

3   On the **Printer Tasks** menu, click **Add a printer** to open the **Add Printer Wizard**, and then click **Next**.

4   On the **Local or Network Printer** page, click **Local printer attached to this computer**.

5   Clear the **Automatically detect and install my Plug and Play printer** check box, and then click **Next**.

6   On the **Select a Printer Port** page, confirm that your printer is connected to the rec-ommended printer port, or click the correct port in the drop-down list, and click **Next**.

7   On the **Install Printer Software** page, insert the installation CD-ROM or floppy disk, click **Have Disk**, and follow the instructions on the screen.

8   When the installation is complete, click the **Close** button to close the Printers and Faxes window.

89   **To install a local printer without an installation CD-ROM or disk**

1   Connect the printer to the appropriate port.

2   On the **Start** menu, click **Printers and Faxes**.

3   On the **Printer Tasks** menu, click **Add a printer** to open the **Add Printer Wizard**, and then click **Next**.

4   On the **Local or Network Printer** page, click **Local printer attached to this computer**.

5   Clear the **Automatically detect and install my Plug and Play printer** check box, and then click **Next**.

6   On the **Select a Printer Port** page, confirm that your printer is connected to the recommended printer port, or click the correct port in the drop-down list, and click **Next**.

7   In the **Manufacturer** list on the **Install Printer Software** page, click the name of the manufacturer of your printer.

8   In the **Printers** list, select the model of your printer, and then click **Next**.

9   On the **Name Your Printer** page, type a name for your printer in the **Printer name** box, or accept the default name, and then click **Next**.

10   On the **Print Test Page** page, click **Yes**, and then click **Next**.

11   Click **Finish** to print the test page, and then click **OK** to close the confirmation dialog box and the **Add Printer Wizard**.

12   Click the **Close** button to close the Printers and Faxes window.

94   **To connect to a network printer**

1   On the **Start** menu, click **Printers and Faxes**.

2   On the **Printer Tasks** menu, click **Add a printer**.

3   In the **Add Printer Wizard**, click **Next**.

4   On the **Local or Network Printer** page, select **A network printer, or a printer attached to another computer**, and then click **Next**.

5 On the **Specify a Printer** page, select **Connect to this printer**, type the computer name and printer name in the **Name** box, and click **Next**.

6 If prompted, enter a user account name and password, and then click **OK**.

7 If prompted, specify a default printer, and then click **Next**.

8 Click **Finish** to close the dialog box, and then click the **Close** button to close the Printers and Faxes window.

97 **To configure a fax service**

1 On the **Start** menu, click **Control Panel**, and then click **Printers and Other Hardware**.

2 In the Printers and Other Hardware window, click the **Printers and Faxes** icon.

3 On the **Printer Tasks** menu, click **Set up faxing**.

4 When prompted to do so, insert the Windows XP installation CD into the CD-ROM drive, and click **OK**.

5 When the configuration process is complete, click the **Close** button.

98 **To install a Plug and Play scanner or camera**

● Plug your scanner or camera into the appropriate port on your computer.

98 **To access a Plug and Play scanner or camera**

1 On the **Start** menu, click **Control Panel**, and then click **Printers and Other Hardware**.

2 In the Printers and Other Hardware window, click **Scanners and Cameras**.

3 Double-click the icon for your scanner or camera to open the **Scanner and Camera Wizard**.

100 **To install an external storage device**

● Plug the storage device into the appropriate port and into a power source, if necessary.

100 **To install an internal CD-RW drive**

1 Turn off your computer, and disconnect the power cord.

2 Remove the computer's cover, and install the internal device according to the manufacturer's instructions.

3 Replace the cover, and reconnect the power cord.

4 Turn on your computer, and log on to Windows XP.

101   **To burn your own CDs**

   1   Insert a blank CD in the CD-RW drive.

   2   On the **Start** menu, click **My Computer**.

   3   Browse to the folder containing the files you want to copy to CD, and click the **Copy this folder** task.

   4   In the **Copy Items** dialog box, click the CD drive, and then click **Copy**.

   5   On the **CD Writing Tasks** menu, click **Write these files to CD**.

   6   Follow the **CD Writing Wizard's** instructions to complete the process.

102   **To install a software program from a folder on your hard drive**

   1   In Windows Explorer, browse to the folder from which you want to install the program.

   2   Double-click the **Setup** file, and work through the installation process.

102   **To uninstall a software program from your computer**

   1   On the **Start** menu, click **Control Panel**, and click **Add or Remove Programs**.

   2   In the Add or Remove Programs window, click the program you want to remove, and then click the **Change/Remove** button.

   3   Accept the default uninstall options to remove the program from your computer.

107   **To start a program automatically**

   1   On the **Start** menu, point to **All Programs**, right-click **Startup**, and then click **Explore All Users** on the shortcut menu.

   2   Drag the program you want to start automatically into the Startup folder.

110   **To configure your computer to display your Windows desktop on two monitors**

   1   Turn off your computer and remove the cover.

   2   Insert the second video card into an available slot that matches the size of your video card, and then replace the cover.

   3   Secure the video card to the cover with screws.

   4   Plug the additional monitor into the second video out port.

   5   Turn on your computer.

   6   On the **Start** menu, click **Control Panel**.

   7   In the Control Panel window, click the **Appearance and Themes** category.

   8   In the Appearance and Themes window, click the **Display** icon.

   9   On the **Settings** tab, click the secondary monitor.

10 Select the **Extend my Windows desktop onto this monitor** check box, and then click **OK**.

To change your current default middleware

1 On the **Start** menu, click **Set Program Access and Defaults**.

2 Click the double chevrons to the right of the **Custom** option.

3 Change your default middleware applications, and then click **OK**.

Working with Files and Folders

To start Windows Explorer in Folders view

● On the **Start** menu, point to **All Programs**, point to **Accessories**, and then click **Windows Explorer**.

To start Windows Explorer in Tasks view

● On the **Start** menu, click **My Computer**.

To change the way you view files and folders in Windows Explorer

● On the toolbar, click the **Views** button, and then click the desired view.

To display or hide the Address toolbar

1 Right-click the taskbar, and click **Lock the taskbar** to deselect it.

2 On the taskbar shortcut menu, click **Toolbars**, and then click **Address**.

To view the properties of a file or folder

● Right-click the file or folder, and click **Properties** on the shortcut menu.

To create a new folder

1 On the **File and Folder Tasks** menu, click **Make a new folder**.

2 With the default folder name selected, type the name of the folder, and then press **ENTER**.

To create a new text document

1 Right-click in the right pane of Windows Explorer, and on the shortcut menu, point to **New**, and then click **Text Document**.

2 With the default file name selected, type the name of the folder, and then press **ENTER**.

To create a new bitmap image

1 Right-click an empty area of the right pane, and on the shortcut menu, point to **New**, and then click **Bitmap Image**.

2 With the default file name selected, type the name of the folder, and then press **ENTER**.

135 **To create a compressed folder**

1 Select the file(s) you want to include in the folder.

2 Right-click the selection, and on the shortcut menu, point to **Send To**, and then click **Compressed (zipped) Folder**.

140 **To use briefcase**

1 Right-click the desktop, point to **New**, and then click **Briefcase**.

2 Open the briefcase folder, and drag your files into it.

3 Move the briefcase folder to a floppy disk or other portable storage medium.

4 After you make changes, insert the disk containing the briefcase into your main computer, or reconnect your laptop computer to your main computer, and click **Update All** on the **Briefcase** menu to bring your files up to date.

140 **To make a copy of a folder**

1 Select the folder. On the **File and Folder Tasks** menu, click **Copy this folder**.

2 In the **Copy Items** dialog box, browse to the folder where you want to insert the copy, and then click **Copy**.

140 **To rename a folder**

1 Right-click the folder, and click **Rename** on the shortcut menu.

2 With the name selected, type the new name of the folder, and press **ENTER**.

140 **To make a copy of a file**

● Right-click the file, and click **Copy** on the shortcut menu. Then right-click an empty area of the right pane, and click **Paste** on the shortcut menu.

● Select the original file, and on the **Edit** menu, click **Copy**. Then on the **Edit** menu, click **Paste**.

● Select the original file, press **CTRL+C**, and then press **CTRL+V**.

140 **To move a file**

● Drag the file from the right pane to the new folder in the left pane; or

1 Select the file. On the **File and Folder Tasks** menu, click **Move this file**.

2 In the **Move Items** dialog box, browse to the folder where you want to move the file, and then click **Move**.

144 **To start the Search Companion**

● On the **Start** menu, click **Search**.

4 Click the **Settings** button.

5 Click **Browse**.

6 Browse to the folder containing the pictures you want to display, and click **OK**.

7 Click **OK** to close the **My Pictures Screen Saver Options** dialog box, and then click **Preview** on the **Screen Saver** tab to see what your slideshow will look like as a screen saver.

8 Move the mouse or press any key on the keyboard to finish previewing the slideshow.

9 Click **OK** to close the dialog box and apply your settings.

158 **To change your monitor settings**

1 In the Control Panel window, click **Appearance and Themes**, and then click the **Change the screen resolution** task.

2 Point to the marker on the **Screen resolution** slider, hold down the mouse button, and drag the marker all the way to the right to maximum the resolution, or to the left to minimize the resolution.

3 Click **Apply**.

4 Click **Yes** if prompted to confirm your change.

161 **To manually reset your system time**

1 Double-click the clock on the taskbar.

2 In the **Date and Time Properties** dialog box, drag the mouse pointer over the setting you want to change in the digital clock, and then use the spinner to the right of the clock to change the setting.

3 Click **OK** to close the dialog box and update your settings.

163 **To change your regional settings**

1 In the Control Panel window, click the **Date, Time, Language, and Regional Options** icon.

2 Click the **Regional and Language Options** icon.

3 In the **Standards and formats** area, click the current country to open the drop-down list.

4 Click the regional setting you want to use.

5 In the **Location** area, click the current country to open the drop-down list, and click the country.

6 Click **OK** to close the **Regional and Language Options** dialog box, and then close the Date, Time, Language, and Regional Options window.

4 On the **Network Connection Type** page, click **Connect to the Internet**, and then click **Next**.

5 On the **Getting Ready** page, click **Set up my connection manually**, and then click **Next** to display the connection options.

6 If you are connecting using a modem and phone line, select the first option, and click **Next**. When prompted, provide the name and phone number of your ISP, your user account name, and your password.

7 If you are connecting using a password-protected broadband connection, select the second option, and click **Next**. When prompted, provide the name of your ISP, your user account name, and your password.

8 If you are connecting using a dedicated or constant broadband connection, select the third option, and click **Next**.

9 Click **Finish**, and then click the **Close** button to close the Network and Internet Connections window.

183 **To set up your computer so that it can be accessed using Remote Desktop**

1 On the **Start** menu, click **Control Panel**.

2 Click **Performance and Maintenance**, and then click the **System** icon.

3 In the **System Properties** dialog box, click the **Remote** tab.

4 In the **Remote Desktop** area, select the **Allow users to connect remotely to this computer** check box.

5 When the **Remote Sessions** message box appears, read the message, and then click **OK** to close it.

6 You are automatically authorized as a remote user of your own computer. If you want to authorize additional remote users, click **Select Remote Users**, add users in the **Remote Desktop Users** dialog box, and then click **OK**.

7 Click **OK** to close the **System Properties** dialog box, and then close the Performance and Maintenance window.

183 **To turn off Remote Desktop access on your computer**

1 On the **Start** menu, click **Control Panel**.

2 Click **Performance and Maintenance**, and then click the **System** icon.

3 On the **Remote** tab, clear the **Allow users to connect remotely to this computer** check box.

4 Click **OK** to close the **System Properties** dialog box, and then close the Performance and Maintenance window.

183 **To access your computer from another Windows XP computer through Remote Desktop**

1 On the **Start** menu, point to **All Programs**, point to **Accessories**, point to **Communications**, and then click **Remote Desktop Connection**.

2 Click **Options** to expand the dialog box if necessary.

3 Enter the connection information on the **General** tab.

4 Specify the display information on the **Display** tab.

5 Specify any other pertinent information, and then click **Connect**.

185 **To share a folder on your computer**

1 On the **Start** menu, click **My Documents**.

2 Browse to the folder you want to share.

3 On the **File and Folder Tasks** menu, click **Share this folder**.

4 In the **Sharing Properties** dialog box, click **Share this folder**.

5 Click **Permissions**, make the appropriate changes, and click **OK**.

6 Click the **Close** button to close the window.

188 **To share a local printer**

1 On the **Start** menu, click **Printers and Faxes**.

2 In the right pane of the Printers and Faxes window, click the printer you want to share.

3 On the **Printer Tasks** menu, click **Share this printer**.

4 On the **Sharing** tab of the printer's **Properties** dialog box, click **Share this printer**.

5 In the **Share name** box, type a simple name for the printer.

6 Click **OK** to close the dialog box, and then click the **Close** button to close the Printers and Faxes window.

190 **To create a Virtual Private Network connection over the Internet**

1 On the **Start** menu, click **Control Panel**, and then click **Network and Internet Connections**.

2 Click the **Create a connection to the network at your workplace** task.

3 On the **Network Connection** page, select the **Virtual Private Network connection**, and then click **Next**.

4 Type a name for your connection in the **Company Name** box, and click **Next**.

5   Type the remote access server's host name or IP address in the box, and click **Next** to move to the **Connection Availability** page.

6   Specify whether you want to make the connection available to other users of your computer or keep it to yourself, and click **Next**.

7   Select the **Add a shortcut to this connection to my desktop** check box, and then click **Finish** to create the connection.

190   **To connect to a Virtual Private Network**

1   Double-click the VPN icon on your desktop.

2   Enter your user account name and password.

3   Select the **Save this user name and password for the following users** check box, and make sure that the **Me only** option is selected.

4   Click **Connect**.

190   **To close a Virtual Private Network connection**

●   Right-click the network icon, and click **Disconnect**.

Chapter 8   **Communicating with Other People**

Page 197   **To create a Passport account for a computer that is part of a network**

1   On the **Start** menu, click **Control Panel**, and then click **User Accounts**.

2   On the **Advanced** tab of the **User Accounts** dialog box, click **.NET Passport Wizard**.

3   Follow the instructions in the **.NET Passport Wizard**.

4   When you are finished, click **OK** to close the **User Accounts** dialog box, and then click the Control Panel window's **Close** button to close it.

208   **To exit Windows Messenger**

●   In the notification area, click the **Windows Messenger** icon, and then click **Exit** on the shortcut menu.

208   **To add people to your Windows Messenger Contact list**

1   Sign in to Windows Messenger.

2   Click **Add a Contact**.

3   Follow the instructions of the **Add a Contact Wizard**.

213   **To create a group and add contacts to it**

1   Sign in to Windows Messenger.

2   Click **Add a Group**.

3   Create a name for the group, and then drag a contact to the new group.

To send an instant message

1 Sign in to Windows Messenger.

2 Double-click the name of the contact you want to chat with.

3 Type your message in the input box, and click **Send**.

To add another person to an in-progress instant message

● Click **Invite Someone to this Conversation**. Select the contact's name from the **Add Someone to this Conversation** dialog box, and click **OK**.

To leave an instant message conversation

● Click the conversation box's **Close** button.

To disable emoticons in Windows Messenger

● On the **Tools** menu, click **Options**, and then on the **Personal** tab of the **Options** dialog box, in the **My Message Text** area, clear the **Show graphics (emoticons) in instant messages** check box.

● On the **View** menu, click **Enable Emoticons** to clear the check mark.

To change the length of inactive time that triggers the Away setting

● On the **Tools** menu, click **Options**, and then click the **Preferences** tab.

To change your online status

● On the **Windows Messenger File** menu, point to **My Status**, and click the setting that indicates your status.

● Right-click the **Windows Messenger** icon in the notification tray, point to **My Status**, and then click the appropriate status setting.

To start Outlook Express

● On the **Start** menu, point to **All Programs**, and then click **Outlook Express**.

To configure Outlook Express to send and receive e-mail messages

1 On the **Start** menu, point to **All Programs**, and then click **Outlook Express**.

2 Enter your name as you want it to appear to recipients of e-mail messages from you, and then click **Next** to display the wizard's second page.

3 Enter the e-mail address you want to display to recipients of your messages, and click **Next** to display the third page.

4 Type the names of your incoming and outgoing mail servers in the boxes. Then select the type of server that handles your incoming mail from the drop-down box, and click **Next**.

5 Enter your e-mail account name and password.

6 Click **Next**, and then click **Finish** to close the wizard.

7 Outlook Express prompts you to download the list of folders from your mail server. Click **Yes**. Double-click the folders you want to display, and click **OK** to download the selected folders to your computer.

8 Click the account name to display the synchronization options.

9 Select the check boxes of the folders you would like to synchronize, and then click **Synchronize Account**.

230 **To send e-mail messages**

1 On the **Start** menu, click **E-mail**.

2 Click **Outlook Express** on the Folder bar to display a list of available folders.

3 Click the **Inbox** folder for your e-mail account.

4 On the toolbar, click the **Create Mail** button.

5 In the **To** box, type the e-mail address of the person to whom you want to send a message.

6 After you have written your message in the e-mail message form, on the message form's toolbar, click the **Send** button.

230 **To reply to e-mail messages**

1 Double-click the message to open it.

2 On the message window's toolbar, click the **Reply** button.

3 After you have written your message in the e-mail message form, on the message form's toolbar, click the **Send** button.

230 **To delete e-mail messages**

● Click the e-mail message to select it, and click the **Delete** button.

235 **To create e-mail stationery**

1 On the **Start** menu, click **E-mail**.

2 On the toolbar, click the down arrow to the right of the **Create Mail** button, and click **Select Stationery**.

3 Click the **Create New** button.

4 Click **Next** to move to the wizard's **Background** page.

5 Customize the look of your stationery as you like, clicking **Next** until you reach the wizard's **Complete** page.

6 In the **Name** box, type a name for your stationery, and then click **Finish**.

261 **To change the visual representation of a song in Windows Media Player**

1 Start Windows Media Player, and on the taskbar, click **Now Playing** to display the current playlist.

2 Start a song from the music selector drop-down list.

3 Click the **Select Now Playing** options button, point to **Visualizations**, point to a category, and then click a visualization.

265 **To watch a DVD with Windows Media Player**

1 Insert the DVD into the DVD-ROM drive.

2 Start Windows Media Player.

3 Click **Play DVD**.

266 **To make a movie with Windows Media Player**

● On the **Start** menu, point to **All Programs**, point to **Accessories**, and then click **Windows Movie Maker**.

266 **To change the Windows Media Player skin**

1 Start Windows Media Player in full mode.

2 On the taskbar, click **Skin Chooser**.

3 Click the new skin, and then click **Apply Skin**.

268 **To play a CD with Windows Media Player**

1 Insert a music CD into your CD-ROM drive.

2 If the **Audio CD** dialog box prompts you to select an action, click **Play Audio CD using Windows Media Player**, and then click **OK**.

268 **To copy a song track to your hard disk**

1 On the taskbar, click **Copy from CD**.

2 Select the check boxes of the songs you want to copy and clear the check boxes of the songs you don't want to copy.

3 Click **Copy Music**.

4 If the **Copy Music Protection** dialog box opens, giving you the option to turn off the automatic protection of your copied CD files, ensure that the **Add copy protection to your music** check box is selected, and then click **Next**.

5 Select **Keep my current format settings**, and then click **Finish**.

268 **To copy audio tracks from the Media Library to portable device**

1   Open Windows Media Player.

2   On the taskbar, click **Copy to CD or Device**.

3   In the **Items to Copy** pane's drop-down list, select the album or type of music from which you want to make your selection, and then clear the check boxes of any tracks you don't want to copy.

4   In the **Items on Device** pane's drop-down list, select the destination drive.

5   Click **Copy**.

272 **To locate and listen to a radio station over the Internet**

1   Start Windows Media Player.

2   On the taskbar, click **Radio Tuner**.

3   In the **Featured Stations** list, select a station, and then click **Play**.

275 **To create your own playlist**

1   On the **Start** menu, click **My Documents**.

2   Browse to the location of the songs you copied to your hard disk.

3   Right-click a song, and click **Add to Playlist** on the shortcut menu.

4   Click **New**, type a name for the new playlist, and click **OK**.

5   Click **Add to Media Library**, and then click **Add File or Playlist**.

277 **To publish photos from your hard disk on the Web**

1   On the **Start** menu, click **My Documents**.

2   Browse to the location of the photo files on your hard disk.

3   On the **File and Folder Tasks** menu, click **Publish this folder to the Web**, and click **Next**.

4   On the wizard's **Change Your File Selection** page, select or clear each file's check box to indicate whether you want to publish it, and click **Next**.

5   Click **MSN Groups**, and then click **Next**.

6   On the **Select where you want your files stored** page, click **Create a new MSN Group to share your files** (if it is not already selected), and then click **Next**.

7   Select the **Shared** option, and then click **Next**.

8   On the **Create your new Group** page, type a name for your MSN group, and enter your e-mail address. Read the code of conduct, select the **Yes** option, and click **Next**.

9   In the text box, describe the purpose of your new MSN group.

10   If you want to include your MSN group in the online Group Directory, select the **Yes** option; otherwise accept the default **No** option.

11   Choose a home page language from the drop-down list, and click **Next**.

12   Accept the default **Yes** option to add the URL to your **Favorites** list, and click **Next**.

13   If you want to change the names of either or both of the upload folders, click the **Change** button, click the **Or create a new folder** link, type a name for your new folder in the text box, and click the **Done** button twice to return to the upload folder page.

14   Click the **Next** button, resize your photo if you want, and then click **Next**.

15   On the last page of the wizard, make sure that the **Open this site when I click Finish** check box is selected, and then click the **Finish** button.

16   To look at the photos you uploaded, click **Pictures** on the menu at the left side of the screen.

Chapter 10   Solving Problems

Page 285   **To automatically deliver important updates to your computer**

1   On the **Start** menu, click **Control Panel**, and then click **Performance and Maintenance**.

2   In the Performance and Maintenance window, click the **System** icon.

3   On the **Automatic Updates** tab of the **System Properties** dialog box, click **Download the updates automatically and notify me when they are ready to be installed**.

4   Click **OK** to close the dialog box and save your changes, and then click the **Close** button to close the Performance and Maintenance window.

288   **To gather general, status, hardware, or software diagnostic information about your computer**

1   On the **Start** menu, click **Help and Support**.

2   In the Help and Support Center, select the **Automatic** option.

3   Click the day and time to run the automatic updates, and then click **OK**.

288   **To view general system information about your computer**

1   On the **Start** menu, click **Help and Support**.

2   Click **Use tools to view your computer information and diagnose problems**.

3   Click **My Computer Information**.

4   Click **View general system information about this computer**.

5   When you are finished looking at the report, click the **Close** button to close the Help and Support Center.

288   **To view the status of your system hardware and software**

1   On the **Start** menu, click **Help and Support**.

2   Click **Use tools to view your computer information and diagnose problems**.

3   Click **My Computer Information**.

4   Click **View the status of my system hardware and software**.

5   Click **Back**, and then click **Find information about the hardware installed on this computer**.

6   Click **Back**, and the click **View a list of Microsoft software installed on this computer**.

7   When you are finished looking at the report, click the **Close** button to close the Help and Support Center.

288   **To gather network diagnostic information about your computer**

1   On the **Start** menu, click **Help and Support**.

2   In the Help and Support Center, click **Use tools to view your computer information and diagnose problems**.

3   On the **Tools** menu, click **Network Diagnostics**.

4   Click **Set scanning options**, select the options that interest you, and then click **Scan your system**.

5   When you are finished looking at the report, click the **Close** button to close the Help and Support Center.

293   **To run the Disk Cleanup utility on your computer**

1   On the **Start** menu, point to **All Programs**, point to **Accessories**, point to **System Tools**, and then click **Disk Cleanup**.

2   Select the check boxes of all the types of temporary files you want to delete, and then click **OK**.

3   Click **Yes** to confirm that you want to proceed with the deletion.

295   **To run the Disk Defragmenter utility on your computer**

1   On the **Start** menu, point to **All Programs**, point to **Accessories**, point to **System Tools**, and then click **Disk Defragmenter**.

2   In the **Disk Defragmenter** dialog box, click the volume you want to defragment, and then click **Analyze**.

3   Click **View Report** to see information the program collected about the volume.

4   If defragmentation is recommended and you want to do it at this time, click **Defragment**. Otherwise, click **Close** to close the report window.

5   If you choose to defragment the volume, click **Close** to close the **Disk Defragmenter** dialog box when the defragmentation process is complete.

298   **To open the Help and Support Center**

●   Click **Help and Support** on the **Start** menu.

●   Press **F1**. Depending on what area of Windows you are in, this might open the Help and Support Center to a page that is specific to that area. For example, if you press **F1** from within the Control Panel window, the Help and Support Center opens to the Control Panel topic.

303   **To open a new Online Assisted Support Incident report for Windows XP**

1   On the **Start** menu, click **Help and Support**.

2   On the toolbar, click the **Support** button.

3   On the **Support** menu, click **Get help from Microsoft**.

4   Enter your Passport sign-in name and password, and click **Sign In**.

5   If prompted to do so, enter the requested information, select the **I accept the License Agreement for the use of this site** check box, and click **Submit**.

6   On the **Microsoft Online Assisted Support** page, click **Ask a Microsoft Support Professional for help**.

7   If the EULA is displayed, read it, and then click **I Agree**.

8   Select the option that identifies the computer with the problem, and click **Next**.

9   In the drop-down list, click the version of Windows XP that is installed on the computer, and then click **Next**.

10   Select the support option you want and then click **Next**.

11   Fill out and submit the incident form.

307   **To request and receive Remote Assistance from another person**

1   On the **Start** menu, point to **All Programs**, and click **Remote Assistance**.

2   On the **Remote Assistance** page of the Help and Support Center, click **Invite someone to help you**.

3   Click the name of the person you are going to invite to help you; or type his or her e-mail address in the **Type an e-mail address** box, and then click **Invite this person**.

4 When the remote assistance invitation opens, type an explanatory message in the **Message** box, and then click **Continue**.

5 Specify the duration of your invitation.

6 If you want to use a password, enter the password in the **Type password** and **Confirm password** boxes, and then communicate that password to your Remote Assistance buddy.

7 When you are ready to send the invitation, click **Send Invitation**.

8 When the invitation is accepted, click **Yes** to allow your buddy to view your screen and to chat with you.

9 In the chat session, tell your buddy to take control of your computer.

10 When you receive a message asking if you would like to share control of your computer, click **Yes**.

11 Click **Stop Control** to regain exclusive control of your computer.

12 Click **Disconnect** to end the Remote Assistance session.

311 **To enable or disable Remote Assistance**

1 On the **Start** menu, click **Control Panel**.

2 Click **Performance and Maintenance**, and then click the **System** icon.

3 In the **System Properties** dialog box, click the **Remote** tab, and then click the **Advanced** button.

4 In the **Remote Assistance Settings** dialog box, click the **Allow this computer to be controlled remotely** check box to enable Remote Assistance, or clear the check box to disable Remote Assistance.

5 Click **OK** to close the **Remote Assistance Settings** dialog box, and then click **OK** to close the **System Properties** dialog box and save your changes.

311 **To back up files from your computer**

1 On the **Start** menu, point to **All Programs**, point to **Accessories**, point to **System Tools**, and then click **Backup**.

2 In the **Backup and Restore Wizard**, click **Next**.

3 On the **Backup or Restore** page, click **Back up files and settings**, and click **Next**.

4 On the **What to Back Up** page, select the **Let me choose what to back up** option, and then click **Next**.

5 On the **Items to Back Up** page, browse to the folder you want to back up. Select the check box preceding the folder, and then click **Next**.

6   On the **Backup Type, Destination, and Name** page, specify the backup destination and file name, and then click **Next**.

7   Click **Finish** to start the backup.

8   When the backup is complete, click **Close**.

311   **To restore a backup file**

1   On the **Start** menu, point to **All Programs**, point to **Accessories**, point to **System Tools**, and then click **Backup**.

2   In the **Backup and Restore Wizard**, click **Next** to begin the process of backing up your files.

3   On the **Backup or Restore** page, click **Restore files and settings**, browse to and select the backup file, click **Next**, and then click **Finish**.

315   **To start the System Restore Wizard**

●   On the **Start** menu, point to **All Programs**, point to **Accessories**, point to **System Tools**, and then click **System Restore**.

●   On the **Start** menu, click **Help and Support**, and then click **Undo changes to your computer with System Restore**.

●   On the **Start** menu, click **Control Panel**, click **Performance and Maintenance**, and then click **System Restore** on the **See Also** menu.

315   **To restore your computer system to a previous state**

1   Close any open programs.

2   Start the **System Restore Wizard**.

3   Select the **Restore my computer to an earlier time** option, and then click **Next**.

4   On the **Select a Restore Point** page calendar, click a specific restoration checkpoint, click **Next**, and then click **Next** again.

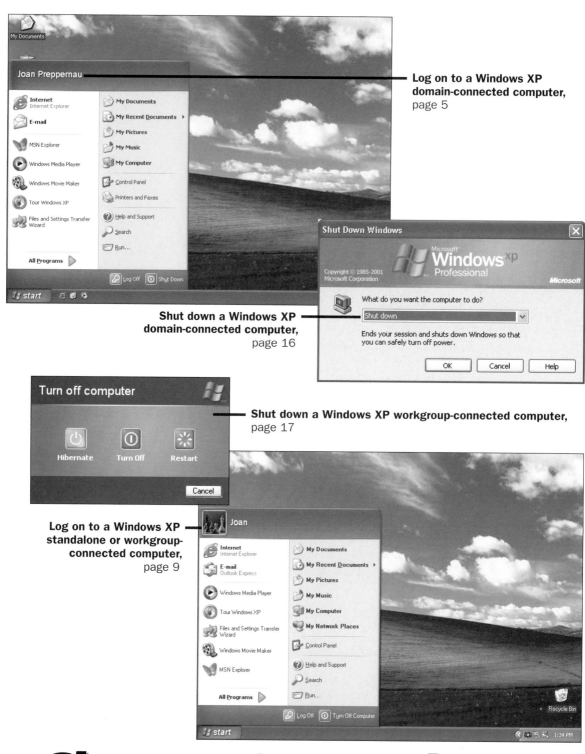

Log on to a Windows XP
domain-connected computer,
page 5

Shut down a Windows XP
domain-connected computer,
page 16

Shut down a Windows XP workgroup-connected computer,
page 17

Log on to a Windows XP
standalone or workgroup-
connected computer,
page 9

Chapter 1 at a Glance

1 Getting Started with Windows XP

In this chapter you will learn to:
- ✔ Talk knowledgeably about the Windows XP operating system.
- ✔ Log on to your computer.
- ✔ Update and safeguard your computer system.
- ✔ Log off of your computer.
- ✔ Shut down your computer.

Microsoft Windows XP is the latest in the line of Windows operating systems for personal computers. Windows XP is the successor to Microsoft Windows 2000 and Microsoft Windows Millennium Edition (Windows Me), and it is the first operating system expressly designed by Microsoft to fill the needs of both business and personal users.

This chapter provides an overview of Windows XP and takes you through the process of logging on to a computer that is running either Windows XP Professional or Windows XP Home Edition and ensuring that your operating system is up to date. Whether you are new to Windows or familiar with an earlier version, you will find useful information in this chapter. Note that many of the features introduced in Windows XP run behind the scenes and are not obvious to the casual observer, or they are used to set up and maintain (administer) a network. We don't cover these features in this book because most people never have to deal with them.

> **See Also** For an explanation of the different editions of the Windows XP operating system and how they are addressed in this book, refer to "What's New in Microsoft Windows XP" at the beginning of this book.

Unlike most of the exercises in this book, some of the exercises in this chapter are specific to Windows XP Home Edition or Windows XP Professional because of differences in the procedures for logging on and off and shutting down your computer. You can work through the exercises that are designated for the version of Windows XP you have installed, and skip the exercises designed for the other version. For all the exercises, we assume Windows XP Professional or Windows XP Home Edition is already installed on your computer, and that you know your user name and password (if you need them).

See Also   Do you need only a quick refresher on the topics in this chapter? See the Quick Reference entries on pages xx–xxi.

There are no practice files for this chapter.

Understanding Windows XP Basics

Windows XP is a *computer operating* system. The operating system functions as your computer's brain; it tells your computer what to do and how to do it. An operating system is required by every computer in order to enable it to perform basic functions such as receiving input from the keyboard and mouse, sending output to the monitor, accessing files and programs, and controlling data storage devices and peripheral devices.

A Windows-based operating system, such as Windows XP, also acts as the interface between you and your computer. You tell your computer what to do by means of a graphical *user interface (UI)* that helps you work in an intuitive, visual way, such as choosing commands by clicking graphic representations. The Windows XP operating system provides an easy way for you to work with your computer without knowing anything about its inner workings.

The *operating system* interacts with *software programs* installed on your computer and enables your computer to communicate with other computers and peripheral devices such as printers, scanners, and modems. Windows XP includes several basic programs such as Calculator, Notepad, Outlook Express, Paint, WordPad, and a variety of games. Programs such as these are not part of the operating system and are not essential to the operation of your computer; instead, they build on the basic operating system functionality so you can perform more complex operations. You can purchase or download from the Internet other programs such as Microsoft Office Word, Microsoft Office Excel, and Adobe Acrobat Reader to add further functionality to your computer.

Windows XP is designed to be very reliable and has been visually redesigned to give you a personalized, task-focused computing experience. If you are accustomed to one of the previous Windows user interfaces, such as Microsoft Windows 98 or Windows 2000, you might at first be somewhat surprised by the changes, but the increased capabilities of Windows XP will quickly win you over.

So what exactly can you expect from your new operating system? First and foremost, you can expect a smooth way of carrying out common computer tasks and communicating with your programs. For those of you who are already somewhat familiar with other versions of Windows, here are the Windows XP features that both Professional and Home Edition users are most likely to take advantage of:

new for
WindowsXP

Updated user
interface

■   The operating system's updated look uses graphics to simplify moving around and completing common tasks.

■   Its task-focused design and dynamic menus display options specifically associated with the task or file you are working on.

Upgrading to Windows XP

Upgrading is the process of updating your computer's operating system files to a newer version, without disturbing other files, such as documents, spreadsheets, and data files, that are stored on your computer. You can upgrade your computer's operating system to Windows XP Home Edition from Windows 98 or Windows Me. You can upgrade to Windows XP Professional from Microsoft Windows NT Workstation or Windows 2000.

Upgrading to Windows XP should not affect your personal files and settings. However, it is always a good policy to back up important files before upgrading.

new for
WindowsXP

Fast User
Switching

■ The Fast User Switching feature makes it easy for multiple users to share a single stand-alone computer without interfering with each other's programs.

Important Fast User Switching is not available for computers logged on to a network domain.

new for
WindowsXP

Redesigned
Start menu

■ The redesigned **Start** menu can be customized by each user so that frequently used files, folders, and programs are grouped together for easy access.

■ The Welcome screen can be personalized and secured with a password for each person who has an account on the computer.

new for
WindowsXP

Search
Companion

■ The Search Companion feature identifies what kind of help you need and retrieves search information relevant to your current task.

■ The file management system makes it easy for you to arrange files according to your own needs, and includes optional *thumbnail* images for easy scanning of folder contents.

new for
WindowsXP

Album view
thumbnail
images and
photo
management

■ The My Music folder is a place where you can organize and view your music files, and create lists of songs (called *playlists*) to play.

■ The My Pictures folder is a specialized place where you can store and organize photos, view images as thumbnails or a slideshow, publish pictures to the Internet, compress photos so that they are easier to e-mail, order photo prints from the Internet, and optimize print settings to make the best use of high-quality photo paper.

■ The **Scanner and Camera Wizard** makes it easy to scan single or multiple images into one or more image files.

■ The **Web Publishing Wizard** takes you through the process of publishing pictures and other files to the Web so that you can share them with other people.

■ The **Network Setup Wizard** takes you through the key steps of setting up a network, including sharing files, printers, and devices; sharing an Internet connection; and configuring *Windows Firewall*, which protects your computer from intrusion when you are connected to the Internet.

■ Internet Connection Sharing makes it easy for multiple computers to share a single Internet connection.

■ Microsoft Internet Explorer 6, the Web browser that comes with most configurations of Windows XP, includes new and enhanced features that simplify your daily Internet tasks while helping you to maintain the privacy of your personal information on the Web. (You can choose to install a different browser if you want.)

new for
WindowsXP
Help and
Support Center

■ The Help and Support Center combines features such as Search, Index, and Favorites with up-to-the-minute online content, including help from other Windows XP users and online support professionals.

new for
WindowsXP
Remote
Assistance

■ The Remote Assistance feature enables you to share control of your desktop with another Windows XP user who can see your screen and control the keyboard and mouse from his or her computer.

new for
WindowsXP
Automatic
updates

■ The Windows Update Web site is where you can find Windows XP improvements, including new device drivers and security updates. With your permission, updates can be automatically *downloaded* in the background while you are connected to the Internet.

■ Application compatibility improvements enable many programs that don't run on Windows 2000 to run on Windows XP, and you can use the **Program Compatibility Wizard** to run an incompatible program as if it were in an earlier version of Windows.

■ The System Restore feature enables you to restore a Windows XP computer to a previous state without losing personal data or document files.

■ Windows Installer helps you install, configure, track, upgrade, and remove software programs correctly.

■ Multilingual support helps you easily create, read, and edit documents in many languages with the English version of Windows XP Professional.

■ The Windows XP environment adapts to the way you work, enabling you to easily find crucial information and programs.

■ Increased virus protection helps block the execution of e-mail attachments; your system administrator can remotely manage whether certain types of programs are allowed to run on your computer.

■ Troubleshooters available through the Help and Support Center help you or an administrator configure, optimize, and troubleshoot numerous Windows XP Professional functions.

■ ClearType triples the horizontal resolution available for text displayed on a computer screen, making it crisper and easier to read.

■ Up to 4 gigabytes (GB) of RAM and one or two processors can be installed in your computer.

■ Audio and video conferencing now include improved audio and video quality, reduced audio response time, and support for new cameras, synchronization of video and voice, and larger video sizes.

■ Hibernate mode saves the computer's memory to the *hard disk* when power is shut down so that when you restore power, all your applications are reopened exactly as you left them.

■ Peer-to-peer networking support facilitates interaction with computers running earlier versions of Windows. Networked computers can share resources such as folders, printers, and peripherals.

■ Most of the situations in which you had to restart your computer in Windows NT 4.0, Windows Me, Windows 98, and Microsoft Windows 95 have been eliminated.

Logging On to a Windows XP Domain-Connected Computer

Many computers running Windows XP Professional are connected to a *local area network (LAN)* and are configured as part of a *network domain*. Others might be connected to a *workgroup*, or they might be stand-alone computers. This section applies to the first kind of computer.

Tip The easiest way to check whether your Windows XP computer is connected to a network domain is to click the **Start** button: If your computer is not connected to a domain, a small picture appears to the left of the user name at the top of the **Start** menu.

The process of starting a computer session is called *logging on*. To log on to a network domain, you must have a valid *user account*, and you must know your *user account name* and *password*. You must also know the *domain name*. You can get all this information from your network administrator.

Tip Each user account is associated with a *user profile* that describes the way the computer environment looks and operates for that particular user. This information includes such things as the color scheme, desktop background, fonts, shortcuts, and what you can do on the computer.

When Windows XP is installed on a computer, an account is created with the *administrative privileges* required to control that particular computer. Someone—usually a *network administrator*—can use that account to create other accounts on the computer. These accounts are generally for specific people, and they might have more restricted privileges that prevent the account owners from changing some of the settings on the computer.

In this exercise, you will log on to a computer that has Windows XP Professional installed and is part of a network domain.

Activating Windows XP

When you upgrade your computer's operating system to Windows XP Professional or Windows XP Home Edition, or the first time you start a new computer on which Windows XP has been installed by the original equipment manufacturer (OEM), you are prompted to activate your copy of Windows XP.

new for
WindowsXP

Windows
Product
Activation

Windows Product Activation is a security measure instituted by Microsoft to help prevent the distribution and use of unlicensed (or pirated) versions of Windows. *Software piracy* is a multi-billion dollar industry that is harmful to software creators and software users for these reasons:

- Unlicensed software is ineligible for technical support or product upgrades.

- Abuse of software licenses can result in financial penalties and legal costs, as well as a bad reputation for you or for your company. Individual company executives can be held criminally and civilly liable for copyright infringements within their organization.

- Pirated software can contain harmful viruses with the potential to damage individual computers or entire networks.

- The counterfeit software manufacturing industry stifles the potential growth of the high tech industry and contributes to loss of tax revenue.

For more information on software piracy, see *www.microsoft.com/piracy/*.

The goal of Windows Product Activation is to reduce a form of software piracy known as *casual copying* or *softlifting*, which is when people share software in a way that infringes on the software's *end user license agreement*. Each copy of Windows XP must be activated within 30 days of the first use. You can activate Windows XP over the Internet or by telephone. You don't have to give any personal information about yourself or your computer, although you are given the option of registering to receive information about product updates, new products, events, and special offers.

BE SURE TO know your user account name, your password, and your domain name before beginning this exercise.

Important   This exercise assumes that your computer is physically connected to a network and logging on to a domain, rather than dialing in or connecting over the Internet.

Follow these steps:

1   Start your computer.

After the computer starts, or *boots*, a **Welcome to Windows** screen appears.

2   Hold down both the **CTRL** and **ALT** keys, and press **DELETE**.

Windows XP displays a *dialog box* and waits for you to give it the information it needs to proceed. Dialog boxes are the main means of communication between the computer and the computer user in Windows and in Windows- based programs. Each dialog box presents all the possible options associated with an action, and you set the options to indicate how you want the action carried out.

In this case, the **Log On to Windows** dialog box appears.

Important   When you press **CTRL**+**ALT**+**DELETE**, Windows temporarily halts any other programs that are running on your computer. This precaution ensures that your password remains secure because it prevents programs called *Trojan horses*, which might have been planted on your system by *hackers*, from capturing your user account name and password. The requirement to press **CTRL**+**ALT**+**DELETE** is turned on by default. A user with administrative privileges can change this requirement, but making this change is definitely not recommended.

3   Enter your user account name in the **User name** box.

4   Enter your password in the **Password** box.

5   If the **Log on to** box is not shown, click **Options** to expand the dialog box. Then click the down arrow to the right of the **Log on to** box, and click the correct domain name in the drop-down list.

Troubleshooting   If your domain is not available in the drop-down list, contact your network administrator.

6   Click **OK** to log on to Windows XP Professional and your network domain.

The Windows XP Professional desktop appears. If you are logging on to Windows XP for the first time, the **Start** menu opens automatically.

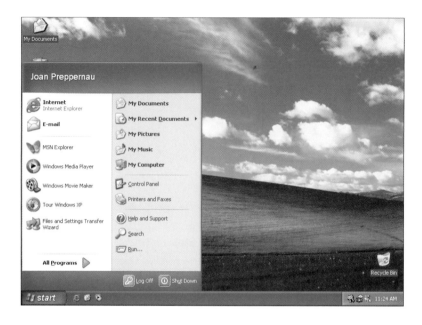

Using Your Mouse

For new computer users who are not familiar with the standard Windows mouse actions, we'll briefly summarize them here:

- *Clicking* an object involves moving the mouse pointer over it and quickly pressing and releasing the primary mouse button once. (By default, the primary mouse button is the left one.)

- *Double-clicking* an object involves moving the mouse pointer over it and pressing and releasing the primary mouse button twice in rapid succession.

- *Right-clicking* an object involves moving the mouse pointer over it and clicking the secondary mouse button once. This displays the object's *shortcut menu*, which is a set of actions that can be performed with the object you right-clicked. Specify the action you want by clicking it on the shortcut menu.

- *Dragging* an object involves moving the mouse pointer over it, holding down the primary mouse button, moving the mouse until the pointer is in the location where you want the object to appear, and releasing the mouse button. You can also drag to select multiple objects from a list.

If you prefer to click, double-click, and drag with the right mouse button, you can switch the buttons by adjusting the **Mouse** settings in Control Panel. (You can access Control Panel by clicking the **Start** button and then clicking **Control Panel** on the **Start** menu.)

Important Don't worry if your Windows XP desktop looks different from the ones shown in this and subsequent chapters. The desktop varies depending on whether Windows XP is installed on a brand new computer or as an upgrade on a computer that has been running a previous version of the Windows operating system. In the latter case, Windows XP will retain many aspects of the previous desktop. Windows XP might also carry over some of the settings made in a previous version, which can alter the look of the screen slightly. These differences affect the way Windows XP looks but do not affect your ability to successfully complete the exercises in this book. If you prefer to have the desktop icons that appeared in previous versions of Windows available, you can right-click the desktop, and click **Properties** on the shortcut menu. Then in the **Display Properties** dialog box, click the **Desktop** tab, click **Customize Desktop**, select the check boxes of the icons you want, and click **OK**.

Logging On to a Windows XP Standalone or Workgroup-Connected Computer

Your computer might be used by only you, or it might be used by several people. If only you use your computer, it needs only one configuration, or *user account*. If other people use your computer, everyone can use the same account, or you can set up a separate user account for each person. Each account is associated with a *user profile* that describes the way the computer environment looks and operates for that particular user. This information includes such things as the color scheme, desktop background, fonts, and shortcuts, and it can vary from profile to profile. Individual user profiles link to individual My Documents folders to restrict other people from accessing your private files.

The process of starting a computer session is called *logging on*. When you start the computer, Windows XP prompts you to select your user profile and, if your account has been password-protected, to enter your password.

Tip By default, Windows XP Home Edition creates a special account called *Guest*. Users who do not have their own accounts can log on to the computer using the Guest account. The Guest account can be disabled if you don't want to allow people without accounts to log on to your computer.

Each user has a *user account name* and a *user account picture*. Each user can change his or her account name and account picture; users with administrative privileges can change any user's account name and picture.

In this exercise, you will log on to a standalone computer that has Windows XP Home Edition installed and that has been configured to include multiple accounts (with or without passwords).

BE SURE TO know your user account name and password before beginning this exercise.

Follow these steps:

1 Start your computer.

After the computer boots, a logon screen appears.

The logon screen displayed by Windows XP Home Edition is called the Welcome screen. This screen displays graphic representations of all the user accounts on the computer. These accounts can be created during setup or later to keep each user's data separate.

new for
WindowsXP

Welcome
screen

2 Move the mouse pointer over the available user names.

Notice that the selected user name is bright, whereas the other user names are dimmed.

3 Click your user account name or user account picture.

4 If your account is password-protected, enter your password in the **Type your password** box, and then click the arrow button to continue.

Tip If you forget your password, click the question mark button to see any password hint that was specified when your password was set.

5 While Windows XP is loading your profile, your user account name and user account picture move to the center of the screen, and the other options disappear. When you are logged on to your account, the Windows XP Home Edition desktop appears. If you are logging on to Windows XP for the first time, the **Start** menu open automatically:

Logging On to a Windows XP Domain-Configured Computer While Offline

Windows XP Professional is generally used in a networked environment, but you do not have to be connected to a network domain to run it. For example, you might have Windows XP Professional installed on a laptop computer that you use both at the office and at home; or you might travel with your Windows XP Professional computer, *work offline*, and connect to your network over a remote connection.

When you log on to a Windows XP Professional computer that is not currently connected to a network domain, you log on in the ordinary manner, and your user information is validated against information that was stored on the computer the last time you logged on to the domain. If your Windows XP Professional computer is not currently configured to work on a network, the process of logging on is identical to that of Windows XP Home Edition. Valid user accounts are displayed on a central logon screen, and the Fast User Switching option is available and turned on by default.

Updating and Safeguarding Your Computer System

If your computer is running Windows XP Professional or Home Edition without Service Pack 2 (SP2), it is a good idea to install the service pack to ensure that you have the latest functionality and security updates. Depending on when and where you purchased your computer, Services Pack 1 or 2 might already be installed as part of the Windows XP operating system.

See Also   For information about Windows XP service packs, refer to "What's New in Microsoft Windows XP" at the beginning of this book.

Although it is not mandatory to install service packs, it is a very good idea to do so. Each service pack includes all the security updates released to date, as well as fixes for any problems discovered since the software was released.

In this exercise, you will check to see whether your computer is running Windows XP SP2, and install the service pack and any other necessary updates.

Important   The graphics shown in the rest of this book assume that SP2 is installed on your computer. If you choose not to install the service pack, you might notice slight variations between the graphics shown in this book and what you see on your computer screen.

BE SURE TO log on to Windows and establish an active Internet connection before beginning this exercise.

Follow these steps:

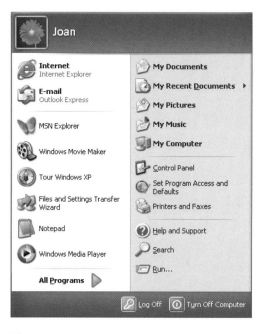

1 If the **Start** menu is not displayed, click the **Start** button.

The **Start** menu opens. Your user information appears at the top of the menu. Depending on the programs installed on your computer, the **Start** menu looks something like this:

Tip Windows XP Home Edition displays the user account name and user account picture at the top of the **Start** menu. Windows XP Professional displays only the user name.

2 On the **Start** menu, click **Control Panel**.

Control Panel opens:

3   At the top of the window, on the **Help** menu, click **About Windows**.

The **About Windows** message box appears, looking something like this:

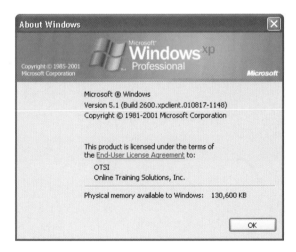

The **Help** menu and **About Windows** message box can be accessed from any Windows system window. Similar options are available from within all Windows-based applications such as Word, Excel, and other Microsoft Office applications.

The second line of text in the lower section of the message box displays the version and build numbers of your Windows XP installation. If the build number contains the phrase *Service Pack 2*, you already have SP2 installed. If the build number contains the phrase Service Pack 1, you have SP1 installed. If the build number doesn't include a service pack version, neither service pack is installed on your computer.

If the build number doesn't include neither, service pack is installed on your computer.

4   Click **OK** to close the **About Windows** message box, and then click **Windows Update** on the **See Also** menu in Control Panel.

The Windows Update Web site opens in your default Internet browser. The Web site changes from time to time and might look slightly different from that shown here:

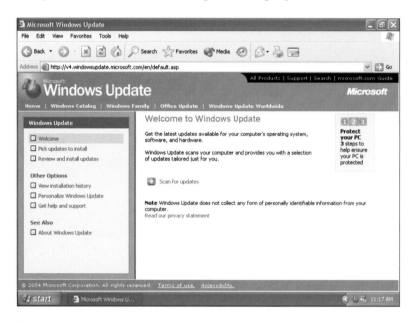

Important   The first time you access the Windows Update Web site, you might be prompted to install a special Windows Update control, or to choose from Express Install and Custom Install options.

5   If the site looks as shown, click **Scan for updates**; otherwise, click **Custom Install** to check your computer for available updates that haven't yet been installed and review the updates before installing them.

Depending on the version of Windows Update, updates are classified as Critical Updates and Service Packs, Windows XP, and Driver Updates; or as high-priority updates, optional software updates, and optional hardware updates. Service packs and security-related updates are automatically selected for installation. You can select updates from other categories if you want.

Important You must be logged on to your computer as an administrator or a member of the Administrators group to install updates from the Windows Update Web site.

See Also For more information about computer administrators, refer to Chapter 3, "Managing Computer Security."

---

6 Review the available updates, select any optional updates that you want to install, and then follow the procedure indicated on the Web site to install SP2 and any other important updates that are available.

7 When the installation completes, restart your computer if instructed to do so, or close any open dialog boxes and the Windows Update Web site.

See Also For more information about Windows Update, refer to "Keeping Your Computer Up to Date" in Chapter 10, "Solving Problems."

Logging Off of Windows XP

The process of ending a computer session is called *logging off*. Logging off ends the Windows session for your account but leaves the computer turned on. It is important to log off when you leave for the day, or even when you leave your computer for an extended period of time, to safeguard against other people accessing your personal information. For example, if your account has administrative privileges and you go out to lunch without logging off or otherwise protecting your computer against intrusion, someone could create a local user account with administrative privileges for themselves and later use that account to log on to your computer.

In this exercise, you will log off of your Windows XP user account. Both Windows XP Professional and Windows XP Home Edition users can complete this exercise.

BE SURE TO log on to Windows before beginning this exercise.

Follow these steps:

1 Click the **Start** button.

The **Start** menu opens. Your user information appears at the top of the menu.

2 At the bottom of the **Start** menu, click **Log Off**.

The **Log Off Windows** dialog box appears.

Tip When your current Windows XP configuration includes Fast User Switching, that option is shown in the **Log Off Windows** dialog box.

3 Click **Log Off** to complete the process and display the Welcome screen or logon screen.

Tip If bubble notes appear above the notification area while you are working, read them, and then click the **Close** button in the bubble's upper-right corner.

Shutting Down a Windows XP Domain-Connected Computer

Rather than simply logging off of your computer, you might want to *shut down* and turn off the computer to conserve energy. Shutting down closes all your open applications and files, ends your computing session, and shuts down Windows so that you can safely turn off the computer's power. This process ensures that your data is safely stored and any external connections are appropriately disconnected. The process of shutting down a Windows XP computer varies slightly depending on whether your computer is connected to a network domain or to a workgroup.

Important Always shut down Windows XP before turning off your computer; otherwise, you could lose data.

In this exercise, you will shut down your Windows XP domain-connected computer.

BE SURE TO log on to Windows before beginning this exercise.

Follow these steps:

1 Click the **Start** button.

2 At the bottom of the **Start** menu, click **Shut Down**.

The **Shut Down Windows** dialog box appears:

The most recently selected shut-down option is displayed in the option box, and a description of that option appears below the box.

3   Click the down arrow to display the other options, and select each option in turn to display its description.

4   Select **Shut down** as the option, and click **OK** to end your Windows session.

Shutting Down a Windows XP Workgroup-Connected Computer

Rather than simply logging off of your computer, you might want to *shut down* and *turn off* the computer to conserve energy. Shutting down closes all your open applications and files, ends your computing session, and quits Windows so you can safely turn off the computer's power. This process ensures that your data is safely stored and all your external sessions are appropriately disconnected. The process of shutting down a Windows XP computer varies slightly depending on whether your computer is connected to a network domain or to a workgroup.

Important   Always shut down Windows XP before turning off your computer; otherwise, you could lose data.

In this exercise, you will turn off your Windows XP workgroup-connected computer.

BE SURE TO log on to Windows before beginning this exercise.

Follow these steps:

1   Click the **Start** button.

2   At the bottom of the **Start** menu, click **Turn Off Computer**.

Tip   The **Turn Off Computer** command is also available on the Welcome screen.

This **Turn off computer** dialog box appears:

Tip When connected to a workgroup rather than a domain, the Windows XP Professional **Turn off computer** dialog box displays the **Standby**, **Turn off**, and **Restart** options. Press the **SHIFT** key to display the **Hibernate** option.

3 Click **Turn Off** to end your Windows session and turn off your computer.

Other Shut Down Options

In addition to logging off and shutting down your computer, the Windows XP **Shut Down** or **Turn off computer** dialog box presents some or all of these options (depending on your installation):

- *Hibernate* **saves** your session and turns off your computer. The next time you start the computer, your session is restored to the place where you left off.

- *Restart* ends your session, shuts down Windows, and then starts Windows again without turning off the computer.

- *Stand by* maintains your session (the programs that are open and any work you are doing in them) and keeps the computer running on low power with your data still in the memory. To return to a session that is on standby, press **CTRL+ALT+DELETE**.

Key Points

■ The Windows XP operating system offers a number of new features designed to simplify your computing experience.

■ There are some small differences between working with Windows XP Professional and working with Windows XP Home Edition.

■ It is important to keep your computer up to date with the most current service packs and updates. Windows Update makes it easy to do this.

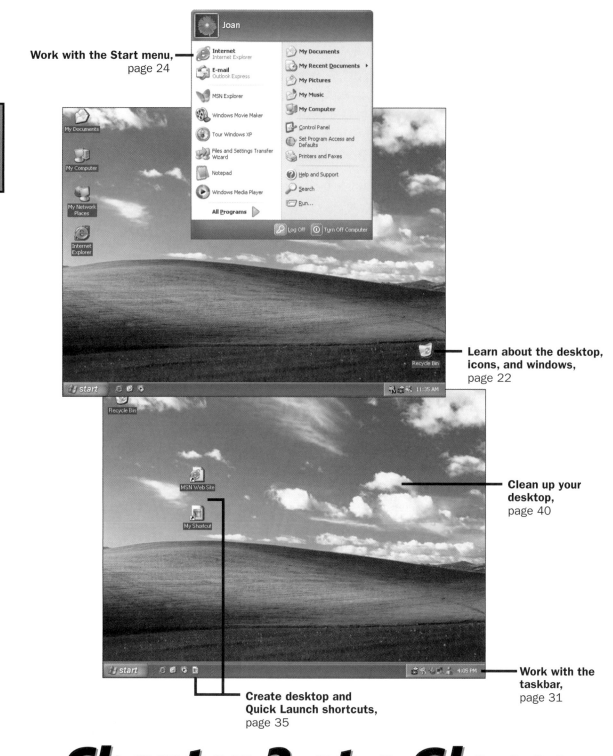

Work with the Start menu, page 24

Learn about the desktop, icons, and windows, page 22

Clean up your desktop, page 40

Work with the taskbar, page 31

Create desktop and Quick Launch shortcuts, page 35

Chapter 2 at a Glance

2 Working Efficiently in Windows XP

In this chapter you will learn to:

✔   Work comfortably on the Windows XP desktop.

✔   Work with the Start menu and taskbar.

✔   Create and arrange shortcuts on the desktop and Quick Launch toolbar.

✔   Clean up your desktop.

Working in the Microsoft Windows environment is a lot like working in a real-world office environment. You have a *desktop* where all your work tools are displayed, and you have *folders* in which to organize all your *files*. Windows incorporates all these elements into its *user interface*, which is the means by which you and your computer communicate with each other.

Windows XP presents its tools, commands, and structure through a graphical user interface. Each type of file is represented by a picture and description, and each command is represented by a button. Programs are arranged on a series of menus to make it easy to locate them.

In this chapter, you will explore some of the elements of the Windows user interface and the various ways in which you can look at the information on your computer. You will then see how to tailor some of these elements to suit the way you work.

See Also   Do you need only a quick refresher on the topics in this chapter? See the Quick Reference entries on pages xxi–xxiii.

 Important   Before you can use the practice files in this chapter, you need to install them from the book's companion CD to their default location. See "Using the Book's CD-ROM" on page xv for more information.

Getting to Know the Windows Desktop

When you start Windows XP, your computer screen looks something like this:

Desktop

Icon

Quick launch toolbar — Taskbar — Notification area —

The most basic element of the Windows user interface is a background screen called the desktop. All your other programs are opened over this background screen. The *taskbar* at the bottom of the screen displays information about what's going on with your computer. You can also use it to easily open and close programs.

You might have one or more *icons* visible on your desktop, depending on how the programs that are installed on your computer are set up, and on your Windows XP settings. Icons are graphic representations of programs. When an icon appears on the desktop, you can double-click it to start the associated program.

Below the icon is the name of the element it represents. If the name is too long, it is truncated by an ellipsis (...) when it is not selected, and displayed in full when you click it. Positioning the mouse pointer over an icon usually displays a box, called a *ScreenTip*, containing a few words that tell you something about the program.

Some icons are placed on the Windows desktop when you install the programs they represent. If the icon has an arrow overlaid on its lower left corner, it is a *shortcut*. Shortcuts are links to items that are stored in another location. If you delete a shortcut, you aren't actually deleting the file, folder, or program to which it points. Many programs create shortcuts when you install them. You can also create your own shortcuts to programs; to specific files, folders, or network locations; or to Web sites. Windows XP assigns graphics to each shortcut based on the type of element it represents, so you can easily locate the one you are looking for.

One of the icons on the desktop is the *Recycle Bin*, which is where Windows temporarily stores files you have deleted. It is also the place where you manage deleted files. You can recover deleted files from the Recycle Bin, or you can empty the Recycle Bin and permanently delete the files to free up space on your hard disk.

When you purchase a new computer, the *original equipment manufacturer (OEM)* might have installed programs and created icons and shortcuts for you. If you upgrade to Windows XP from a previous version of Windows, your existing icons and shortcuts will still be available.

In this exercise, you will open, resize, and close the Recycle Bin.

BE SURE TO log on to Windows before beginning this exercise.

Follow these steps:

1   On the Windows desktop, double-click the **Recycle Bin** icon.

The Recycle Bin opens in a *window*, something like this:

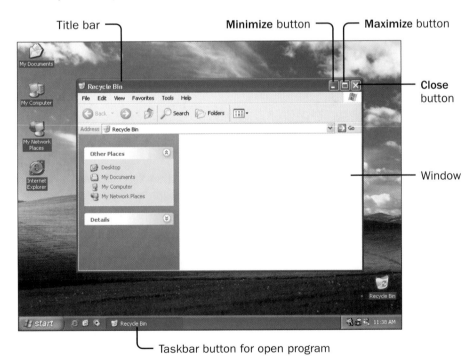

The program's title appears on the *title bar* at the top of the window. If the content of the window is too large to fit in the window, a *scroll bar* is displayed down the right side and/or across the bottom of the window. A button representing the program is displayed on the taskbar to indicate that it is open.

Minimize

2 Click the **Minimize** button near the right end of the title bar.

The window is minimized so that it is no longer visible on the desktop. The program is still running and is represented by a button on the taskbar.

3 Click the Recycle Bin's taskbar button to redisplay the window.

4 Click the **Maximize** button.

Maximize

The window expands to fill your entire screen.

5 Click the **Restore Down** button.

Restore Down

The window returns to its original size. The **Restore Down** button is available only when the window is maximized.

Tip   You can manually resize a window by positioning the mouse pointer over the window's frame and, when the pointer changes to a double-headed arrow, dragging the frame to make the window smaller or larger. You cannot manually resize maximized windows; you must first restore the window to its non-maximized state.

Close

6 Click the **Close** button.

Closing the window closes the program and removes the corresponding button from the taskbar.

Working with the Start Menu

The *Start menu* is a list of options that is your central link to all the programs installed on your computer, as well as to all the tasks you can carry out with Windows XP. The first time you start Windows XP, the **Start** menu is displayed until you click something else. Thereafter, you open the **Start** menu by clicking the **Start** button at the left end of the taskbar.

The **Start** menu has been significantly redesigned in Windows XP so you can more easily access your programs. When it first opens, it looks something like this:

Current user —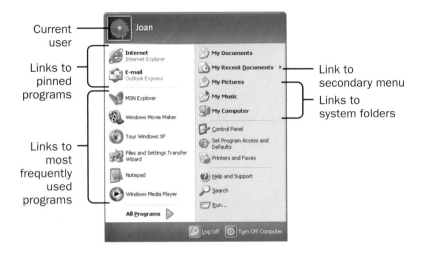

Links to pinned programs

Links to most frequently used programs

Link to secondary menu

Links to system folders

Tip   If you are accustomed to the previous menu style, which is now called the *Classic* menu, you might find that the change takes a little getting used to. If you are unable to adjust, you have the option of changing back to the Classic version. However, the new menu is designed to increase efficiency, so we recommend that you at least give it a try!

new for
WindowsXP

Pinning programs

You can pin links to your favorite programs to a special area at the upper left side of the Start menu to make the programs easy to find and start. You can rearrange the pinned programs by dragging them into whatever order you want. By default, Microsoft Internet Explorer and Microsoft Outlook Express are pinned to the *Start* menu. If you change your default Web browser or e-mail program, the pinned programs area is updated to reflect that change.

Tip   If your computer came pre-installed with Windows XP SP1 or Windows XP SP2, the OEM might have stipulated alternate default programs.

See Also   For more information about Windows XP service packs, refer to "What's New in Microsoft Windows XP" at the beginning of this book, and "Changing Your Default Middleware Applications" in Chapter 4, "Working with Hardware, Software, and Middleware."

Below the first horizontal line on the left side of the **Start** menu is a list of links to your most frequently used programs, which by default includes the last six programs you started. (You can adjust that number if you want.) The first time you start Windows XP, the list displays some of the new programs that are available, such as MSN Explorer, Windows Media Player, Windows Movie Maker, **File and Settings Transfer Wizard**, and Tour Windows XP. (The tour is somewhat long and sales-oriented, but it does introduce you to new features of Windows XP that you will work with in this book.)

On the right side of the **Start** menu are links to the locations where you are most likely to store the files you create, a link to a directory of other computers on your network, and links to various tools that you will use while running your computer. If you are running Windows XP SP1 or Windows XP SP2, you also see a **Set Program Access and Defaults** shortcut, which connects you to that page of the Add or Remove Programs window. The commands you will use to log off of or shut down your computer are located at the bottom of the **Start** menu.

In this exercise, you will first clear the list of most frequently used programs links from the **Start** menu. Then you will pin links to two programs to the top of the menu, rearrange them, and remove them from the pinned programs area.

BE SURE TO log on to Windows before beginning this exercise.

Follow these steps:

1   Close any open windows so that no buttons appear on the taskbar.

2   Click the **Start** button to open the **Start** menu, and note which programs currently appear in the most frequently used programs list.

> **Tip**   If your most frequently used programs list is empty, you can still follow along with this exercise so that you will know how to clear the list later.

3   Right-click the blue stripe at the bottom of the **Start** menu, and click **Properties** on the shortcut menu.

The **Taskbar and Start Menu Properties** dialog box appears, like this:

This is where you have the option to change to the Classic **Start** menu.

4   Make sure that the **Start menu** option is selected, and then click **Customize**.

The **Customize Start Menu** dialog box appears. The default settings are shown here:

5   Click the **Clear List** button to clear the list of most frequently used programs.

6   Click the **Advanced** tab to display the advanced **Start** menu options:

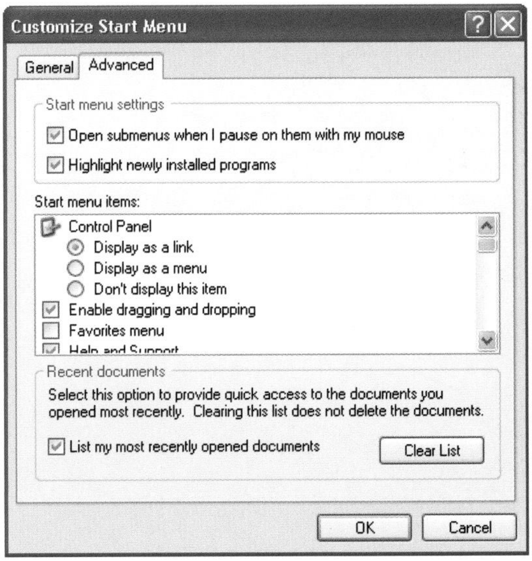

27

7 Scroll through the list of options to see what is available, but don't change any of the default settings at this time.

8 Click **Cancel** to close the **Customize Start Menu** dialog box without making any changes, and then click **OK** to close the **Taskbar and Start Menu Properties** dialog box.

9 Click the **Start** button to open the **Start** menu.

The most frequently used programs list has been cleared.

10 Point to **All Programs**.

The **All Programs** menu expands with your currently installed programs listed, something like this:

> Installed with
> Service Pack 1 or 2.

> Recently installed
> programs are highlighted.

As with other types of menus in Windows XP, the right-pointing arrows indicate that clicking the menu entry, or simply hovering the mouse pointer over it for a few seconds, will open a secondary menu.

11 On the **All Programs** menu, point to **Accessories**.

The secondary **Accessories** menu expands. All the programs on this menu come with Windows XP:

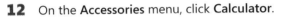

12 On the **Accessories** menu, click **Calculator**.

The menus close, Calculator opens, and a **Calculator** button appears on the taskbar.

13 Click the **Start** button to open the **Start** menu.

Calculator now appears in the most frequently used programs list, like this:

14 Now you'll pin a program to the **Start** menu. Point to **All Programs**, and then point to **Games**.

See Also For more information about playing games on your Windows XP computer, refer to Chapter 9, "Having Fun with Windows XP."

Tip   You can pin programs to the **Start** menu from the **All Programs** menu or from the most frequently used programs list.

The secondary **Games** menu expands:

🎮 FreeCell
♥ Hearts
🎲 Internet Backgammon
⚪ Internet Checkers
💗 Internet Hearts
🔴 Internet Reversi
♠ Internet Spades
💣 Minesweeper
⚫ Pinball
🃏 Solitaire
🕷 Spider Solitaire

All the games on this menu come with Windows XP.

15   On the **Games** menu, right-click **FreeCell**, and click **Pin to Start menu** on the shortcut menu. Then click a blank area of the **Start** menu to close the **Games** and **All Programs** menus.

FreeCell is added to the pinned programs area of the **Start** menu:

FreeCell has been pinned to the **Start** menu for easy access.

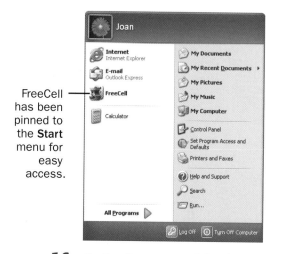

16   On the **Start** menu, right-click **Calculator**, and click **Pin to Start menu** on the shortcut menu.

Calculator is moved from the most frequently used programs area to the pinned programs area.

Tip   When the most frequently used programs list is empty, the horizontal line separating it from the pinned programs area disappears.

17 Drag the Calculator link to the top of the pinned programs list.

While you are dragging the link, a thick black line indicates where it will appear if you release the mouse button.

18 Drag the FreeCell link above the Calculator link.

19 Right-click the Calculator link, and click **Unpin from Start menu** on the shortcut menu.

The Calculator link is moved from the pinned programs area back to the most frequently used programs area. You could have clicked **Remove from This List** to remove it entirely.

20 Right-click the FreeCell link, and click **Unpin from Start menu** on the shortcut menu.

The FreeCell link disappears from the pinned programs area and (because it was never on the most frequently used programs list) from the **Start** menu.

21 Click away from the **Start** menu to close it.

22 On Calculator's title bar, click the **Close** button.

Calculator closes, and its button disappears from the taskbar.

Close

Using the Taskbar

The *taskbar* is your link to current information about what is happening on your Windows XP computer. In addition to the **Start** button, the taskbar displays a button for each open program. You click a taskbar button to activate the window of the program it represents. The taskbar buttons are resized depending on the number of programs that are currently open, and they disappear when you close the programs they represent.

Tip The taskbar does not display buttons for open dialog boxes, message boxes, or warnings.

new for
WindowsXP

Grouped
taskbar
buttons

If you start the same program more than once so that several instances of the program are open at the same time (for example, three instances of Internet Explorer, or two Microsoft Office Word documents), and the taskbar is becoming crowded, similar windows are grouped onto one button that is labeled with the name of the program. A number following the *program icon* on the button indicates the number of open windows represented by the button. You can click the button to display a pop-up list of the open windows and then click the one you want to activate. This new feature makes it easier to work with your open windows.

Tip When multiple windows are grouped on a taskbar button, you can close all the windows in the group by right-clicking the button and clicking **Close Group** on the shortcut menu.

By default, the taskbar displays one row of buttons and is *docked* at the bottom of the desktop, but you can control its size and position:

- You can dock the taskbar at the top, bottom, or on either side of the desktop.

- When the taskbar is docked at the top or bottom, you can expand the taskbar to be up to half the height of your screen by dragging its border up or down.

- When the taskbar is docked on the left or right, you can adjust its width from nothing (only the border is visible) to up to half the width of your screen.

- You can stipulate that the taskbar should be hidden when you're not using it, or that it should always stay on top of other windows so that it is not accidentally hidden.

- You can lock the taskbar to prevent it from being changed.

Troubleshooting   You cannot move or change the taskbar while it is locked. To lock or unlock the taskbar, right-click an empty area of the taskbar, and click **Lock the Taskbar** on the shortcut menu. A check mark indicates when this option is selected.

Windows XP taskbar buttons change size so that they fit on the taskbar as programs are opened and closed. The maximum number of buttons that can fit on the taskbar varies based on your monitor and display settings. When you exceed the maximum, Windows either tiles the buttons or displays a scroll bar, depending on the current taskbar configuration.

The *notification area* is located at the right end of the horizontal taskbar or at the bottom of the vertical taskbar. By default, the notification area displays the current time. Icons appear temporarily in the notification area when activities such as the following take place:

- The printer icon appears when you send a document to the printer.

- A message icon appears when you receive new e-mail messages.

- The Windows Automatic Update icon appears to remind you to look online for updates to the operating system.

- Information icons appear to give you information about various program features.

- Network connections and Microsoft Windows Messenger icons appear when those features are in use. (Inactive connections are indicated by the presence of a red X on the icon.)

In addition to the items that are visible by default, the taskbar can also display its own set of toolbars. The most frequently used of these is the *Quick Launch toolbar*, which displays single-click links to programs and commands. (This toolbar is hidden by default.)

Tip   The Quick Launch toolbar might be hidden or visible, depending on your taskbar settings.

Windows XP installs links to Internet Explorer, Microsoft Windows Media Player, and the Show Desktop command on the Quick Launch toolbar. You can add more program shortcuts to the Quick Launch toolbar at any time by dragging a program or shortcut icon onto it.

In this exercise, you will open several windows and use the taskbar to move among them.

BE SURE TO log on to Windows before beginning this exercise.

Follow these steps:

1   Close any open windows so that no taskbar buttons appear on the taskbar.

> **Tip**   To close an open window, click the Close button at the right end of its title bar, or right-click its taskbar button, and then click Close. You are prompted to save changes to documents before they close.

2   Click the **Start** button to open the **Start** menu.

3   On the **Start** menu, click **My Documents**.

The My Documents folder opens, and a button appears on the taskbar. The button label is preceded by a folder icon to indicate that the button represents a folder.

Minimize

4   Click the **Minimize** button to hide the folder's window under its taskbar button.

5   On the **Start** menu, click **My Pictures**.

The My Pictures folder opens in a new window, and another button appears on the taskbar. The button label is preceded by a folder icon to indicate the type of window it represents.

6   On the **Start** menu, click **My Music**.

The My Music folder opens in a new window, and a button appears on the taskbar. The button label is again preceded by a folder icon.

You now have three open folder windows, each represented by a taskbar button. The taskbar looks something like this:

The active window's taskbar button ─┘
is indicated by a darker color.

7   On the **Start** menu, click **Calculator**.

Calculator opens, and the **Calculator** button appears on the taskbar.

> **Tip** If your taskbar is getting full, the existing buttons are resized so that there is room for the new button.

8 On the taskbar, click the **My Pictures** button to make the window for the My Pictures folder active.

The My Pictures window comes to the top of the stack of open windows. On the taskbar, the **My Pictures** button is active instead of the **Calculator** button.

9 If the Quick Launch toolbar is not currently visible, right-click an empty area of the taskbar, point to **Toolbars** on the shortcut menu, and then click **Quick Launch**.

Show Desktop

10 On the Quick Launch toolbar, click the **Show Desktop** button.

All open windows are minimized.

11 On the desktop, double-click the **Recycle Bin** icon.

The Recycle Bin folder opens in a new window. There is not enough room to add the **Recycle Bin** button to the taskbar, so the four folder windows are grouped onto one button. The taskbar now looks like this:

This button's label indicates that it represents four Windows Explorer folder windows.

12 Click the **Windows Explorer** button to display a pop-up list of the windows represented by the button:

```
Recycle Bin
My Music
My Pictures
My Documents
```

13 Click **My Music** in the window list.

The My Music window appears, and the list closes.

14 Right-click the **Windows Explorer** button, and then click **Close Group** on the shortcut menu.

All four folder windows close, and the **Windows Explorer** button disappears. Calculator is now the only open program.

15 Click the **Calculator** button to display Calculator, and then click its **Close** button.

Calculator closes, and the last taskbar button disappears.

Close

Creating Shortcuts

Shortcuts are icons on your desktop or the Quick Launch toolbar that are linked to files, folders, and programs in other locations. Many programs give you the option of creating one or more shortcuts during installation, or in some cases, they create the shortcuts without asking. You can also create your own shortcuts, and you can delete any shortcut.

Important   Deleting a shortcut does not delete the program or file that the shortcut is linked to.

In this exercise, you will create a desktop shortcut for an existing program, a desktop shortcut for a Web site, and a Quick Launch shortcut.

BE SURE TO log on to Windows before beginning this exercise.
USE the Sunset image in the *My Documents\Microsoft Press\Microsoft Windows XP SBS\Working \Shortcuts* folder.

Follow these steps:

Show Desktop

1   On the Quick Launch toolbar at the left end of the taskbar, click the **Show Desktop** button to minimize any open windows.

Tip   If the Quick Launch toolbar is not displayed on the taskbar, right-click an empty area of the taskbar, point to **Toolbars** on the shortcut menu, and then click **Quick Launch**.

2   Right-click an open area of the desktop.

3   On the shortcut menu, point to **New**, and then click **Shortcut**.

The first page of the **Create Shortcut Wizard** appears:

> **Create Shortcut** ⊠
>
> This wizard helps you to create shortcuts to local or network programs, files, folders, computers, or Internet addresses.
>
> Type the location of the item:
>
> [   ] [Browse...]
>
> Click Next to continue.
>
> [< Back] [Next >] [Cancel]

Tip   *Wizards* are series of pages, similar to dialog boxes, that walk you through the steps necessary to accomplish a particular task. In this case, the wizard will prompt you for the information Windows needs to create a shortcut.

35

4 Click **Browse** to open the **Browse For Folder** dialog box:

You use this dialog box to tell the wizard which file or folder you want the shortcut to link to (its target), and where the file or folder is located.

5 Click **My Documents**, then **Microsoft Press**, then **Microsoft Windows XP SBS**, then **Working**, and finally **Shortcuts**. Then click the **Sunset** file, and click **OK** to close the dialog box and return to the wizard.

The location, called the path, of the selected file is entered in the **Type the location of the item** box.

6 Click **Next** to move to the **Select a Title for the Program** page:

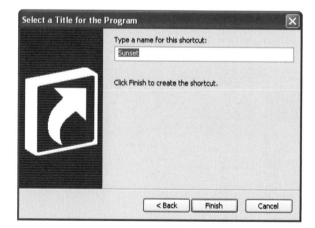

Using information saved with the selected file, the wizard has suggested a name for the shortcut.

7 With the current name selected, type **My Shortcut**.

8 Click **Finish** to create the shortcut and close the wizard.

A shortcut is created on the desktop in approximately the place you originally right-clicked. The shortcut is named *My Shortcut*. It is represented by a graphic icon with an arrow in the lower-left corner.

9   Double-click **My Shortcut** to open the Sunset photo that the shortcut links to.

The photo opens in the Windows Picture and Fax Viewer, a photo viewer that comes with Windows XP.

Close

10   Click the photo window's **Close** button to close the window.

11   Right-click **My Shortcut**, and click **Properties** on the shortcut menu.

The **My Shortcut Properties** dialog box appears.

12   Click the **General** tab, and look at the information and available options.

13   Return to the **Shortcut** tab, and click the **Change Icon** button.

This **Change Icon** dialog box appears:

14   Scroll through the list to see all the available icons.

15   Click your favorite icon and then click **OK** to change the icon and close the **Change Icon** dialog box, or click **Cancel** to keep the current icon.

16   Click **OK** to close the **My Shortcut Properties** dialog box and apply your change.

The shortcut's icon changes if you selected a new one.

17   Now you'll create a shortcut for a Web site. Right-click an open area of the desktop, point to **New** on the shortcut menu, and then click **Shortcut**.

The **Create Shortcut Wizard** appears.

18   In the **Type the location of the item** box, type http://www.msn.com.

19 Click **Next** to move to the **Select a Title for the Program** page.

The suggested shortcut name is *New Internet Shortcut*.

20 With the current name selected, type MSN Web Site.

21 Click **Finish** to close the dialog box and create another shortcut.

22 If you are connected to the Internet, double-click the new **MSN Web Site** shortcut to open the MSN Web site in your default Web browser.

23 Click the Web site window's **Close** button to close the window.

24 Right-click **My Shortcut**, and drag it to the left of the Quick Launch toolbar.

A thick black line behind the shortcut indicates where it will appear when you release the mouse button.

25 Release the right mouse button when the shortcut is in position on the Quick Launch toolbar, and then click **Copy Here** on the shortcut menu.

A copy of the shortcut appears on the Quick Launch toolbar. Double chevrons appear at the right end of the toolbar to indicate that more shortcuts are available than can fit on the toolbar.

26 Position the mouse pointer over the new toolbar shortcut.

A ScreenTip displays the shortcut's name.

27 Click the chevrons to view the other available Quick Launch shortcuts.

28 Right-click the taskbar. If **Lock the Taskbar** is checked on the shortcut menu, click it to unlock the taskbar. If **Lock the Taskbar** is not checked, click away from the short-cut menu to close it.

When the taskbar is unlocked, the Quick Launch toolbar is bordered by movable left and right borders, represented by double dotted lines:

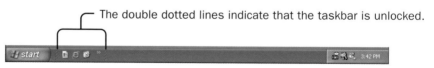

The double dotted lines indicate that the taskbar is unlocked.

29 Position the mouse pointer over the double dotted lines to the right of the Quick Launch toolbar so that the pointer turns into a double-headed arrow.

30 Drag the double-headed arrow to the right until all the Quick Launch toolbar short-cuts are visible.

31 On the Quick Launch toolbar, right-click your new shortcut, and click **Delete** on the shortcut menu.

The **Confirm File Delete** dialog box appears:

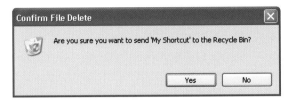

32 Click **Yes**.

The shortcut is deleted from the Quick Launch toolbar.

33 Right-click the taskbar, and then click **Lock the Taskbar** on the shortcut menu.

The two shortcuts you created are still on your desktop. They are used in the next two exercises.

Rearranging Your Desktop

After you have installed several programs and created shortcuts to put the programs, folders, and files you use most often at your fingertips, your desktop might start to get pretty messy. To cope with the clutter, some people like to line up their icons and short-cuts in regimented rows, some like to arrange them as a sort of frame around the perim-eter of their screen, and others like to group them by type in various discrete locations. You can organize your icons and shortcuts manually, or if you are happy with simple arrangements, you can have Windows XP arrange them for you.

In this exercise, you will rearrange the items on your desktop.

BE SURE TO log on to Windows and minimize any open windows before beginning this exercise. USE the desktop shortcuts you created in the previous exercise, or copy the files from the *My Documents\Microsoft Press\Microsoft Windows XP SBS\Working\Arranging* folder.

Follow these steps:

1 Drag your desktop shortcuts to random positions on the desktop.

2 Right-click an open area of the desktop, point to **Arrange Icons By** on the shortcut menu, and then click **Auto Arrange**.

> **Tip** A check mark indicates when the Auto Arrange option is selected.

Windows XP neatly arranges your shortcuts and icons on the left side of the desktop.

3 Now try to drag a shortcut to a different position on the desktop.

You can move the shortcuts up and down, but not away from the left edge of the screen.

4 If you don't like the Auto Arrange feature, right-click an open area of the desktop, point to **Arrange Icons By** on the shortcut menu, and then click **Auto Arrange** to turn it off.

Cleaning Up Your Desktop

new for
WindowsXP

Desktop
Cleanup
Wizard

The **Desktop Cleanup Wizard** helps you clean up your desktop by moving rarely used shortcuts to a desktop folder called **Unused Desktop Shortcuts**. The Unused Desktop Shortcuts folder is a temporary holding area for the shortcuts you are not using. You can restore shortcuts from this folder to your desktop, or you can delete the entire folder.

In this exercise, you will use the **Desktop Cleanup Wizard** to clean up your desktop, and you will then delete some desktop shortcuts.

BE SURE TO log on to Windows and minimize any open windows before beginning this exercise.
USE the desktop shortcuts you created in the previous exercise, or copy the files from the *My Documents\Microsoft Press\Microsoft Windows XP SBS\Working\Cleaning* **folder.**

Follow these steps:

1 Right-click any open area of the desktop, point to **Arrange Icons By** on the shortcut menu, and then click **Run Desktop Cleanup Wizard**.

The first page of the **Desktop Cleanup Wizard** appears.

2 Click **Next** to open a **Shortcuts** page like this one:

Desktop Cleanup Wizard	☒

Shortcuts
The shortcuts selected below will be moved to the Unused Desktop Shortcuts folder.

To leave a shortcut on your desktop, clear its check box.

Shortcuts:

Shortcut to Clean Up	Date Last Used
☑ 🌐 Internet Explorer	Never
☐ 🖳 MSN Web Site	8/25/2001
☐ 🖳 My Shortcut	8/25/2001

This list varies depending on your desktop shortcuts.

[< Back] [Next >] [Cancel]

3 If you created the desktop shortcuts in the earlier exercise, select the **MSN Web Site** and **My Shortcut** check boxes. If you copied the shortcuts from the Cleaning folder, select the **MSN Web Site** and **FreeCell** check boxes. Clear all other check boxes, and then click **Next**.

The selected shortcuts are displayed on the **Completing the Desktop Cleanup Wizard** page.

4 Click **Finish**.

Windows XP creates a new folder on the desktop called *Unused Desktop Shortcuts* and moves the selected shortcuts into the folder. Notice that the folder icon on the desktop does not have a bent arrow in its bottom left corner, indicating that the icon represents the actual folder rather than a shortcut to the folder.

5 On the desktop, double-click the **Unused Desktop Shortcuts** folder to open it:

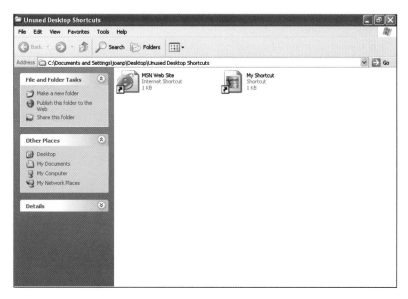

6 Click the **MSN Web Site** shortcut.

7 On the **File and Folder Tasks** menu, click **Move this file**.

The **Move Items** dialog box appears:

This list varies depending on your installed hardware and programs.

8 If necessary, use the scroll bar to move to the top of the list.

9 Click **Desktop**, and then click the **Move** button.

The **MSN Web Site** shortcut is moved from the Unused Desktop Shortcuts folder to your desktop.

10 In the Unused Desktop Shortcuts folder, click the remaining shortcut.

11 On the **File and Folder Tasks** menu, click **Delete this file**.

12 In the **Confirm File Delete** dialog box, click **Yes** to delete the shortcut.

13 Click the **Close** button to close the Unused Desktop Shortcuts folder and return to the desktop.

The **MSN Web Site** shortcut has been restored to your desktop.

14 On the desktop, right-click the **MSN Web Site** shortcut, and then click **Delete** on the shortcut menu.

15 In the **Confirm File Delete** box, click **Yes** to delete the shortcut.

16 Right-click the **Unused Desktop Shortcuts** folder, and then click **Delete** on the shortcut menu.

This **Confirm Folder Delete** dialog box appears:

17 Click **Yes** to delete the folder.

Key Points

- The Windows XP user interface is designed to provide simple and intuitive access to the functionality you want.

- You can personalize the Windows desktop to make your most frequently used programs quickly accessible.

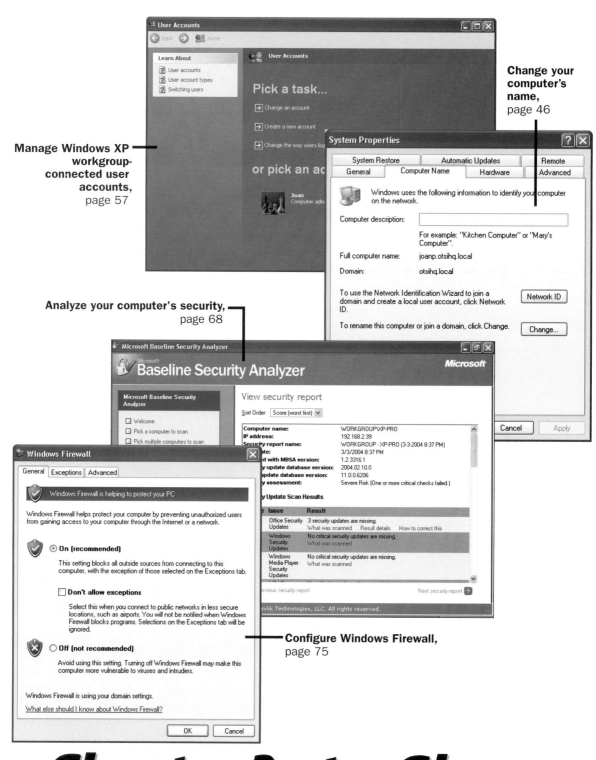

Change your computer's name, page 46

Manage Windows XP workgroup-connected user accounts, page 57

Analyze your computer's security, page 68

Configure Windows Firewall, page 75

Chapter 3 at a Glance

3 Managing Computer Security

In this chapter you will learn to:

- ✓ Change your computer's name.
- ✓ Create, modify, and delete user accounts.
- ✓ Set user account passwords.
- ✓ Represent user accounts with pictures.
- ✓ Enable multiple people to log on simultaneously.
- ✓ Analyze your computer's security.
- ✓ Configure Internet security zones.
- ✓ Configure Windows Firewall

In the old days, computers were isolated, and the only way to get information from one to another was to transfer it on a floppy disk. With the advent of *networks*, information transfer became easier, but so did the possibility that the information stored on a computer would be accessed inappropriately or even illegally from another computer. As networks have grown from small to large and worldwide access to local area networks has become simple and commonplace concerns about information security have also increased.

Most people think of security in terms of protecting against *viruses* and intruders, or *hackers*. Many commercial software packages that detect and treat computer viruses are available. Apart from the use of special software, the most common way of addressing security concerns in a networked computer environment has been through a system of *user accounts* and *passwords*. Microsoft Windows XP extends this account and password system to single stand-alone computers so that more than one person can use the same machine. For example, if you manage your family's financial records on a home computer that is also used by your children to do their homework, you can set up separate accounts for your children so that they can't view confidential information or change your files.

The great thing about user accounts and passwords is that they help to keep your information private; that is, you can prevent other users from reading or altering your documents, pictures, music, and other files. You can choose to *share* files by placing them in a folder that is available to other users, but you don't have to. With Windows XP, each user can personalize his or her own working environment and have easy access to frequently used files and applications without worrying about other people making changes.

In this chapter, you will learn how to rename your computer, how to manage user accounts on Windows XP Professional and Windows XP Home Edition computers, and how to analyze and manage some of your computer's security settings.

See Also   Do you need only a quick refresher on the topics in this chapter? See the Quick Reference entries on pages xxiii–xxvi.

Important   Before you can use the practice files in this chapter, you need to install them from the book's companion CD to their default location. See "Using the Book's CD-ROM" on page xv for more information.

Important   Because management processes vary depending on whether your computer is part of a workgroup or on a network domain, we address these options separately, and you should follow the steps for your particular installation. The exercises assume that you have *administrative privileges* on your computer. This means that you are allowed to change basic settings that control access to your computer and the items stored on it. If your computer is connected to a network domain, your network administrator might have set up your computer so that you cannot change some settings. If this is the case, you can read through the exercises, but you won't be able to follow the steps.

Changing Your Computer's Name

Every computer has a name. That might seem like something out of a science fiction story in which computers take over the world, but there is nothing sinister about it. Your computer was named during the Windows XP initial setup process. It might have been named after its user (you), after its make or model (for example, *HP* or *Laptop*), or based on what it is most commonly used for (for example, *Media*); or it might have been given a whimsical name to give it some sort of personality.

In this exercise, you will locate and change your computer's name.

Important   Many corporations have standard naming conventions for computers on their network to help employees easily locate and identify network resources. If your computer is connected to a network, check with your network administrator before attempting to change your computer's name.

BE SURE TO log on to Windows before beginning this exercise.

Follow these steps:

Troubleshooting   If your computer is configured to log on to a network domain, you should change the computer name only while you are connected to the domain. Otherwise you might inadvertently change the name to one that is already in use in the domain, which would result in an error the next time you tried to connect to the domain.

1   On the **Start** menu, click **Control Panel**.

The Control Panel window appears:

Tip   Control Panel is a central place where you can access many of your computer's settings. These settings are grouped according to category. Clicking a category name or icon displays a window with specific options or starts a wizard that leads you through the process of making changes.

2   Click the **Performance and Maintenance** icon.

The Performance and Maintenance window appears, looking something like this:

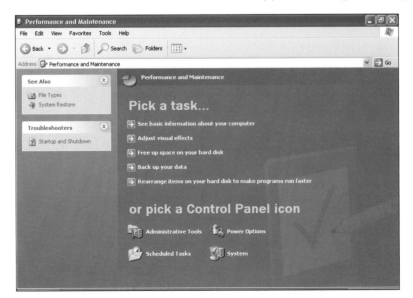

3 Click the **See basic information about your computer** task.

The **System Properties** dialog box appears:

4 Click the **Computer Name** tab to display it:

The names of your computer and, if applicable, your domain or workgroup are displayed in the center of the tab. If you are logged on to a domain, your computer name is represented as *computer name.domain*.

5 Click **Change** to open the **Computer Name Changes** dialog box:

Your current computer name is selected.

6 Type your new computer name in the **Computer name** box, and click **OK**.

Troubleshooting Computer names cannot be longer than 15 characters and must consist of standard characters, which include uppercase or lowercase letters (A–Z or a–z), digits (0–9), and hyphens (-).

If your computer is connected to a network domain, you will be prompted for the user account name and password of a network administrator who has permission to rename the computer in the domain.

7 If you are prompted to do so, enter your user account name and password, and then click **OK**.

8 When a dialog box appears informing you that you must restart the computer for the changes to take effect, click **OK**.

9 Click **OK** to close the **System Properties** dialog box, and then click **Yes** to restart your computer.

Your computer now has a new name.

Working with User Accounts in a Domain

If your computer is connected to a network domain, your network administrator must set up a user account or accounts for the computer to be able to access the network. User accounts can be established during the setup process or at any time from Control Panel.

If you have administrative privileges, you can create *local computer* user accounts that other people can use to access your computer. For example, you might want to create a local user account for a friend so that he can log on to your computer to check his e-mail. Each user account belongs to a *group* with *permissions* to perform certain operations on the computer. The most common groups are:

- *Administrators*, who have unrestricted access to the computer.

- *Power Users*, who have most administrative capabilities but with some restrictions.

- *Users* and *Guests*, who are restricted from making system-wide changes.

- *Backup Operators*, who can override security restrictions for the purpose of backing up or restoring files.

Other groups are available for support personnel, network administrators, and remote users. There are also special groups that might be created when a computer is upgraded from other versions of Windows to Windows XP Professional. And finally, anyone assigned to the Administrators group can create custom groups.

In this exercise, you will create a local computer user account, change its privileges, and then delete it.

Tip You cannot delete the account of a user who is currently logged on to the computer.

BE SURE TO log on to Windows and know your computer's name before beginning this exercise.

Tip To find out your computer's name, open Control Panel, click **Performance and Maintenance**, click **See basic information about your computer**, and in the **System Properties** dialog box, click the **Computer Name** tab.

Follow these steps:

1 Click the **Start** button, and on the **Start** menu, click **Control Panel**.

2 In the Control Panel window, click the **User Accounts** icon.

Troubleshooting You must be a member of the Administrators group on your domain-connected computer to access the User Accounts settings.

This User Accounts window appears:

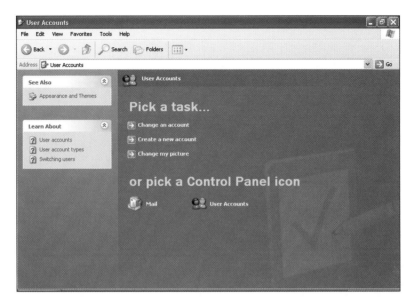

3 In the User Accounts window, click the **User Accounts** icon to open the **User Accounts** dialog box.

4 Click the **Advanced** tab.

5 In the **Advanced user management** area, click **Advanced** to open the Local Users and Groups window.

6 In the left pane of the Local Users and Groups window, click the **Users** folder to display a list of the current user names:

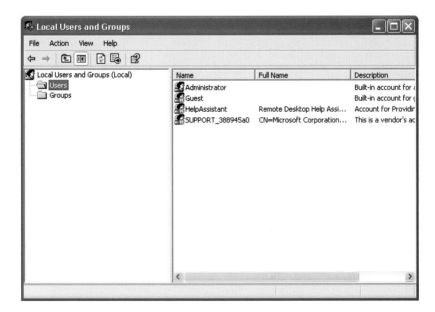

7 On the **Action** menu, click **New User** to open the **New User** dialog box:

8 In the **User name** box, type **Joe**.

9 In the **Full name** box, type **Joe the Dog**.

10 In the **Description** box, type **Man's best friend**.

11 In the **Password** box, type **Woof!**.

Tip Your corporate network policy might require that passwords conform to a minimum length or meet other guidelines. A common guideline for creating a secure password is to use a combination of numeric and alphabetic characters with at least one punctuation mark.

12 Type the password again in the **Confirm password** box.

13 Ensure that the **User must change password at next logon** and the **Account is disabled** check boxes are cleared, and then click **Create**.

Tip You clear the first check box because you don't want the user to have to change the password, and you clear the second because you want the account to be active and available.

The account is created, and the input screen is cleared.

14 Click **Close** to return to the Local Users and Groups window.

Joe has been added to the list of users:

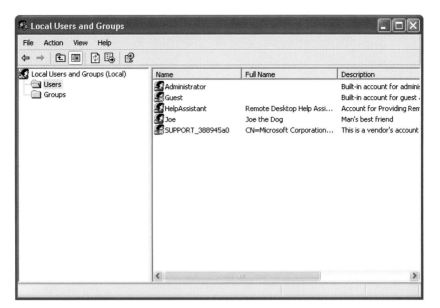

15 In the right pane of the Local Users and Groups window, double-click **Joe** to open the **Joe Properties** dialog box.

16 Click the **Member Of** tab.

Joe is currently shown as a member of the Users group, the default group for new users.

17 Click **Cancel** to close the **Joe Properties** dialog box.

18 To add Joe to another group, click the **Groups** folder to display a list of the available groups in the right pane of the Local Users and Groups window:

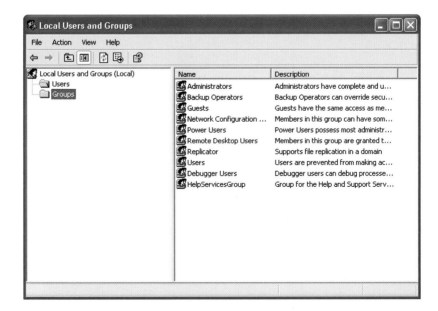

19 In the right pane of the Local Users and Groups window, double-click **Power Users** to open the **Power Users Properties** dialog box.

20 Click **Add**.

21 If you are connected to a network domain, click the **Locations** button, if necessary click your computer name, and then click **OK**.

22 In the **Enter the object names to select** box, type Joe, and click **Check Names**.

Tip   To enter multiple user names, separate the names with a semicolon.

The **Select Users** dialog box looks something like this:

The name you typed is replaced by the *computer name\user name* combination.

Tip   If there are a lot of people named Joe on your network, you might be asked to select the one you want from a list.

23 Click **OK** to add Joe to the Power Users group, and then click **OK** to close the **Power Users Properties** dialog box.

Close

24 Click the **Close** button to close the Local Users and Groups window, and click **OK** to close the **User Accounts** dialog box. Then click the **Close** button to close the User Accounts window.

Log Off

25 On the **Start** menu, click the **Log Off** button, and then click **Log Off** in the **Log Off Windows** dialog box.

You are logged off of Windows and returned to the logon security screen.

26 Press **CTRL+ALT+DELETE** to access the **Log On to Windows** dialog box.

27 In the **User name** box, type Joe.

28 In the **Password** box, type Woof! (or the secure password you created in step 11).

The characters of the password are displayed as dots as you type.

29 Click the down arrow to the right of the **Log on to** box, and click your computer in the drop-down list.

30 Click **OK**.

Joe is now logged on to your computer, but not your network domain. The **Start** menu expands, with Joe's full name shown at the top:

Because this is the first time that Joe has logged on to this computer, the desktop is in its default state.

31 On the **Start** menu, click **Log Off**, and then click **Log Off** in the **Log Off Windows** dialog box to log Joe's account off of the computer. Then log back on as yourself, changing the **Log on to** setting to your domain if necessary.

32 Now you'll change the group to which Joe is assigned again. Open Control Panel, and click the **User Accounts** icon to open the **User Accounts** dialog box.

33 In the **Users for this computer** list, click **Joe**, and then click **Properties** to open the **Joe Properties** dialog box.

34 On the **Group Membership** tab, click **Other**, and click **Administrators** in the drop-down list.

35 Click **OK** to change Joe's group membership to Administrators.

36 Now that you've completed this exercise, you don't need this account on your computer, so in the **Users for this computer** list, click **Joe**, and then click **Remove**.

A message box warns you that Joe will no longer be able to use this computer.

37 Click **Yes**.

Joe is removed from the list of users.

38 Click **OK** to close the **User Accounts** dialog box.

39 Click the **Close** button to close Control Panel.

Working with User Accounts in a Workgroup

When your computer is part of a workgroup rather than connected to a domain, Windows XP supports two levels of user privileges: computer administrator and limited. Users with computer administrator accounts have permission to do everything, including:

- Create, change, and delete accounts.
- Make system-wide changes.
- Install and remove programs.
- Access all files.

Users with limited accounts have permission to do things that affect only their own account, including:

- Change or remove their password.
- Change their user account picture.
- Change their theme and desktop settings.
- View files they created and files in the Shared Documents folder.

Important   Users with limited accounts can run into difficulties when trying to install new software, because administrative privileges are required to install or remove certain some programs. Be sure you have the appropriate privileges before attempting to install or remove new software.

On the logon screen, each user account is represented by the *user account name* and also by a *user account picture*. Windows XP comes with 23 user account pictures, representing a variety of animals, sports, and interests. You can select the picture that most closely matches your personality or interests. If none of the default pictures is to your liking, you can add a picture you like better.

Tip   Computer administrators can assign or change the picture for any user. Limited account and guest account users can change only their own picture.

You can use *bitmap (BMP)* files, *Graphic Interchange Format (GIF)* files, *Joint Photographic Expert Group (JPEG)* files, or *Portable Network Graphics (PNG)* files as user account pictures. The orginal graphic can be any size, but the user account picture is always displayed at 48 *pixels* high by 48 pixels wide. If you select a graphic that does not have the same height and width, it will be stretched or compressed to the standard size when displayed.

In this exercise, you will create a new user account with administrative privileges, change its privileges, create a password, and choose a custom graphic to represent the user. You will then delete the account.

Tip You can never delete the account of a user who is currently logged on to the computer.

BE SURE TO log on to Windows before beginning this exercise.
USE the *Joe* picture in the practice file folder for this topic. This practice file is located in the *My Documents\Microsoft Press\Microsoft Windows XP SBS\Computer\UserAcct* folder.

Follow these steps:

1 On the **Start** menu, click **Control Panel**.

2 Click the **User Accounts** icon.

The User Accounts window appears:

3 Click **Create a new account** to open the **Name the new account** screen.

You are prompted to enter a name for the new account.

4 Type **Joe**, and then click **Next** to move to the **Pick an account type** screen.

You are prompted to specify the account type.

5 Select the **Computer administrator** option, and then click **Create Account**.

Windows XP creates a new account called *Joe*, and assigns a user account picture to the account, which now appears at the bottom of the User Accounts window.

6   Now you'll customize Joe's account. In the User Accounts window click **Joe's account**.

The options for changing the account are displayed:

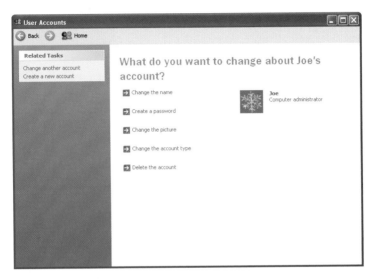

7   Click **Change the picture**.

You are prompted to select from the default pictures:

8   Click **Browse for more pictures**.

9 In the Open window, click the down arrow to the right of the **Look in** box, and browse to *My Documents\Microsoft Press\Microsoft Windows XP SBS\Computer \UserAcct*.

10 Click the picture named **Joe**, and then click **Open**.

A picture of Joe (an American Eskimo dog) is added to the available pictures, Joe's user account picture is changed, and you are returned to the account options screen.

11 Click **Change the account type**.

12 On the **Pick a new account type for Joe** screen, select the **Limited** option, and then click **Change Account Type**.

In the account options screen, the *Limited account* type is now indicated to the right of Joe's user account picture.

13 Click **Create a password**.

You are prompted to enter a password for Joe's account.

14 In the **Type a new password** box, type BowWow!, and then press the **TAB** key to move to the next field.

To ensure the secrecy of the password, the characters are displayed as dots as you type.

15 In the **Type the new password again to confirm** box, retype BowWow!, and then press the **TAB** key twice to move to the next field.

16 In the **Type a word or phrase to use as a password hint** box, type What does Joe say?.

The screen now looks like this:

17 Click **Create Password** to save the password as part of Joe's user account profile and return to the account options screen.

The *Password protected* status is now indicated to the right of Joe's user account picture.

18 Now you'll delete Joe's account. Click **Delete the account**.

Troubleshooting   If the account you are trying to delete is currently logged on to the computer, you must switch to that user account and log it off before you can delete it.

You are asked whether you want to keep or delete any files that Joe might have created on the desktop or in the My Documents folder.

19 Joe has not created any files that you care about, so click **Delete Files**, and then click **Delete Account** to delete Joe's account and return to the main **User Accounts** screen.

Joe's account no longer appears among the active accounts.

20 Click the **Close** button to close the User Accounts window, and then close Control Panel.

Close

Switching Quickly Among Users

When you're using Windows XP Professional on a network domain, there is only one way to log on to your computer: by entering your user account name and your password. If you are not on a network domain, whether you are using Windows XP Professional or Home Edition and whether you are working on a network (with no domain) or on a stand-alone computer, you have two logon options:

■   You can select from pictorial representations on the Windows XP Welcome screen.

■   You can use the classic logon prompt that requires you to enter your user account name as well as your password (if the account is password-protected).

The Welcome screen is the default.

new for
WindowsXP

Fast User
Switching

Another option available in Windows XP on a stand-alone computer is Fast User Switching, which makes it possible for multiple users to log on to their user accounts without logging previous users off. This feature saves time and decreases frustration for all users, because open applications don't need to be closed when switching between user accounts.

In this exercise, you will turn on Fast User Switching on your computer.

Tip Fast User Switching is not available when your Windows XP Professional computer is connected to a network domain.

BE SURE TO log on to Windows before beginning this exercise.

Follow these steps:

1 On the **Start** menu, click **Control Panel**.

The Control Panel window appears.

2 Click the **User Accounts** icon.

The User Accounts window appears.

If the user account names aren't displayed at the bottom of the window, click the secondary **User Accounts** icon.

Important If you have only one user account on your computer, you will need to create at least one other account to be able to use Fast User Switching.

See Also For more information about creating user accounts, refer to "Working with User Accounts in a Domain" and "Working with User Accounts in a Workgroup" in this chapter.

---

3 Click the **Change the way users log on or off** task.

The **Select logon and logoff options** screen appears.

4 Select the **Use Fast User Switching** check box, and click **Apply Options**.

The change is applied, and you return to the main User Accounts window.

Log Off

5 With the User Accounts and Control Panel windows still open, click **Log Off** on the **Start** menu.

This **Log Off Windows** dialog box appears:

6 Click the **Switch User** button. The Welcome screen appears with the current user accounts shown.

Switch User

7 Click one of the account names to log on with that account.

If the account is password-protected, a password box appears.

Tip If you don't remember your password, you can click the blue question mark button to see the password hint.

8 If an account password is required, type the password and click the green arrow button to continue.

You are now logged on to the account, and that account's personal settings are loaded. The **Start** menu expands, with the account's user name and user account picture displayed at the top:

Joe

Internet Internet Explorer	My Documents
E-mail Microsoft Office Outlook	My Recent Documents ▶
MSN Explorer	My Pictures
Windows Media Player	My Music
Windows Messenger	My Computer
Tour Windows XP	Control Panel
Windows Movie Maker	Set Program Access and Defaults
Files and Settings Transfer Wizard	Printers and Faxes
	Help and Support
All Programs ▷	Search
	Run...

Log Off   Turn Off Computer

If this is the first time this account has logged on, all the settings are the default settings, and there are no open applications.

9 On the **Start** menu, click **Log Off**.

10 In the **Log Off Windows** dialog box, click **Switch User**.

11 On the Welcome screen, click your own user name, and if your account is password-protected, enter your password.

Your own user account is displayed, and the User Accounts and Control Panel windows are still open. (They might be minimized.)

12 Click the **Close** button to close each of the open windows.

Close

Analyzing Your Computer's Security

Computer security is a hot topic these days. The proliferation of Internet access and e-mail in homes and workplaces around the world has provided a new (and relatively simple) avenue for malicious intrusion into our lives. It is important to be aware of the possible security vulnerabilities of each computer you work on, whether it is at home, at school, at work, or in a public place such as an Internet café. It is also important to protect these computers through correct network setups, appropriate virus scanning software, and informed computer use practices.

Any computer that is connected to the Internet, whether full-time or intermittently, is exposed to the risk of attack by a computer virus. This sounds dangerous, and the potential risk should always be taken seriously, but there are a number of things you can do to protect your system from infection:

■ Work behind a *firewall*. A firewall is a secure bridge between the external Internet and your computer (if you have a direct Internet connection) or the intranet to which your computer is connected (if you're working on a network). In a networked business environment, the corporate intranet should sit behind a firewall that protects the network from intrusion. In a home environment, the firewall can be installed on the computer through which your home network accesses the Internet, or it can be part of your computer's operating system. Windows XP Service Pack 2 includes Windows Firewall software that monitors the information communicated from the Internet to your computer or network. Windows Firewall ensures that only authorized communications reach your system, thus protecting you from malicious intrusions.

Tip Windows Firewall can prevent you from doing things like sharing resources across a network or hosting network games. If you experience difficulties when trying to connect to other computers, refer to "Configuring Windows Firewall" later in this chapter.

See Also For more information about Windows Firewall, refer to "Configuring Windows Firewall" later in this chapter.

■ Install all available security upgrades. Use Windows Update to automatically keep your Windows XP computer up to date with Microsoft-issued product updates.

See Also For more information about Windows Update, refer to "Keeping Your Computer Up to Date" in Chapter 10, "Solving Problems."

- Utilize third-party antivirus software. Select a program that monitors your hard disk drive and external drives, as well as all incoming and outgoing files.

- Do not open unidentified e-mail attachments.

See Also For more information about e-mail security, refer to "Sending and Receiving E-Mail Messages" in Chapter 8, "Communicating with Other People."

- Analyze your system security from time to time to ensure that your computer system is as secure as possible. Microsoft Baseline Security Analyzer is a free tool you can download from the Microsoft Web site that scans your system for security vulnerabilities and leads you through the process of optimizing your system security.

In this exercise, you will install and run the Baseline Security Analyzer.

BE SURE TO log on to Windows and start your Internet connection before beginning this exercise. You might also need to know your computer's IP address.

Tip Here's a simple way to find your computer's IP address. On the **Start** menu, click **Run**. Type **cmd** in the **Open** text box and then click **OK**. In the command window, type **ipconfig** and press the **ENTER** key. Your computer's IP address is printed on the screen along with other related information. Write down the IP address and then click the command window's **Close** button to close the window.

Follow these steps:

1 Click the **Start** button, and then click **Internet** at the top of the **Start** menu.

Your default Internet browser starts. If you are using Internet Explorer and this is the first time you've started it, you will be required to specify your location.

2 If necessary, click the browser window's **Maximize** button.

Maximize

3 Click in the **Address** box to select the current Web page address, and then press the **DELETE** key to clear the **Address** box content.

4 In the **Address** box, type http://www.microsoft.com/technet/security/tools/mbsahome.mspx, and then press the **ENTER** key or click the **Go** button.

An article about the Microsoft Baseline Security Analyzer opens in a new window. If you are interested, you can learn the technical details of the Baseline Security Analyzer here.

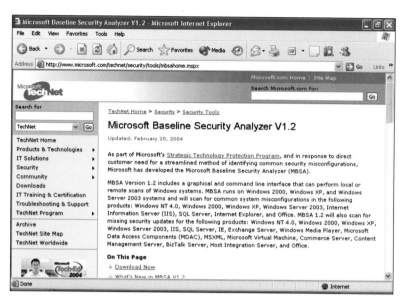

5 Click in the vertical scroll bar at the right side of the window to scroll down to the *Download Now* heading. Under this heading, click the link to download the English version of the program.

A **File Download** dialog box appears.

6 Click the **Run** button.

The **Microsoft Baseline Security Analyzer Setup Wizard** file is downloaded to a temporary folder on your hard disk and then opened.

7 Click the **Next** button to move to the wizard's **License Agreement** page.

8 Read the license agreement, select the **I accept the license agreement** option, and click the **Next** button.

9 On the **Destination Folder** page, keep the default settings and click the **Next** button.

10 On the **Start Installation** page, click the **Install** button.

11 When the installation is complete, click **OK**, and then click the browser window's **Close** button to close window.

Close

12 On your desktop, double-click the **Microsoft Baseline Security Analyzer** program shortcut installed by the setup wizard.

13 Maximize the Baseline Security Analyzer window if necessary to display a Welcome screen:

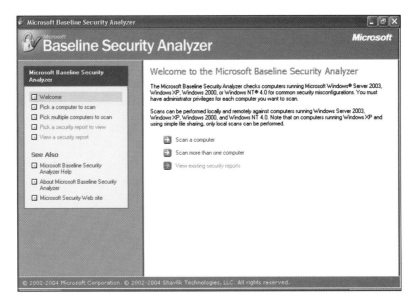

14 Click **Scan a computer** to move to the next step:

The computer you are working on is selected in the **Computer name** drop-down list. All scanning options are selected by default.

15 Click **Start scan**.

The Baseline Security Analyzer scans your computer for the selected scanning options, and creates an interactive security report:

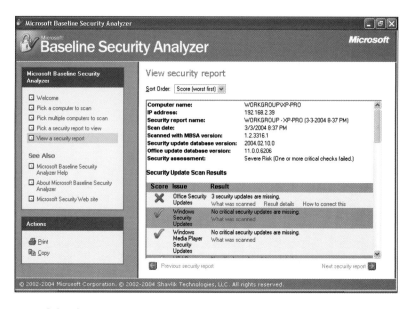

Troubleshooting   If you see a message that the computer was not found, click **Continue** to return to the Welcome screen, and then repeat steps 14 and 15, but enter your computer's IP address in the **IP address** text boxes before clicking **Start scan**.

You can print the report by clicking **Print** in the **Actions** box in the lower-left corner of the window.

16 Scroll through the report to see how your computer scored.

17 If the report points out any critical issues (indicated by a red X in the Score column), click the **How to correct this** link for the issue to display information describing the issue and how to fix it. If you like, fix each of the reported issues and then rerun the Baseline Security Analyzer to ensure that your system is secure.

18 When you're done with the Baseline Security Analyzer, click its **Close** button to close the window.

Configuring Internet Security Zones

With Internet Explorer, you can set different levels of security for different types of Web sites. For instance, you might not want to allow certain types of programs to run on your computer when you're surfing the Web, but you might feel perfectly comfortable running programs that originate from your organization's intranet site or from specific Web sites that you trust (such as your own).

Internet Explorer divides the types of Web sites you visit into four security zones:

- *Internet.* All external Web sites that are not in the trusted or restricted site lists.

- *Local intranet.* All Web sites that are part of your organization's local network.

- *Trusted sites.* Specific Web sites that you have designated as trustworthy; you believe that content from these sites will not damage your computer or data.

- *Restricted sites.* Specific Web sites that you believe might contain content that will damage your computer or data.

You must specifically designate Web sites as part of the Trusted sites and Restricted sites zones; otherwise these zones are empty.

You can set the security level for each zone at one of four predefined levels, or you can customize the security level for your own or your organization's needs. The predefined security levels are:

- *High.* This level is appropriate for any Web sites that you don't trust, or if you want to have full control over the content that is downloaded to and run on your computer. This is the default security level for the *Restricted sites* zone. Internet Explorer prevents potentially harmful content from running on your computer, which might mean that certain Web sites function or are displayed improperly.

- *Medium.* This level is appropriate for most Internet sites, and it is the default security level for the *Internet* zone. Internet Explorer prompts you before downloading any potentially unsafe content, and it does not download unsigned ActiveX controls.

- *Medium-low.* This level is appropriate for intranet sites, and it is the default security level for the *Local intranet* zone. Internet Explorer does not download unsigned ActiveX controls, but most other content runs without prompts.

- *Low.* This level is only appropriate for sites that you absolutely trust, and it is the default security level for the *Trusted sites* zone. Internet Explorer provides only minimal safeguards and warnings, and it downloads and runs most content without prompting you for permission.

Most people will find that the default settings are adequate for their needs, but from time to time you might want or need to customize a setting. Even if you never do, it's good to know what your options are so you can feel confident that your Web browsing is done in a secure and sensible manner. The following sections describe the security setting categories and show the default setting for each of the four standard security levels. A discussion of the meaning of each of these security options is beyond the scope of this book, but you will get a general idea of the settings you can control. For most of the security options you have the option to enable, disable, or prompt for approval when Internet Explorer encounters that particular option.

Important The settings shown here reflect the default options for each security level in its default security zone.

You can set the following options for ActiveX controls and plug-ins:

Security option	High	Medium	Medium-low	Low
Download signed ActiveX controls	Disable	Prompt	Prompt	Enable
Download unsigned ActiveX controls	Disable	Disable	Disable	Prompt
Initialize and script ActiveX controls not marked as safe	Disable	Disable	Disable	Prompt
Run ActiveX controls and plug-ins	Disable	Enable	Enable	Enable
Script ActiveX controls marked safe for scripting	Disable	Enable	Enable	Enable

You can set the following options for downloading files and fonts from Web pages:

Security option	High	Medium	Medium-low	Low
File download	Disable	Enable	Enable	Enable
Font download	Prompt	Enable	Enable	Enable

You can set the following miscellaneous options:

Security option	High	Medium	Medium-low	Low
Access data sources across domains	Disable	Disable	Prompt	Enable
Allow automatic prompting for file and code downloads	Enable	Enable	Enable	Enable
Allow META REFRESH	Disable	Enable	Enable	Enable
Allow windows to be opened without security restrictions	Disable	Disable	Enable	Enable
Display mixed content	Prompt	Prompt	Prompt	Prompt
Don't prompt for client certificate selection when no certificates or only one certificate exists	Disable	Disable	Enable	Enable

Security option	High	Medium	Medium-low	Low
Drag and drop or copy and paste files	Prompt	Enable	Enable	Enable
Installation of desktop items	Disable	Prompt	Prompt	Enable
Launching programs and files in an IFRAME	Disable	Prompt	Prompt	Enable
Navigate sub-frames across different domains	Disable	Enable	Enable	Enable
Open files based on content, not file extension	Enable	Enable		Disable
Software channel permissions	High safety	Medium safety	Medium safety	Low safety
Submit nonencrypted form data	Prompt	Enable	Enable	Enable
Userdata persistence	Disable	Enable	Enable	Enable
Web sites can open new windows in a less restrictive Web content zone	Disable	Disable	Enable	Enable

You can set the following scripting options:

Security option	High	Medium	Medium-low	Low
Active scripting	Disable	Enable	Enable	Enable
Allow paste operations via script	Disable	Enable	Enable	Enable
Scripting of Java applets	Disable	Enable	Enable	Enable

You can set the following option for authenticating you as a user on Web sites that require you to log on:

Security option	High	Medium	Medium-low	Low
Logon	Prompt for user name and password	Automatic logon only in Intranet zone	Automatic logon only in Intranet zone	Automatic logon with current username and password

---

See Also For more information about Internet Explorer security settings, refer to "Setting Up Security Zones" on the Microsoft Web site at *www.microsoft.com/windows/ie/using /howto/security/setup.asp* and "Working with Internet Explorer 6 Security Settings" on the Microsoft Web site at *www.microsoft.com/windows/ie/using/howto/security/settings.asp*.

In this exercise, you will examine your current Internet Explorer security zone settings, experiment with changing your security options, and add and remove Web sites from the trusted and restricted sites lists.

OPEN Control Panel.

Troubleshooting To complete this exercise as written, you must be running Internet Explorer as your default Web browser. If you do not have a working Internet connection, the dialog box settings you see might look slightly different from the ones shown here, but you will still be able to complete the exercise.

Follow these steps:

1 In **Control Panel**, click the **Security Center** icon.

new for **Windows**XP

Security Center

The **Security Center** window appears:

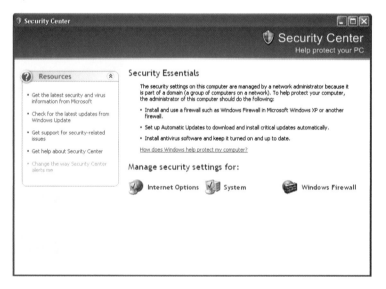

The contents of this window may change depending on whether you are connected to a network domain.

2 Click the **Internet Options** icon.

The **Internet Properties** dialog box appears.

3 Click the **Security** tab, which looks something like this:

Depending on your current security settings, the **Security level for this zone** area displays either a slide control like the one shown here or a custom setting.

4   If your screen shows a custom setting, click the **Default Level** button to return the Internet zone to the default Medium security level.

5   Drag the slide control down one mark to **Medium-low**.

A message box warns you that you have selected a security level lower than the recommended minimum.

6   Click **OK** to retain the default Medium security level.

Next you'll try customizing the security options.

7   Click the **Custom Level** button to display this **Security Settings** dialog box:

The default security level is displayed in the **Reset custom settings** area. You can change this to Low, but it is not recommended.

8 Scroll through the options and change a few to see how changing security levels works. When you're finished making changes, click **OK**.

A message box prompts you to confirm your changes.

9 Click **Yes** to customize your security options and close the **Security Settings** dialog box.

In the **Internet Options** dialog box, the security level is now shown as *Custom*.

10 Click the **Restricted sites** icon, and then click the **Sites** button.

This **Restricted sites** dialog box appears:

11 In the **Add this Web site to the zone** box, type the name of a Web site to experiment with, such as www.microsoft.com, and then click the **Add** button.

The Web site you entered moves to the **Web sites** list; if you visit the Web site now it will be as a restricted site.

Tip If you want to experiment with the restricted sites setting, you can click **OK** to close the **Restricted sites** dialog box, and then click **OK** to close the **Internet Properties** dialog box and apply your changes. If you do this, be sure to return to the **Internet Properties** dialog box and reset your security levels when you're done.

12 In the **Web sites** list, select your practice site, click the **Remove** button to clear the list, and then click **OK** to close the **Restricted sites** dialog box.

13 Click the **Internet** icon, and then click the **Default Level** button to return the Internet zone to the default security level.

14 To implement this security level, click **OK**; otherwise, click **Cancel** to close the **Internet Properties** dialog box without implementing any of the changes.

CLOSE Security Center and Control Panel.

Ensuring Effective Virus-Checking

The Windows XP System Restore feature utilizes a series of checkpoints and restoration points that are created when certain events occur or at certain time intervals. You can also manually create restoration points. Each of these restoration points is the equivalent of a large-scale file backup. If a virus-infected file is stored as part of a restoration backup, it could be restored along with the rest of your system settings if you choose to restore your system to that particular restoration point.

While the System Restore feature is enabled, the backup files are protected from detection or cure by virus scanning programs. Prior to running a system-wide virus checker, disable the System Restore feature to ensure that all files are checked and cured or deleted as appropriate.

To disable System Restore, right-click **My Computer** (on the desktop or **Start** menu), and then click **Properties** on the shortcut menu. In the **System Properties** dialog box, click the **System Restore** tab. Select the **Turn off System Restore** check box, and then click **OK** to close the dialog box and save your changes. If you are prompted to restart the computer, close any open program windows and then click **Yes**.

After running the virus scanner, repeat the above process and clear the **Turn off System Restore** check box to restart System Restore.

See Also   For more information about the System Restore feature, refer to "Restoring Your Operating System" in Chapter 10, "Solving Problems."

Configuring Windows Firewall

Windows XP (prior to SP2) includes Internet Connection Firewall (ICF). Service Pack 2 updates ICF to the new Windows Firewall. Windows Firewall protects your computer from receiving any unwanted connections, such as connections made by certain kinds of computer viruses. With Windows Firewall, the only connections that can be made to your computer are those either initiated or approved by you.

Unlike ICF, Windows Firewall is enabled by default for all users and all connections to your computer, including local area network (LAN), Virtual Private Network (VPN), and dial-up connections. You can make changes to the configuration of Windows Firewall for your own user profile without affecting other users' configurations.

new for
WindowsXP

Security Center

Windows Firewall settings are controlled from the Security Center window installed with Service Pack 2.

In this exercise, you will examine your Windows Firewall setting options.

OPEN Control Panel.

Follow these steps:

1 In Control Panel, click the **Security Center** icon.

2 In the Security Center window, click **Windows Firewall**.

The Windows Firewall dialog box appears:

3 Read the descriptions of the three basic options: **On** (with exceptions allowed), **Don't allow exceptions**, and **Off**.

When you are connecting to an unsecured or questionable network such as free connections in public locations, you should return to this dialog box and select the **Don't allow exceptions** check box.

4 At the bottom of the **General** tab, click the **What else should I know about Windows Firewall** link.

The Help and Support Center opens to the Windows Firewall topic:

You can consult this Help file at any time if you want further information about Windows Firewall.

5 Read through the topics, and then click the Help and Support Center window's **Close** button.

Close

6 In the **Windows Firewall** dialog box, click the **Exceptions** tab to display the list of programs and services that you can choose to allow to bypass the firewall:

Remote Assistance is the only exception enabled by default.

See Also For more information about Remote Assistance, refer to "Asking for Help from Someone Else" in Chapter 10, "Solving Problems."

By clicking the buttons below the list, you can grant access to additional programs, and specify whether those programs can access the entire Internet, your local network only, or a specific list of computers. Or, if the program you want to use requires access to a specific port, you can open that port through the firewall.

7 Click the **Advanced** tab to display the network connection setting options:

Note that you can configure individual settings for each of your network connections. You can enable logging and network information sharing, and if you are concerned that your firewall protection might be compromised by settings you've changed, you can restore the default Windows Firewall settings at any time.

8 Click the **Cancel** button to close the **Windows Firewall** dialog box without making any changes.

CLOSE the Security Center and Control Panel windows.

Key Points

- Every computer has a name that uniquely identifies it within a workgroup or network domain.

- Multiple people can log on to one Windows XP computer with their own user accounts. The user account type governs the tasks that a person can perform on the computer.

- Each computer user can control the look and feel of his or her Windows XP computing experience.

- User accounts can have associated passwords to protect the privacy of each person's data.

- Windows XP Service Pack 2 enables certain security settings by default to protect your computer from unwanted traffic.

- You can easily analyze and optimize your computer's security settings. You can also set different levels of security for different types of Web sites.

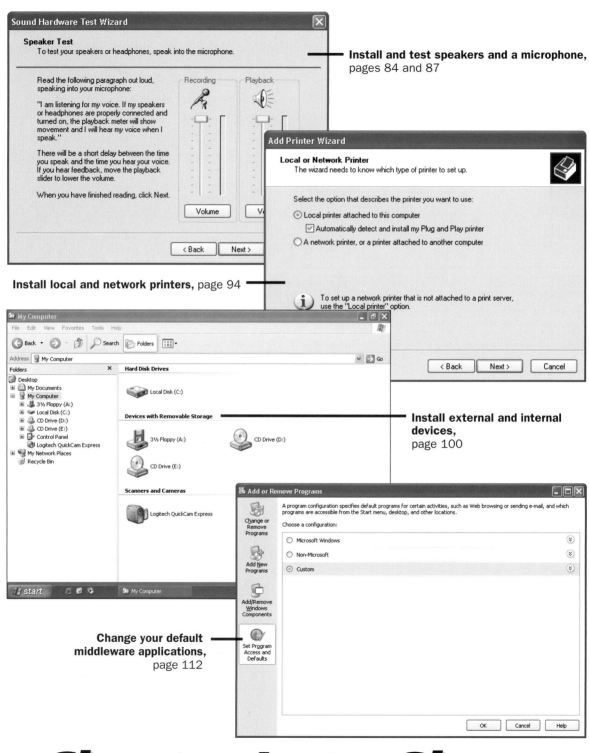

Install and test speakers and a microphone, pages 84 and 87

Install local and network printers, page 94

Install external and internal devices, page 100

Change your default middleware applications, page 112

Chapter 4 at a Glance

4 Working with Hardware, Software, and Middleware

In this chapter you will learn to:

✔ Install speakers and a microphone.

✔ Install local and network printers.

✔ Install a scanner or camera.

✔ Install storage devices.

✔ Install internal devices.

✔ Install programs and Windows components, and have them start automatically.

✔ View your Windows XP display on multiple monitors.

✔ Expand your laptop with peripheral devices.

✔ Change your default middleware applications.

People discuss computers in terms of *hardware* and *software*. As you probably know, physical items such as computers and monitors are hardware, and all the programs that you use to do things with that hardware are collectively known as software.

Software and hardware are terms that have been around for a while, but *middleware* is a relatively new term that is slowly becoming known to computer users. Middleware is software that connects two or more otherwise separate applications, which could be software programs or system applications. Middleware programs are freestanding programs and therefore differentiated from importing or exporting functions within applications. Common types of middleware include transaction processing monitors and terminal emulation, messaging, and database access programs. Many middleware applications are Web-based.

In the context of Microsoft Office, middleware refers to the software programs that provide standard features such as Internet browsing, e-mail, instant messaging, video display, and audio playback. The standard Office middleware applications are Microsoft Internet Explorer, Microsoft Outlook Express, Microsoft Windows Media Player, and Microsoft Windows Messenger.

Whether you're working in an office or at home, you will eventually want to install one or more bits of extra hardware, called *peripheral devices*, on your computer. Some devices, such as the keyboard, monitor, and mouse, usually come with the computer, but you will purchase others separately. The most common devices are speakers and a printer. Other popular devices include scanners, storage devices such as Zip drives, and fax machines. These devices are all *external*—meaning that you can install them without having to open up your computer—but others, such as a CD-ROM burner or a tape backup drive, might be *internal*—meaning that they have to be installed inside your computer's case.

Many peripheral devices fall into a category called *Plug and Play*, which quite literally means that you can plug them in and use them—no setup is required. Others might require that you supply some kind of information, usually through a wizard, or they might require a specific *device driver* in order to work properly. Device drivers enable peripheral devices to "talk" to your computer, but they are unfortunately not universal. To hook up a printer, for example, you might need a driver that is not only specific to the printer but also specific to Microsoft Windows XP.

Device Drivers

Device drivers are files containing information that Windows needs to communicate with your printer, fax machine, scanner, camera, or other device. Drivers can be specific to an individual device or to a family of devices (such as all HP LaserJet printers), and they are often specific to a certain version of Windows.

Device drivers can be found on the Web site of the device manufacturer or on certain Web sites that centralize driver information. If you are looking for current device drivers, try these Web sites:

Manufacturer	Driver download
Apple	*www.info.apple.com/support/downloads.html*
Brother	*www.brother.com/E-ftp/softwin1.html*
Canon	*www.usa.canon.com/html/cprSupportDetail.jsp?navfrom=DrivD*
Citizen America	*www.citizen-america.com/drivers*
Compaq	*www.compaq.com/support/files*
Epson	*support.epson.com/filelibrary.html*
Fujitsu	*www.fcpa.com/download*
Hewlett-Packard	*welcome.hp.com/country/us/en/support.html*
IBM	*www-1.ibm.com/support/us/all_download_drivers.html*
Kodak	*www.kodak.com/global/en/service/software/driverSupport.jhtml*

Manufacturer	Driver download
Konica	*www.konica.com/downloads*
Lexmark	*downloads.lexmark.com*
Minolta (business products)	*bpg.minoltausa.com/eprise/main/minoltausa/musaBPG /support_center/downloads/searchdownload*
NEC	*printers.necsam.com/printers/drivers/drivers.cfm*
Panasonic	*www.panasonic.com/support*
Ricoh	*ricoh-usa.com/download/?usa*
Toshiba	*copiers.toshiba.com/support/swdrivers.shtml*
Xerox	*www.xerox.com/go/xrx/template/drivermain.jsp*

Other device driver resources include:

Resource	Website
Drivers Headquarters	*www.drivershq.com*
The Driver Guide	*www.driverguide.com*
Totally Drivers	*www.totallydrivers.com*
WinDrivers	*www.windrivers.com*

Nowadays you can pretty much walk into a computer store, purchase a computer, plug it in, and start working without installing any additional software. New name-brand computers usually come with the operating system (in this case, Windows XP) already installed. They might also include software programs that you'll use to carry out specific tasks, such as word processing. Sooner or later, however, you will want to install additional programs, either from a floppy disk, a CD-ROM, a network server, or the Internet. You might also need to install some of the optional components of Windows XP that did not get set up during the operating system's installation.

In this chapter, you will learn how to install hardware and software on your Windows XP computer, and how to specify your preferred middleware options.

See Also   Do you need only a quick refresher on the topics in this chapter? See the Quick Reference entries on pages xxvi–xxx.

 Important   Before you can use the practice files in this chapter, you need to install them form the book's companion CD to their default location. See "Using the Book's CD-ROM" on page xv for more information.

Installing Speakers and a Microphone

A basic computer system consists of a computer, monitor, keyboard, and mouse. Computer systems that are equipped with sound cards usually come with a set of external speakers so that you can listen to music and other audio files. If you're a real enthusiast, you might want to purchase fancy surround-sound speakers for your computer. Or if you want to listen to audio output privately, you might want to use speakers that have headphone jacks.

Most standard speaker systems consist of two speakers with one cord that connects them to each other, another that connects them to the computer, and a power cord that connects them to the power source. One speaker might have a volume control (independent of the computer-controlled volume control) and a headset jack.

With the rapid evolution of Internet-based communications, digital video, and speech-to-text technologies, microphones are being used more commonly with business and home computer systems. Microphones come in a variety of options: freestanding microphones, microphones that attach to your computer, headset microphones with built-in headphones that allow more private communication and consistent recording quality, boom microphones with a single headset speaker, and many others.

If you will be recording a lot of speech, it is worthwhile to invest in a good-quality microphone. Anything less and you are likely to find yourself making a return trip to the store. To get the best quality, it is also critical that you choose the type of microphone that best fits your needs. Headset and boom microphones maintain a constant distance between the microphone and your mouth, which helps to maintain a more consistent sound level than a stationary microphone. The headphones built into headset and boom microphones provide the same privacy of conversation as a telephone, because the audio output is heard only by the wearer.

In this exercise, you will connect a stereo speaker system and a microphone to your Windows XP computer. You will then test the connection and adjust the audio input and output levels appropriately.

BE SURE TO log on to Windows and obtain a set of computer speakers and a microphone before beginning this exercise.

Follow these steps:

1   Remove the audio devices from their packaging, if you have not already done so.

   Tip   If you are using an alternate audio configuration, such as a boom microphone, connect the input and output cables appropriately and then skip to step 8.

2   Link the two speakers using the connector cable.

3   Position the speakers to the left and right of your monitor to provide stereo sound quality.

4   Plug the speakers into a nearby power outlet using the AC adapter cord.

5   Plug the speakers into the speaker jack on the sound card at the back of the computer using the connector cable.

> **Tip**   The speaker jack might be indicated by a small speaker icon or the words *Audio* or *Audio/Out*.

6   Plug the microphone connector cable into the audio input jack on the sound card on the back of your computer.

> **Tip**   The audio input jack might be indicated by a microphone icon or the word *Mic* or *Microphone*.

7   Click the **Start** button, and then on the **Start** menu, click **Control Panel**.

The Control Panel window appears.

8   Click **Sounds, Speech, and Audio Devices** to open this window:

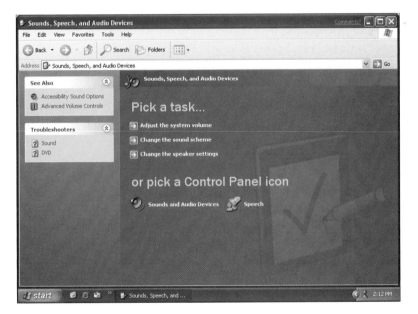

9   Click the **Sounds and Audio Devices** icon.

The **Sounds and Audio Devices Properties** dialog box appears:

10   Click each of the tabs, and explore the options available.

11   On the **Voice** tab, click **Test hardware**.

The **Sound Hardware Test Wizard** appears:

12 Make sure no programs are open, and then click **Next**.

The wizard runs an automated test of your sound hardware. You will not hear any sounds during this process.

13 After completing the automated test, the wizard prompts you to test the microphone:

14 Read the microphone test paragraph aloud in your normal speaking voice. Just for fun, you might try singing a couple of lines from your favorite song!

You will not hear any sound from the speakers during the microphone test.

As you speak (or sing), the **Recording** indicator moves in response to your voice. When your voice volume is in an acceptable recording range, the meter is green. If your voice is too loud for the current **Recording** setting, the indicator enters a yellow or red zone, and the **Recording** setting adjusts to a lower level. If your voice is too quiet, the setting adjusts to a higher level to pick up your voice at the most appropriate level for recording.

Troubleshooting   If the **Recording** indicator does not move, your microphone might be incorrectly connected, or it might not be compatible with your computer. If this happens, hold the microphone close to your mouth and scream loudly—if the recording meter moves slightly, the connection is good, and the problem is between your microphone and your computer. You might be able to solve this problem by downloading new device drivers from the microphone manufacturer's Web site, or it might be simpler to replace the microphone.

87

15   When you have finished reading the paragraph, click **Next** to begin the speaker test:

```
Sound Hardware Test Wizard                                      ⊠

  Speaker Test
    To test your speakers or headphones, speak into the microphone.

  Read the following paragraph out loud,        Recording      Playback
  speaking into your microphone:

  "I am listening for my voice. If my speakers
  or headphones are properly connected and
  turned on, the playback meter will show
  movement and I will hear my voice when I
  speak."

  There will be a short delay between the time
  you speak and the time you hear your voice.
  If you hear feedback, move the playback
  slider to lower the volume.

  When you have finished reading, click Next.
                                              [ Volume ]    [ Volume ]

                          [ < Back ]  [ Next > ]    [ Cancel ]
```

16   Read the speaker test paragraph aloud in your normal speaking voice.

As you speak, the **Recording** and **Playback** indicators will move in response to your voice, and you will hear yourself speaking, with a short delay between your words and the sound. (This can be somewhat distracting.) As with the microphone test, the **Recording** level adjusts to the volume of your voice.

17   Adjust the **Playback** slider control to a comfortable listening level.

Tip   If you are using speakers with a volume control, you can also adjust the volume on the speakers themselves.

18   When you have finished making adjustments, click **Next**, and then click **Finish** to close the **Sound Hardware Test Wizard**.

Close

19   Click **OK** to close the **Sounds and Audio Devices Properties** dialog box, and then click the **Close** button to close the Sounds, Speech, and Audio Devices window.

Installing a Local Printer

A *local printer* is a printer that is connected directly to your computer. The software to run the printer is installed on and run from your computer. When you connect a printer to your Windows XP computer, Windows XP often recognizes that a printer has been connected. It then searches through its database of drivers to locate the appropriate software to run the printer. If Windows XP doesn't have the current driver for your particular printer, it asks you to provide the driver.

Troubleshooting   Many printers come with a CD-ROM or floppy disk containing installation files and drivers that were current at the time the printer was manufactured. If you don't have the current *printer drivers*, you can usually locate them on the printer manufacturer's Web site.

In this exercise, you will install a local printer and then test the installation by printing a test page.

BE SURE TO log on to Windows and obtain a printer and any necessary printer drivers before beginning this exercise.

Follow these steps:

1   Connect the printer to the appropriate plug, or *port*, on the back of your computer. Then turn on the printer.

At this point, three things might happen:

- Windows XP might detect the printer and display a **Found New Hardware** alert in the notification area at the right end of the taskbar. In this case, Windows knows what printer drivers to install, so wait while Windows finishes the installation process, and skip the rest of the steps.

- Windows XP might detect the printer but not have all the information it needs to install it, in which case it displays the **Found New Hardware Wizard**. Skip to step 10 to complete the instructions.

- Windows XP might not detect the printer, in which case it does nothing. Go to step 2.

2   If the **Found New Hardware Wizard** does not appear, click **Start**, and then click **Printers and Faxes**.

The Printers and Faxes window appears:

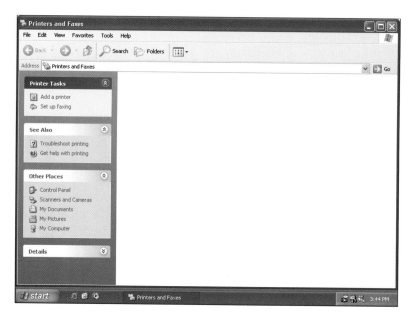

3   On the **Printer Tasks** menu, click **Add a printer**.

The **Add Printer Wizard** starts:

4   Click **Next** to move to the wizard's **Local or Network Printer** page:

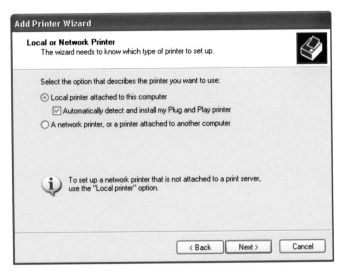

5   Select the **Local printer attached to this computer** option.

6   Clear the **Automatically detect and install my Plug and Play printer** check box.

7   Click **Next** to move to the wizard's **Select a Printer Port** page:

8   Confirm that your printer is connected to the recommended printer port, or select the correct port from the drop-down list, and click **Next** to move to the wizard's **Install Printer Software** page:

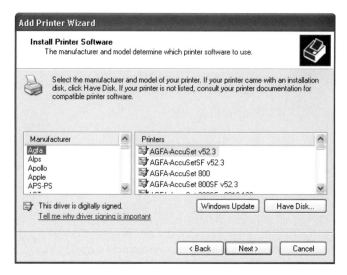

9   If you have an installation CD-ROM or floppy disk, insert it, click **Have Disk**, and follow the instructions on the screen to install your printer.

Important   Your installation CD-ROM or floppy disk must contain updated drivers that are compatible with Windows XP. If your drivers are out of date, download the current drivers from the printer manufacturer's Web site.

10   In the **Manufacturer** list, click the name of the manufacturer of your printer.

The **Printers** list changes to reflect a list of the printer drivers that Windows XP has stored for that manufacturer.

11   In the **Printers** list, select the model of your printer.

Troubleshooting   If your specific model is not listed, select a similar model; or download the necessary drivers from the manufacturer's Web site, return to the **Install Printer Software** page, and click **Have Disk** to install the printer manually.

12   Click **Next** to move to the wizard's **Name Your Printer** page.

13   Type a name for your printer in the **Printer name** box, or accept the default name, and click **Next**.

Tip   Keep the printer name short and easily recognizable, because a long name might not fit in the space provided in some dialog boxes. It's a good idea to use the printer model name or your name to clearly identify the printer, in case you end up with more than one.

14 If you are connected to a network and are asked if you want to share the printer, make sure the **Do not share this printer** option is selected, and click **Next** to open the wizard's **Print Test Page** page:

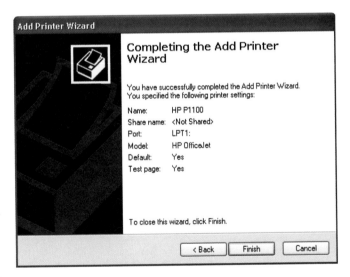

15 Select the **Yes** option, and then click **Next**.

A completion page something like this one appears:

16 Click **Finish** to print the test page.

After the test page has printed, a confirmation dialog box appears.

17 Click **OK** to close the dialog box and the **Add Printer Wizard**.

Your printer connection is displayed in the Printers and Faxes window:

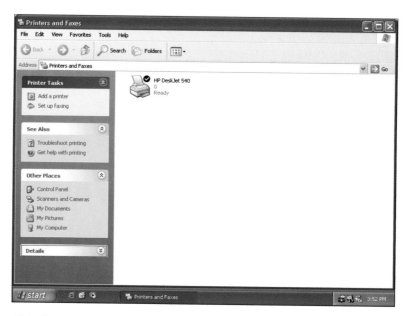

Close

18 Click the **Close** button to close the Printers and Faxes window.

Installing a Network Printer

A *network printer* is a printer that is not connected directly to your computer. Instead, you access the printer over the network as a free-standing networked printer, through someone else's computer, through a print server, or through a printer hub.

If the printer you are connecting to is available to everyone on the network, you will not need specific permission to connect to it. If the printer has been made available only to specific people or groups, you will have to ask the printer's "owner" or your network administrator to make the printer available to you.

In this exercise, you will connect to a network printer.

BE SURE TO log on to Windows and know the name of an available printer on your network before beginning this exercise.

Follow these steps:

1 On the **Start** menu, click **Printers and Faxes**.

The Printers and Faxes window appears with your currently installed printers shown in the right pane.

2   On the **Printer Tasks** menu, click **Add a printer** to open the **Add Printer Wizard**.

3   Click **Next** to move to the wizard's **Local or Network Printer** page.

4   Select **A network printer, or a printer attached to another computer**, and then click **Next**.

You move to the wizard's **Specify a Printer** page:

Add Printer Wizard

Specify a Printer
If you don't know the name or address of the printer, you can search for a printer that meets your needs.

What printer do you want to connect to?

⊙ Find a printer in the directory

○ Connect to this printer (or to browse for a printer, select this option and click Next):

   Name: [   ]

         Example: \\server\printer

○ Connect to a printer on the Internet or on a home or office network:

   URL: [   ]

         Example: http://server/printers/myprinter/.printer

[< Back] [Next >] [Cancel]

5   Select **Connect to this printer**, and click **Next**.

6   On the **Browse for Printer** page, select the printer you want to use, and click **Next**.

If not everyone on your network is allowed to use this printer, at this point you might be asked for your user account name and password. Enter them, and click OK. If you are allowed to use the printer, you then see the wizard's next page. If you are not, you will have to specify a different printer.

7   If necessary, enter your user account name and password, and then click **OK** to close the dialog box and make the connection.

If you have more than one printer installed, you are prompted to specify whether you would like this one to be the printer Windows XP uses unless you specify differently:

8   If this page appears, make your selection, and then click **Next**.

A completion page appears:

The name of the computer to which the printer is attached would be shown here.

9   Click **Finish** to close the wizard.

Tip   If you are prompted to print a test page, do so because this is a good opportunity to test your connection.

10   Your new printer connection is now displayed in the Printers and Faxes window:

The check mark identifies
the default printer.

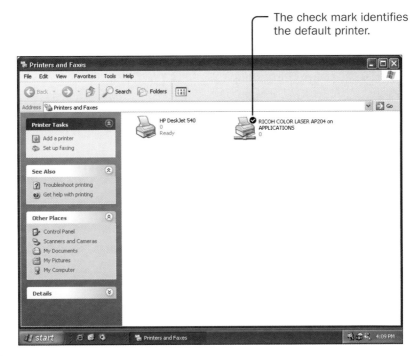

11 Click the **Close** button to close the Printers and Faxes window.

Close

When you print anything from one of your applications, your computer will use the default printer unless you specifically select a different printer.

Configuring the Fax Service

new for
WindowsXP

Fax service

Good news: You no longer need to spend money on a free-standing fax machine to send and receive faxes! You can now use the Microsoft Fax service to send and receive faxes using a fax modem or a fax board installed in your computer, or via your corporate LAN. You can fax a document from any application, send a cover fax page, and track and monitor your fax activity. New wizards make configuring and sending faxes simple. To configure the Fax service:

1 On the **Start** menu, click **Control Panel**, and then click **Printers and Other Hardware**.

2 In the Printers and Other Hardware window, click the **Printers and Faxes** icon.

3 On the **Printer Tasks** menu, click **Set up faxing**.

4 When prompted to do so, insert the Windows XP installation CD into the CD-ROM drive, and click **OK**.

Tip If the Windows installation option page appears after you insert the CD-ROM, click Exit.

Troubleshooting Windows XP might display a Security Alert dialog box warning you that Windows Explorer is trying to access the Internet. If you see this warning, select the Unblock this program option, and then click OK.

Close

5 When the configuration process is complete, click the **Close** button to close the Printers and Faxes window.

6 Remove the Windows XP installation CD from the CD-ROM drive and return it to its protective sleeve or jewel case.

Installing a Scanner or Camera

Scanners are devices you use to convert printed information–words, drawings, photographs, and so on–into digital data that can be processed by your computer. If you have an *optical character recognition (OCR)* program, scanned documents can often be converted to word processor or spreadsheet files. Scanned photos, drawings, and graphics can be saved as graphic files for use on a Web site or in other documents. The digital image can be opened and enhanced in a graphic-processing program.

Computer-compatible cameras come in various shapes and sizes, including handheld digital cameras and digital video cameras (such as "eyeball" cameras).

Most modern scanners and digital video cameras are Plug and Play peripheral devices. To install a scanner or camera, you can simply plug it into the appropriate port on your computer. Windows XP recognizes the device and installs it on your computer. However, some peripheral devices come with special software that enables the features of the hardware, and some manufacturers recommend that you install the software before connecting the hardware to your computer; this is one case where it's a good idea to read the manual first!

new for
WindowsXP

Scanner and
Camera Wizard

After the scanner or camera is installed, you can use the **Scanner and Camera Wizard** in Windows XP to easily create, download, and process images from a scanner, digital camera, or video camera.

In this exercise, you will install and access a Plug and Play scanner or camera.

BE SURE TO log on to Windows and obtain a scanner or camera before beginning this exercise.

Follow these steps:

1 Plug your scanner or camera into the appropriate port on your computer.

Windows XP detects the device and displays a *Found New Hardware* message in the notification area of the taskbar while it installs the hardware.

Important The installation of the scanner or camera might take several minutes. Wait for the notification to go away before continuing with this exercise.

2　On the **Start** menu, click **Control Panel**.

3　In the Control Panel window, click the **Printers and Other Hardware** icon.

4　In the Printers and Other Hardware window, click the **Scanners and Cameras** icon.

　　Your installed scanners and cameras are displayed in the right pane of the Scanners and Cameras window.

5　Double-click the icon for your scanner or camera to open the **Scanner and Camera Wizard**.

　　You can now start working with your installed device.

Need More Ports?

Most computers come equipped with a standard set of *ports* that you use to connect a keyboard, mouse, monitor, or printer. If your computer has a sound card and a network card, you also have audio and network ports. Most desktop and laptop computers have *USB* ports to handle the growing number of devices that are designed to work with this method of connection. Many computers also have *IEEE 1394* (Fire Wire) ports for the highspeed transfer of audio and video data.

When you install several peripheral devices on the same computer, you might find that you don't have enough ports to connect them all. All is not lost! Here are three options for expanding your connection capacity:

■　Install extra ports. After turning off your desktop computer, you can remove its cover and insert a card with more ports, which you can purchase in any computer store, into one of the available *expansion slots*. When you turn the power back on, Windows XP detects and installs the new ports without further ado.

■　Daisy-chain multiple devices. Many devices that connect to the computer via its *parallel port* can be "daisy-chained" together to form a linked network of devices. For example, you might connect a Zip drive to your computer's parallel port and then connect a printer to the parallel port on the Zip drive. Data you send to the printer will pass through the Zip drive.

■　Use a hub. Multiple devices can be connected to a hub that is in turn connected to your computer, enabling all the devices to share that single connection. Hubs are available for network, peripheral, and USB devices. If you want to make a physical connection to multiple peripheral devices, but you don't need to use more than one at a time, you can use a switch box, which looks similar to a hub but allows only one active connection at a time.

Installing a Storage Device

A variety of *data storage devices* are available; the most common are hard disk drives and floppy disk drives. Every computer has at least one hard disk drive, and almost all computers come with a floppy disk drive installed. However, when you need extra storage space, you don't have to buy a new computer or even upgrade your hard disk. It is quite simple to install an internal or external storage device on your Windows XP computer, and there are plenty of options to choose from, such as *Zip disk drives*, *Jaz disk drives*, and *tape drives*. For portable data storage, new *USB flash drives* as small as a finger plug directly into your USB port. You can use these drives to easily transport up to 2 GB of data in your pocket.

To install an external Plug and Play storage device, plug the storage device into the appropriate port and, if necessary, into a power source. Windows XP detects the device and displays a *Found New Hardware* message in the notification area of the taskbar while it installs the hardware.

Installed storage devices are listed as available storage locations when you open, save, or look for a file on your computer in Windows Explorer.

Installing Internal Devices

Although many hardware components can be added to your system through the somewhat simple use of ports and cables, other devices require that components be installed inside the computer's case. The internal component might be in the form of a card that provides a new connection at the back of the computer, or it might be a new hard disk drive, floppy disk drive, CD-ROM drive, or tape backup drive that is accessed from the front of the computer.

To install an internal device, you need to remove the cover from your computer and delve into its innards. This is not a book on hardware configuration, but we do want to demonstrate the manner in which Windows XP assimilates new hardware as it is added to your system.

In this exercise, you will install an internal CD-RW drive.

BE SURE TO log off of Windows, shut down and turn off your computer, and obtain an internal CD-RW drive and an appropriate screwdriver before beginning this exercise.

Follow these steps:

1   Disconnect the power cord from your computer.

2   Remove the computer's cover, and install the internal device according to the manufacturer's instructions.

3   Replace the cover, and reconnect the power cord.

4   Turn on the computer and log on to Windows XP.

Windows detects and installs the internal device.

Troubleshooting   If Windows XP does not detect the device, it is likely that you need to download updated device drivers from the manufacturer's Web site.

5   Right-click the **Start** button, and then click **Explore** on the shortcut menu.

6   In the left pane, click **My Computer**.

Windows displays a list of the internal and external storage devices installed on your computer, something like this:

A camera is installed.   The CD-RW drive is installed as drive E.

Burning Your Own CDs

new for
WindowsXP

CD burning

With CD-Recordable (CD-R) burners and CD-ReWritable (CD-RW) drives now becoming more budget-friendly options, Windows XP includes easy CD burning feature with which you can copy (or *burn*) your files, photos, music, and software to a compact disc (CD) without the need for third-party software. Most CDs have a data capacity of approximately 650 MB.

To burn data to your installed CD-RW drive:

1   Insert a blank CD in the CD-RW drive.

2   On the **Start** menu, click **My Computer**.

3   Browse to the folder containing the files you want to copy to CD, and click the **Copy this folder** task.

4   In the **Copy Items** dialog box, click the CD drive, and then click **Copy**.

5   Click the balloon note that tells you files are waiting to be copied.

6   On the **CD Writing Tasks** menu, click **Write these files to CD**.

7   Follow the **CD Writing Wizard's** instructions to complete the process.

Installing a Software Program

Software programs can be installed from a variety of sources: a CD-ROM, a floppy disk, a file on your computer, over a network, or over the Internet.

Regardless of the source of the installation files, almost all software programs are installed by running an executable file, which is often named *Setup.exe*. Many software manufacturers use files called autorun files, which are located in the *root* directory of the place from which the program is being installed—usually a CD-ROM. When you insert the CD-ROM into its drive, your computer checks the drive, and if it finds an autorun file, it starts it. The autorun file in turn starts an executable file that either leads you through the setup process or simply starts the program contained on the CD-ROM. Autorun files take the guesswork out of the setup process, because they don't require you to browse to a specific location, find a specific file, run a specific program, or make any sort of decision about which installation action to take.

Troubleshooting   With Windows XP, only a user with *administrative privileges* can install certain programs on your computer. If you do not have administrative privileges for the computer on which you want to install new software, you might find that the installation procedure simply fails. The software setup program might just appear to crash, and you might not suspect that the wrong privileges are the culprit until your third unsuccessful attempt! Check with your network administrator or the person who created your user account if you can't install a program.

Many companies supply free software or software upgrades that can be downloaded or installed from the Web. To install a program from the Internet, click the link that is provided. Depending on the type of installation file, you might be offered two options—to run the installation file from its current location on the Internet or to download the installation file to your own computer and run it *locally*. If you have a high-speed Internet connection through a *DSL* modem or a *cable modem*, it is simplest to run the installation file from the Internet. If your connection is not very fast or is unreliable, it is usually easier to download the file and run it locally.

Depending on the location from which you are installing the program, you might have to enter a unique registration code, called a *product key* or *CD key*, during the setup process:

- If you are installing the program from a CD-ROM, the product key is usually located on a sticker on the back of the CD-ROM jewel case.

- If you work for a company that keeps the most current versions of its licensed software on one or more *servers* rather than distributing it on CD-ROM to its employees, your network administrator will be able to supply the product key.

- If you are installing the program from the Internet, you might not need a product key, but the software supplier might request or require you to register with the company before installing the software. The main purpose of this requirement is to add you to software manufacturers' mailing lists so that they can follow up with marketing materials and other information. In the United States, the E-mail User Protection Act (HR 1910) requires that companies provide you with a means to remove yourself from mailing lists, and you can generally find a removal link or instructions at the bottom of the e-mail messages you receive from the company if you would prefer not to receive further messages.

Product keys are one of the methods software manufacturers use to try to prevent *software piracy*. A program that requires a product key for installation can't be installed without it. If you lose your product key, you won't be able to install the program in the future, unless you have registered your copy of the software and can successfully appeal to the software manufacturer for a replacement product key.

Many programs offer multiple installation options, such as *default, complete,* or *custom.* Some programs that are installed from a CD-ROM offer the option of copying large files to your computer or accessing them from the CD-ROM when needed. You might have the option of waiting to install rarely used program features the first time you need them to save space on your hard disk for the features that you do need. When choosing your installation type, consider the way in which you will use the application, the amount of space required by the application, and how much space is available on your hard disk. Also think about whether the installation source will be available to you later, in case you need to access files that aren't installed to your computer or want to reinstall the application. In most cases, the default installation fits the needs of the average user and is the best choice.

When you start the installation process, most programs offer you the opportunity to accept or change the installation location, which by default is usually a product-specific subfolder within the Program Files folder on your drive C. The program might display a progress bar to keep you informed about what is going on during the installation process, and depending on the program, you might be informed of specific actions and file installations as they occur. When the installation is complete, you might be required to restart your computer; in fact, some large program installations require multiple restarts. Restarting the computer allows the installation program to replace older versions of files that are in use and to clean up after itself.

Tip   You can change a program's settings or remove the program altogether through the **Add or Remove Programs** dialog box, which is available from Control Panel.

In this exercise, you will install and optionally uninstall the Plus! Photo Story 2 Limited Edition program from a folder on your hard disk drive.

Tip   Photo Story is a program that you can use to create cool slideshows of photographs. You can add movement (such as zooming and panning), music, and narration to make a movie-like presentation that you can share on your computer or Pocket PC, through e-mail, or on a Web site.

See Also   For more information about Plus! Photo Story 2, visit the Web site at *www.microsoft.com/windows/plus/dme/Photo.asp*.

USE the *PS2LE* executable file in the practice file folder for this topic. This practice file is located in the *My Documents\Microsoft Press\Microsoft Windows XP SBS\Software\Programs* folder.
BE SURE TO log on to Windows before beginning this exercise.
OPEN the *My Documents* folder, and then browse to the practice file folder.

Follow these steps:

1   Double-click **PS2LE**.

The installation program starts and walks you through the process of installing Plus! Photo Story 2 Limited Edition on your computer.

2   On the wizard's first page, click **Next**.

Troubleshooting   Most software companies require that you agree to the terms of an end-user license agreement (EULA) before installing their software. As with any legal contract, it is a good idea to read the EULA before agreeing to it and before installing the software.

3   On the wizard's second page, read the license agreement, select the **I accept the terms in the license agreement** option, and then click **Next**.

4   On the wizard's third page, click the **Install** button.

5   When the wizard finishes installing the program on your computer, clear the **Start Plus! Photo Story 2 LE now** check box, and then click the **Finish** button.

The Photo Story installation program does not install a desktop shortcut.

6 If you are prompted to restart your computer, save and close any open programs, click **Yes**, and then log on to your computer after it restarts.

Troubleshooting Many computer programs require that you restart your computer when you install or uninstall the program. This allows the temporary files created during the setup or removal process to be cleared from your system. If you would prefer not to restart your computer when prompted, you can close the dialog box and the setup or removal tasks will be completed the next time you start or restart the computer.

Close

7 If you are not prompted to restart your computer, click the **Close** button to close the Software window.

8 On the **Start** menu, point to **All Programs**, and then click **Microsoft Plus! Photo Story 2 LE**.

The program displays this welcome screen:

Clicking either of the links in the lower-right corner opens your default Internet browser and connects you to Web pages giving further information about the Microsoft Plus! Digital Media Edition program, of which Photo Story is a part.

9 Click the **Start Photo Story 2 LE** button.

10 Experiment with the program as you like. When you have finished exploring the program, click the **Close** button to close the program's window, and again to close the thank you screen.

11 If you would like to remove the program, on the **Start** menu, click **Control Panel**.

12 In the Control Panel window, click **Add or Remove Programs**.

The Add or Remove Programs window appears, displaying a list of your currently installed programs.

13   Scroll down if necessary, and click **Microsoft Plus! Photo Story 2 LE**.

The Photo Story program listing expands.

14   Click the **Remove** button.

15   When you are prompted to confirm that you want to remove the program, click the **Yes** button.

The Photo Story uninstall program starts. When it finishes, Photo Story is no longer listed in the Add or Remove Programs window.

16   Click the **Close** button to close the Add or Remove Programs window, and again to close Control Panel.

Installing Windows Components

Windows XP comes with a variety of components that are installed automatically during a typical installation. Others are available but are not installed unless you specifically add them to your system.

The **Windows Components Wizard** walks you through the process of installing, configuring, and removing Windows XP components, which include:

■   Accessories, utilities, and games

■   Function-specific programs including Fax Services, Indexing Service, Internet Information Services (IIS), Message Queuing, Networking Services, and other network file and print services

■   Internet Explorer and MSN Explorer

■   Management and monitoring tools

■   Automatic updating of root certificates

In this exercise, you will use the **Windows Components Wizard** to install and configure the Microsoft Fax Console, an application that is not part of the default Windows XP installation.

BE SURE TO log on to Windows and obtain your Windows XP installation CD-ROM before beginning this exercise.
OPEN Control Panel.

Follow these steps:

1   In Control Panel, click the **Add or Remove Programs** option.

2   In the **Add or Remove Programs** window, click the **Add/Remove Windows Components** button to start the **Windows Components Wizard**.

Add/Remove
Windows
Components

3   In the **Windows Components Wizard**, select the **Fax Services** check box, and then click **Next**.

4   If prompted to do so, insert the Windows XP installation CD into the CD-ROM drive, and then click **OK**.

Tip   If the Windows installation option page appears after you insert the CD-ROM, click **Exit**.

5   In the **Windows Components Wizard**, click **Finish**.

6   Click the **Close** button to close the Add or Remove Program window, and then again to close Control Panel.

Close

7   Remove the Windows XP installation CD from the CD-ROM drive and return it to its protective sleeve or jewel case.

Starting Programs Automatically

If you use certain programs every day, you can easily have Windows start them for you whenever you log on to Windows. For example, some people start their e-mail program first thing in the morning and don't quit it until just before they go home. Other people might work all day in a particular accounting program. You might want to open your company's intranet site each morning to look for updates, or you might want to open your favorite Web site to check your horoscope. Whatever the reason, you shouldn't have to go through a repetitive sequence each day when Windows can do it for you.

Tip   If the program you're starting requires a user account name and password, you will be prompted to enter that information when Windows starts.

To specify that a particular program should start automatically, you place a shortcut to the program in the Startup folder. Each user has his or her own Startup folder, and there is also a Startup folder that applies to all users, so you can choose to make a program start automatically for everyone, or just for you.

You can access the Startup folders through the **Start** menu or through Windows Explorer. You cannot access another user's individual Startup folder, but you can access the folder that pertains to all the people who use your computer.

In this exercise, you will specify that a program be started automatically when anyone logs on to your computer. This example uses *Microsoft Paint*, but you can substitute any other program.

BE SURE TO log on to Windows before beginning this exercise.

Follow these steps:

1   On the **Start** menu, point to **All Programs**, right-click **Startup**, and then click **Explore All Users** on the shortcut menu.

   Tip   You can click **Explore** to open your own Startup folder, or click **Open** to open the Startup folder with the **Folders** list closed.

   Windows Explorer opens to the *C:\Documents and Settings\All Users\Start Menu\Programs\Startup* folder, with the **Folders** list open:

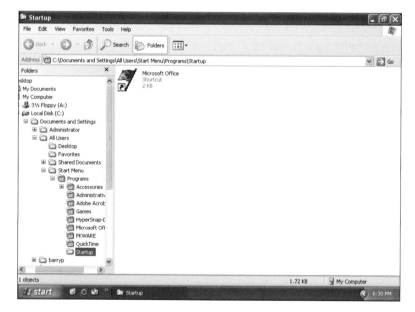

2   In the **Folders** list, click **Accessories** to expand the Accessories folder:

3 If necessary, move the left pane's vertical scroll bar until the Startup folder is visible.

4 In the right pane, point to the shortcut to the **Paint** program, hold down the right mouse button, and drag the program to the **Startup** folder in the left pane.

When you release the mouse button, a shortcut menu appears.

Troubleshooting The shortcut menu appears because you used the secondary mouse button to drag the file, rather than the primary mouse button. If you use the primary mouse button to drag the file, it moves to the folder, and you don't see the shortcut menu.

5 On the shortcut menu, click **Copy Here**.

A copy of the shortcut is created in the Startup folder for all users of your computer to access.

6 In the **Folders** list, click the **Startup** folder to display your new shortcut.

7 Click the **Close** button to close the Startup window.

8 On the **Start** menu, click **Log Off**, and then click **Log Off** in the **Log Off Windows** dialog box. Then log back on again.

After Windows starts, a new Paint window appears.

9 Click the **Close** button to close Paint.

Close

BE SURE TO delete the Paint shortcut from the Startup folder if you don't want Paint to start every time you open Windows.

Using Multiple Monitors

If you often work with multiple open windows or large-format files, such as spreadsheets, that are difficult to see on your monitor because of their width, you might want to consider adding one or more monitors. Windows XP makes it easy to configure up to 10 monitors attached to your computer (which is probably overkill, but certainly enough to handle a pretty tough workload).

In this exercise, you will configure your computer to display your Windows desktop on two monitors.

Troubleshooting   If you are uncomfortable disassembling your hardware, ask a professional for assistance.

BE SURE TO log off of Windows, shut down and turn off your computer, and obtain a monitor, video card, and an appropriate screwdriver before beginning this exercise.

Follow these steps:

1   Remove the cover from your computer.

2   Insert the second video card into an available slot that matches the size of your video card, and then replace the cover.

3   Secure the video card and the cover with screws.

4   Plug the additional monitor into the second video out port.

5   Turn on your computer.

Windows XP detects the second video card and installs the appropriate device drivers.

6   On the **Start** menu, click **Control Panel**.

The Control Panel window appears.

7   In Control Panel, click the **Appearance and Themes** category.

8   In the Appearance and Themes window, click the **Display** icon.

The **Display Properties** dialog box appears.

9   Click the **Settings** tab, which looks like this:

10   On the **Settings** tab, click the secondary monitor.

11   Select the **Extend my Windows desktop onto this monitor** check box, and then click **OK**.

Your display expands to the secondary monitor. The Windows logon screen will always be shown on the primary monitor, as will most application windows when they first open; you can then drag selected windows to the secondary screen.

Expanding Your Laptop with Peripheral Devices

Laptop computers are handy when you want to be able to move around with your computer, either from room to room or when traveling. Although laptops can offer fast computing and large hard disk storage, you usually have to deal with a smaller monitor, a smaller keyboard, and a touchpad or joystick mouse instead of a standard mouse. It is also possible that your laptop computer came without an internal CD-ROM drive or floppy disk drive.

In addition to the frustration caused by these basic differences between laptop and desktop computing, you might find that your wrists become sore because you can't rest them on the keyboard, or you accidentally tap the touchpad when you're typing and move the insertion point without realizing it—which can really mess up the contents of your documents.

Although it probably wouldn't be convenient for you to carry a full-size monitor, keyboard, and mouse everywhere you take your laptop, expanding your laptop computer with full-size peripherals is a great way to improve your laptop computing experience whether you're in your office or at home. If you use a laptop because you need it both at home and at work, you can set up a monitor, keyboard, and mouse at each location for a relatively small sum of money. This gives you the best of both worlds—portable computing and a full-size setup.

You connect peripheral devices to your laptop in the same manner that you would connect them to a standard desktop computer. You might find that your laptop has a limited number of ports, or that it has only a USB port and not a parallel port; inexpensive adaptors are available to help you expand the laptop ports as required. Many newer USB keyboards also incorporate a USB port into the keyboard, so you can plug the keyboard into the laptop and the mouse into the keyboard.

If you attach a full-size monitor to your laptop, you will probably end up seeing the display on both monitors, or only on the laptop—you need to direct the laptop to display only on the external monitor. To do this, look at the function keys at the top of the laptop's keyboard—one of them (usually F5) probably has an alternate monitor function, depicted by a graphic. Hold down the **ALT** key and then press the appropriate function key to switch between laptop display and external display, external display only, and laptop display only.

Tip   If the monitor-switching key is not obvious, consult your laptop owner's manual or the manufacturer's Web site for further information.

Changing Your Default Middleware Applications

new for
WindowsXP

Setting Default
Middleware
Programs

Because middleware applications are merely connectors and not part of the applications they are connecting, different middleware applications are interchangeable. For instance, you might choose to use Internet Explorer or Netscape Navigator to browse the Internet. You might prefer to read your e-mail using Eudora rather than Outlook Express; or you might have a favorite media player that you would like to use by default.

Although you've always been able to install and run your preferred middleware applications on the Windows platform, Windows XP Service Pack 1 (SP1) and Windows XP Service Park 2 (SP2) have made it even simpler to specify your favorite middleware applications as defaults.

If you purchased your computer with the original Windows XP operating system installed or installed the original version yourself, it came with the standard Microsoft middleware applications (Internet Explorer, Outlook Express, Windows Media Player, and Windows Messenger) installed and selected as the default applications. If your computer came pre-installed with Windows XP SP1 or Windows XP SP2, the original equipment manufacturer (OEM) might have stipulated the standard Microsoft middleware applications, or the OEM might have installed other applications and selected them as the default applications for your computer. Regardless of which applications the OEM originally installed and selected as defaults on your computer, the Microsoft middleware applications are available as part of the Windows XP installation, and you can select one or more of them as the default at any time, or use them without selecting them as the default.

After installing SP1 or SP2, you can choose to retain or change the default settings at any time. You have either three or four options when setting your middleware defaults:

- *Computer manufacturer.*   Specifies the original defaults set by the OEM. This option is available only if you purchased your Windows XP computer with SP1 pre-installed by the OEM.

- *Microsoft Windows.*   Specifies all the standard Microsoft middleware applications.

- *Non-Microsoft.*   Specifies the current Web browser, e-mail program, media player, and instant messaging program.

- *Custom.*   Specifies that you will customize your selections to either the Microsoft program or the current program for each of the five middleware options.

See Also   For information about Windows XP service packs, refer to "What's New in Microsoft Windows XP" at the beginning of this book. To find out how to check your operating system version and how to install the most recent service pack, refer to "Updating and Safe-guarding Your Computer System" in Chapter 1, "Getting Started with Windows XP."

In this exercise, you will check your current default middleware applications and change the default applications if desired.

BE SURE TO log on to Windows and install Service Pack 1 or Service Pack 2 before beginning this exercise. If you want to stipulate a non-Microsoft middleware application as a default application, install it on your computer.

Follow these steps:

1   On the **Start** menu, click **Set Program Access and Defaults**. If the **Set Program Access and Defaults** command does not appear in the frequently used programs area of your **Start** menu, click **Control Panel** on the **Start** menu, click **Add or Remove Programs**, and then click **Set Program Access and Defaults**.

The Add or Remove Programs window appears to the **Set Program Access and Defaults** page, shown here:

2 Click the double chevrons to the right of the **Microsoft Windows** and **Non-Microsoft** options and review the expanded description. When you're done, click the double chevrons again to contract the description.

3 Click the double chevrons to the right of the **Custom** option and review the choices. If you have alternate, non-Microsoft middleware applications installed, they will be visible here if their manufacturers have incorporated a special piece of code. If your alternate middleware application isn't shown here, you can still choose it by selecting the **Use my current...** option.

4 If you'd like to make a change to your default middleware applications, make your selection here and then click **OK**. If you don't want to make any changes at this time, click **Cancel**.

Key Points

- Windows XP automatically configures connections to a variety of hardware devices using Plug and Play technology.

- You can instruct Windows XP to automatically start any software program when you start or log on to your computer.

- Windows XP supports multiple-monitor displays, so you can spread your open applications across two screens.

- You can choose the applications that your computer uses when accessing the Internet, watching or listening to media, and communicating by e-mail and instant messaging.

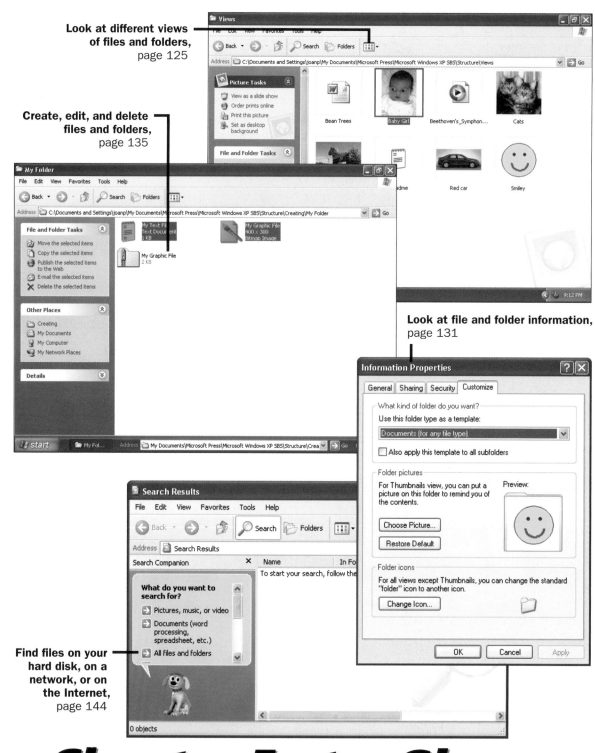

Look at different views of files and folders, page 125

Create, edit, and delete files and folders, page 135

Look at file and folder information, page 131

Find files on your hard disk, on a network, or on the Internet, page 144

Chapter 5 at a Glance

5 Working with Files and Folders

In this chapter you will learn to:

✔ Find your way around your computer.

✔ Look at different views of your files and folders.

✔ Create, edit, delete, move, and rename files and folders.

✔ Find files and folders.

Your computer stores information in the form of files. There are many different types of files. Some are used to run programs, some are created by programs, and some are created by you. The files used or created by programs include *executable files* and *dynamic-link libraries (DLLs)*. These files are sometimes hidden to prevent accidental deletion of important data. The files you create include documents, spreadsheets, graphics, text files, slide shows, audio clips, video clips, and other things that you can open, look at, and change using one of a variety of applications.

Files are organized on your computer in folders. When Microsoft Windows XP is installed on a computer, it creates three *system folders*:

■ *Documents and Settings.*   This folder contains a subfolder for each *user profiles*—each user who has logged on to the computer or who has logged on to a network domain through the computer. Windows XP can create multiple profiles for one person if that person logs on in different ways. For example, you might have one folder for when you are logged on to the domain and another folder for when you are not logged on to the domain.

■ *Program Files.*   This is the folder where most programs install the files they need in order to run. When you install a new program, you are generally given the opportunity to change the installation folder; if you accept the default, the program is installed in this location.

■ *WINDOWS.*   This folder contains most of the critical operating system files. You can look, but unless you really know what you are doing, don't touch! If you upgraded your computer from an earlier version of Windows, the earlier version's WINNT folder might still remain on your computer.

Troubleshooting   If you upgraded your computer from an earlier version of Windows, the earlier version's WINNT folder might still remain on your computer.

Within each profile subfolder in the Documents and Settings folder, Windows XP creates five folders:

- *Cookies.* This folder contains special files that store your Internet account information for various Web sites.

- *Desktop.* This folder contains the files, folders, and shortcuts displayed on the Windows desktop.

- *Favorites.* This folder contains the files, folders, and Web sites that you save as your Favorites.

- *My Documents.* This folder is a convenient place to store documents, spreadsheets, and other files you want to access quickly. This folder contains two subfolders: *My Music* and *My Pictures*, which have special capabilities for handling multimedia files.

- *Start Menu.* This folder contains the program shortcuts displayed on the Start menu.

new for
WindowsXP

Media Folders
(My Music,
My Pictures)

You shouldn't ever need to change the folders that individual programs create and use on your computer, but knowing how to organize the files you create is essential if you want to be able to use your computer efficiently.

All files have names, and all file names consist of two parts: the name and the extension, separated by a period. The type of file or the program in which it was created is indicated by the extension. The extension is a short (usually three letters, sometimes two or four) abbreviation of the file type. By default, Windows XP hides file extensions. If you would prefer to see your file extensions, open My Documents (or any folder) in Windows Explorer, and on the **Tools** menu, click **Folder Options**. On the **View** tab, clear the **Hide extensions for known file types** check box, and then click **OK** to close the dialog box and apply your settings.

Tip When discussing file types, people often refer to them by their extensions only, as in "I'm going to e-mail you some docs for your review."

Files also have icons, which are graphic representations of the file type. Depending on the way you're looking at your files, you might see a large icon, a small icon, or no icon at all.

In this chapter, you will learn how to view and manipulate your files and folders.

See Also Do you need only a quick refresher on the topics in this chapter? See the Quick Reference entries on pages xxx–xxxii.

Important Before you can use the practice files in this chapter, you need to install them from the book's companion CD to their default location. See "Using the Book's CD-ROM" on page xv for more information.

More About Extensions and Icons

Whether or not you can see extensions and icons, every file has one of each assigned to it. Some of the most common file type extensions and icons include the following:

File type	Extension	Icon	File type	Extension	Icon
Bitmap image	.bmp		Microsoft Office Access database	.mdb	
Cascading style sheet	.css		Audio file	.mp3	
Comma-delimited text file	.cvs		Portable Document Format file	.pdf	
Dynamic-link library	.dll		Microsoft Office PowerPoint presentation	.ppt	
Microsoft Office Word document	.doc		Rich Text Format document	.rtf	
Document template	.dot		Plain text file	.txt	
Executable file	.exe		Waveform audio file	.wav	
Graphics Interchange Format image	.gif		Microsoft Office Excel spreadsheet	.xls	
HyperText Markup Language document	.htm or .html		Extensible Markup Language file	.xml	
Joint Photography Experts Group image	.jpg		Compressed (zipped) folder	.zip	

Exploring Your Computer

You can use Windows Explorer to view all the files, folders, drives, and peripherals on your computer, as well as those on any computers you are connected to through a network. Windows Explorer now has two views:

■ *Folders view* displays the hierarchical structure of files, folders and subfolders, drives, and peripheral storage devices on your computer. It also shows any network drives that have been mapped to drive letters on your computer.

Context-
sensitive tasks

■ *Tasks view* displays links to tasks and places that are related to the folder you're currently looking at. The tasks and places are updated automatically based on the contents of the folder.

You can open a specific folder in Windows Explorer by using the **Start** menu options, the Windows Explorer Address Bar, or the Address toolbar on the taskbar.

In this exercise, you will start Windows Explorer in Folders view, explore the files and folders on your computer in different views, and practice navigating between folders.

BE SURE TO log on to Windows before beginning this exercise.

Follow these steps:

1 On the **Start** menu, point to **All Programs, point to Accessories, and then click Windows Explorer.**

Tip You can quickly display Windows Explorer by right-clicking the **Start** button and clicking **Explore**. If you have a **WINDOWS LOGO** key on your keyboard, you can hold down this key and press **E**. You also can create a shortcut to Windows Explorer on your desktop to make it easily accessible. Right-click a blank area of the desktop, point to **New**, and then click **Shortcut**. In the **Type the location of the item** box, type explorer.exe, and click **Next**. In the **Type a name for this shortcut** box, type **Explorer** (or accept the default), and click **Finish**. To make the shortcut accessible when open windows obscure the desktop, you can drag the shortcut to the Quick Launch toolbar on the taskbar.

Windows Explorer opens your My Documents folder in Folders view, looking something like this:

The menus on the menu bar group commands in categories.

The toolbar provides buttons for common actions associated with the window's contents.

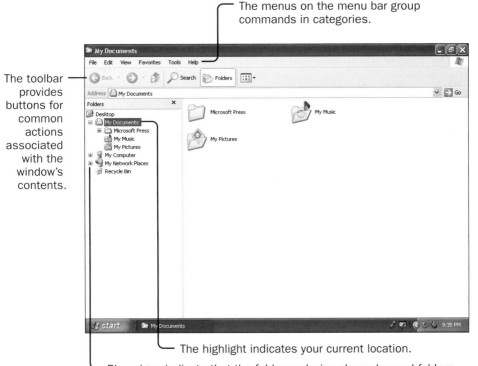

The highlight indicates your current location.

Plus signs indicate that the folder or device shown has subfolders.

Tip The Microsoft Press folder will be visible only if you installed the practice files from this or any other Microsoft Press book in the default folder. If you did not install the practice files, or if you installed them in an alternate location, you will not see them here.

Below the title bar, most windows have a *menu bar* with several categories of actions, called *menus*. Each menu lists a number of *commands* that you can carry out on the files and folders displayed in the window. Below the menu bar you see one or more *toolbars* of various types. These toolbars include *buttons* that you use to carry out common actions, often with a single mouse click.

Folders view displays the folder structure on the left and the contents of the selected folder on the right. For example, in the screen graphic on the facing page, the My Documents folder is selected on the left and its contents are shown on the right. This is the traditional Windows way of looking at things.

2 On the toolbar, click the **Folders** button.

Folders

The My Documents window changes to look like this:

Tip Your specific Windows Explorer display can vary depending on the hierarchical structure of your computer and whether you have explored its contents before. For example, the Address Bar might not be visible in your Windows Explorer window.

The right pane still displays the contents of the current folder, but the left pane now displays a list of tasks and places that are relevant to the currently selected folder or file. This is the Windows XP way of looking at things.

Tip Clicking the **Folders** button toggles the Folders pane open and closed. The Folders pane opens over the Tasks pane. You can close the Folders pane by clicking its **Close** button, revealing the hidden Tasks pane. You cannot click a **Close** button to close the Tasks pane.

3 Click the **Folders** button again to return to Folders view.

4 In the left pane, click **My Computer** to see the list of drives and removable storage devices available to your computer.

5 Click **Local Disk (C:)** to see the list of folders stored there.

Important The folders and files stored directly on a drive are said to be stored in that drive's *root directory*. The first time you attempt to display the contents of the root directory, you might see a warning message telling you to click a link to display the files. This is because the root directory often contains system files that should not be modified or moved in any way.

6   If the right pane does not display the contents of the root directory, click **Show the contents of this folder**.

The Folders pane now lists the available drives and removable storage devices, the default Windows folders, and any other folders you have created in the root directory.

The right pane displays the contents of the root directory. As you can see here, the subfolders displayed in the right pane are the same as those listed in the Folders pane:

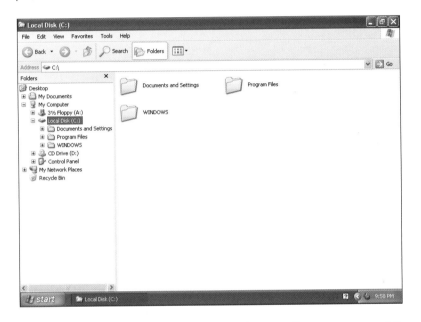

Important   Never delete files from the root directory or any of the system folders created by Windows unless you are absolutely sure you know what you are doing.

7   In the left pane, click **Documents and Settings** to expand the folder.

8   Click **All Users** to expand that folder.

The All Users folder contains four subfolders: *Desktop*, *Favorites*, *Shared Documents*, and *Start Menu*. Files, programs, and shortcuts contained in these folders are available to everyone using this computer.

9   In the left pane, click each of the folders and subfolders in the All Users folder to view the contents of that folder.

10   Click the minus sign next to the All Users folder to contract the folder structure.

11   Click your own name or user name to expand your user profile.

12   In the right pane, double-click the **My Documents** folder.

In Home Edition, click your personalized folder (for example, **Joan's Documents**).

The folder is highlighted in the left pane, and its contents are displayed in the right pane. The folder name appears on the window's taskbar button, and the full path to the folder is displayed in the Address Bar.

Tip The *path* of a folder or file gives the address where the folder or file is stored on your hard disk. A typical path starts with the drive letter and lists the folders and subfolders, separated by backslashes (\), you have to go through to find the folder or file. If the Address Bar is not visible, you can display it by right-clicking the toolbar and clicking **Address Bar** on the shortcut menu. You might then have to right-click the toolbar and click **Unlock the Toolbars** to be able to drag the Address Bar below the toolbar.

13 In the right pane, double-click the **My Pictures** folder.

The folder contains a shortcut to a Sample Pictures folder, whose icon displays previews of up to four pictures in the folder:

In Home Edition, you might not see these pictures.

14 In the right pane, double-click the **Sample Pictures** folder.

The contents of the folder are displayed:

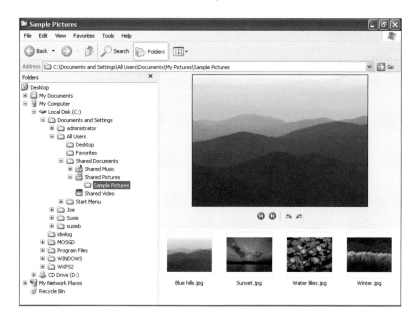

When you double-click the shortcut, you link to the folder to which the shortcut points. In this case, the shortcut links to the All Users folder. The Address Bar reflects the actual location of the folder.

15 On the toolbar, click the **Back** button.

Back

You return to your previous location, your own My Pictures folder.

16 On the toolbar, click the **Forward** button.

Forward

You return to the Sample Pictures folder.

17 On the toolbar, click the **Up** button.

Up

You move up one folder to the *C:\Documents and Settings\All Users\Documents \My Pictures* folder.

18 Click the **Close** button at the right end of the window's title bar to close the window.

Close

Viewing Files and Folders in Different Ways

new for
WindowsXP

New ways of
viewing files
and pictures

On the right side of the Windows Explorer window, you can view your files and folders in several different ways. You can view thumbnails or slide shows of graphic files, display file and folder types as tiles or icons, or view a detailed or not-so-detailed file list. The view options for each folder are available on that folder window's toolbar, and they vary depending on the contents of the folder. Available views include the following:

- *Details view* displays a list of files or folders and their properties. The properties shown by default for each file or folder are Name, Size, Type, and Date Modified. For pictures, the defaults also include Date Picture Taken and Dimensions. You can display a variety of other properties that might be pertinent to specific types of files, including Date Created, Data Accessed, Attributes, Status, Owner, Author, Title, Subject, Category, Pages, Comments, Copyright, Artist, Album Title, Year, Track Number, Genre, Duration, Bit Rate, Protected, Camera Model, Company, Description, File Version, Product Name, and Product Version.

- *Filmstrip view* displays a large version of the currently selected picture at the top of the window above a single row of smaller versions of all the pictures in the current folder. This option is available only for the My Pictures folder and its subfolders. Subfolders containing graphics display miniature versions of up to four of the graphics contained in the folder on top of the folder icon.

- *Icons view* displays the icon and file name for each file or folder in the current folder.

- *List view* displays a list of the files and folders in the current folder, with no information other than the file name and a small icon representing the file type.

■ *Thumbnails view* displays miniature representations of each file in the current folder. Thumbnails of graphics are small versions of the graphics themselves. Other types of files are represented by file type icons. Subfolders containing graphics display miniature versions of up to four of the graphics contained in the folder on top of the folder icon. The file or folder name is displayed below the thumbnail.

■ *Tiles view* displays a large file type icon or folder icon, the file or folder name, and up to two additional pieces of information for each file in the current folder. The additional information varies depending on the type of file.

In this exercise, you will open a folder in Windows Explorer, navigate to another location using the Address Bar, and then view a group of files in several different ways.

BE SURE TO log on to Windows and display the Windows Explorer Address Bar before beginning this exercise.

Tip If the Address Bar is not visible in your current view of Windows Explorer, right-click the toolbar and then click **Address Bar** on the shortcut menu.

USE the image, text, document, and audio files in the practice file folder for this topic. These practice files are located in the *My Documents\Microsoft Press\Microsoft Windows XP SBS\Structure\Views* folder.

Follow these steps:

1 On the **Start** menu, click **My Documents**.

The My Documents folder opens in Windows Explorer.

The right pane displays the folders and files contained in your My Documents folder. The left pane displays a list of tasks and places that are relevant to the My Documents folder.

2 Click in the **Address** box on the Address Bar.

My Documents is highlighted, and anything you type will now replace it.

3 Press **END**, and then type \Microsoft Press\Microsoft Windows XP SBS\Structure \Views. (If you did not save the practice files in the default location, substitute the correct location.)

4 Click the **Go** button or press **ENTER**.

You move to the specified folder.

5   Click **Baby Girl** to preview this picture:

The left pane links to tasks and places related to this folder.

The current view displays the selected file, along with a "filmstrip" of all the other files in the folder.

Tip   If you have changed the default folder view, your window might look different from this one.

6   On the toolbar, click the **Views** button.

A drop-down menu displays the view options available for this folder:

Views

The menu indicates that Filmstrip view is currently selected.

7   On the menu, click **Thumbnails**.

The folder content is displayed in Thumbnails view:

The associated tasks and locations do not change, because you have changed only how you see the folder's content, not the content itself.

8 On the toolbar, click the **Views** button again, and then on the drop-down menu, click **Icons** to switch to Icons view:

9 On the **Views** drop-down menu, click **List** to switch to List view:

10 On the **Views** drop-down menu, click **Details** to switch to that view:

The up arrow indicates that the files are sorted in ascending alphabetical order by name.

11 Move the pointer over the first four column headings (*Name*, *Size*, *Type*, and *Date Modified*).

As the pointer passes over each heading, the heading changes color to indicate that it is currently selected.

12 Click **Size**.

The nine files are re-sorted in ascending order by file size, as indicated by the up arrow next to Size.

13 Click **Size** again.

The files are re-sorted in descending order by file size, and the arrow changes direction to indicate the change of order.

14 Right-click any of the column headings to display this shortcut menu:

The columns currently displayed on the right side of the window are indicated by check marks. *Name* is gray because the file name must be displayed.

15 On the shortcut menu, click **Author**.

A check mark appears next to your selection. When the menu closes, a new column called *Author* is displayed, and the names of the people who created the files are listed, for files that have associated authors.

16 Right-click a column heading, and click **More** at the bottom of the shortcut menu.

The **Choose Details** dialog box appears:

Choose Details

Select the details you want to display for the files in this folder.

Details:

- ☑ Name
- ☑ Size
- ☑ Type
- ☑ Date Modified
- ☑ Author
- ☑ Date Picture Taken
- ☑ Dimensions
- ☐ Date Created
- ☐ Date Accessed
- ☐ Attributes
- ☐ Status
- ☐ Owner
- ☐ Title
- ☐ Subject
- ☐ Category

Move Up
Move Down
Show
Hide

Width of selected column (in pixels):

OK   Cancel

The currently displayed columns appear at the top of the list.

17 Scroll through the list of available columns.

18 Clear the **Author** check box, and then click **OK**.

The **Choose Details** dialog box closes and the *Author* column disappears.

19 Click the **Close** button to close Windows Explorer.

Close

Looking at File and Folder Information

Each file and folder has a variety of information associated with it, including its name, size, author, and many other items. You can view the information for all the files or subfolders in a folder by looking at the folder contents in Details view. You can look at the information for a specific file or folder by viewing its properties. You can also edit some file and folder properties.

Windows XP has a variety of special folder types. By storing files of the corresponding type in one of these folders, you can use features that are desirable for that type, such as playing music clips or viewing photographs. Folder types include:

- Documents
- Pictures
- Photo Album

- Music
- Music Artist
- Music Album
- Videos

In this exercise, you will add the Address toolbar to the taskbar, navigate to a directory using the Address toolbar, view the properties of a file, view the properties of the folder, and change the picture shown on the front of the folder.

BE SURE TO log on to Windows and unlock the taskbar before beginning this exercise.

> **Tip**   To lock or unlock the taskbar, right-click the taskbar and then click **Lock the Taskbar** on the shortcut menu.

USE the image, text, document, and audio files in the practice file folder for this topic. These practice files are located in the *My Documents\Microsoft Press\Microsoft Windows XP SBS\Structure \Information* **folder.**

Follow these steps:

1   Right-click the taskbar. On the taskbar shortcut menu, point to **Toolbars**, and then click **Address**.

The Address toolbar is added to the taskbar. It is currently minimized, like this:

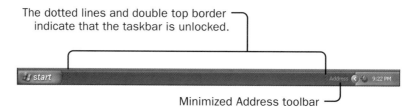

The dotted lines and double top border indicate that the taskbar is unlocked.

Minimized Address toolbar

2   Position the pointer over the double dotted line to the left of the Address toolbar until the pointer changes to a double-headed arrow. Then drag the line to the left until you can see the entire Address toolbar:

3   Click in the **Address** box, and type \My Documents\Microsoft Press\Microsoft Windows XP SBS\Structure\Information.

4   Click the **Go** button or press **ENTER**.

You move to the specified folder, which looks like this:

The left pane displays links to tasks and places related to this folder.

The folder opens in Tiles view.

Troubleshooting   If your folder does not look like this, click the **Views** button on the toolbar, and click **Tiles**.

5   Right-click the **Bean Trees** file, and click **Properties** on the shortcut menu.

This **Bean Trees Properties** dialog box appears:

6   Click each tab, and look at the information. Then click **Cancel**.

7   On the **Other Places** menu, click **Structure** to move up one level.

The subfolders of the **Structure** folder are displayed:

8 Right-click the **Information** folder and then click **Properties** on the short-cut menu.

The **Information Properties** dialog box appears.

9 Look at the information on the **General**, **Sharing**, and **Security** tabs.

Troubleshooting   In Home Edition, the dialog box does not have a **Security** tab.

The information on the tabs is identical to that in a file's **Properties** dialog box.

10 Click the **Customize** tab:

11 Click the down arrow to the right of the **Use this folder type as a template** box to view the list of available folder templates.

12 Click the down arrow again to contract the list.

13 In the **Folder pictures** section, click **Choose Picture**.

The **Browse** dialog box appears, displaying the graphic files contained in the Information folder.

14 Click **Smiley**, and then click **Open** to close the dialog box and apply your selection.

15 Click **OK** to close the **Information Properties** dialog box and save your changes.

Creating, Editing, and Deleting Files and Folders

Each application on your computer creates files of a particular type. For example, Microsoft Office Word creates documents (.doc files), Microsoft Office Excel creates spreadsheets (.xls files), Microsoft Office Access creates databases (.mdb files), and so on. You can also create and edit simple text documents and graphics using the tools that come with Windows XP.

As you create these files, you will want to create folders in which to organize the files for easy retrieval.

new for
WindowsXP

Compressed
(zipped)
folders

When you buy a computer these days, it likely comes with a hard disk that will store several *gigabytes (GB)* of information. A gigabyte is 1 billion *bytes*, and a byte is a unit of information that is the equivalent of one character. Some of your files will be very small—1 to 2 *kilobytes (KB)*, or 1000 to 2000 bytes—and others might be quite large—several *megabytes (MB)*, or several million bytes. If you create enough files that you start to get concerned about running out of hard disk space, you might want to *zip* folders. A zipped folder is a folder whose contents are compressed. The folder can contain files you created, program files, or even other folders. Compressed content takes up less space and is easier to copy or move from one place to another, especially if you are doing the copying via e-mail. Zipped folders are indicated by a zipper on the folder icon. You can protect a zipped folder with a password.

In this exercise, you will create a new folder and two new files: a text document and a picture. You will then compress your two new files into a zipped folder and delete all the files and folders you created in the exercise.

BE SURE TO log on to Windows and display the Address toolbar on the taskbar before beginning this exercise.

Tip If the Address toolbar is not open on the taskbar, open it by right-clicking the taskbar, pointing to **Toolbars** on the shortcut menu, and clicking **Address**. Then resize the toolbar by dragging the dotted line to the left. The taskbar must be unlocked for you to be able to resize the Address toolbar.

Follow these steps:

1   On the taskbar, click in the **Address** box, and type C:\My Documents \Microsoft Press\Microsoft Windows XP SBS\Structure\Creating.

2   Press **ENTER** or click the **Go** button.

The window for the specified folder opens in Windows Explorer. The folder is empty.

Views

3   Click the **Views** button, make sure that **Tiles** is selected on the drop-down menu, and then click away from the menu to close it.

4   Read the list of tasks currently available on the **File and Folder Tasks** menu.

Because the folder doesn't contain any files, all three available options are related to folders.

5   On the **File and Folder Tasks** menu, click **Make a new folder**.

A new folder is created with the name *New Folder*. The file name is selected so that you can change it:

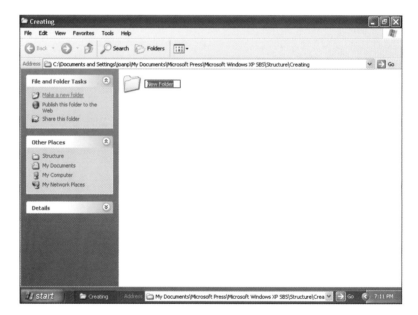

6   Type My Folder, and then press **ENTER**.

7   Double-click your new folder to open it.

8   Right-click the empty right pane, and on the shortcut menu, point to **New**, and then click **Text Document**.

A new text document is created with the name *New Text Document*. The file name is selected so that you can change it.

9   Type My Text File.txt, and then press **ENTER**.

The file is renamed, and the file name, file type, and file size are displayed next to the file's icon. Because the file is empty, the size is 0 KB.

The **File and Folder Tasks** menu changes to reflect the addition of your new file:

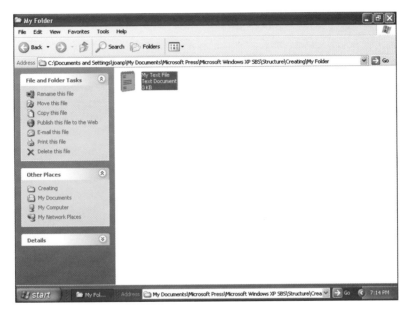

10   Double-click the file icon.

The text document opens in the Microsoft Notepad program, where you can edit it.

Tip   *Notepad* is a text-editing program that comes with Windows XP.

11   Type This is a text file that I created in Microsoft Windows Notepad.

Close

12   Click the file's **Close** button to close the file, and click **Yes** when you are prompted to save your changes.

The file information changes to reflect a new file size of 1 KB.

Tip   This file doesn't really contain 1000 characters. The file size shown in Windows Explorer is rounded up to the nearest whole kilobyte.

13   Right-click an empty area of the right pane, and on the shortcut menu, point to **New**, and then click **Bitmap Image**.

A new graphic file is created with the name *New Bitmap Image*. The file name is selected so that you can change it.

14   Type My Graphic File.bmp, and then press **ENTER**.

The file is renamed, and the file name and file type are displayed next to the file's icon.

15 Right-click the graphic file, and click **Edit** on the shortcut menu.

The file opens in the Microsoft Paint program:

Because it is a new file, the canvas is empty.

16 Click the **Maximize** button to make the window fit the screen.

Maximize

Tip *Paint* is a simple graphics program that comes with Windows XP. You can use Paint to create simple *bitmap* images and to edit graphics in the bitmap format. Bitmaps represent images as dots, or *pixels*, on the screen.

See Also For more information, refer to Chapter 9, "Working with Graphics and Documents."

---

17 Experiment with the Paint tools as you paint a picture of any kind. (Click a tool, move the pointer over the blank canvas, and drag the pointer to use the tool.) When you're done, click the Paint window's **Close** button, and click **Yes** when you are prompted to save your changes.

The file information changes to reflect the size of the graphic; in this case, the file is 400 pixels wide x 300 pixels high.

18 Click the text file to select it, hold down the **CTRL** key, and then click the graphic file to select it as well.

As you select each file or combination of files, the **File and Folder Tasks** menu changes to reflect the currently valid options.

19 Right-click the selection, and on the shortcut menu, point to **Send To**, and then click **Compressed (zipped) Folder**.

20 If you are prompted to associate ZIP files with compressed (zipped) folders, click **Yes**.

A zipped folder named after one of the selected files is created:

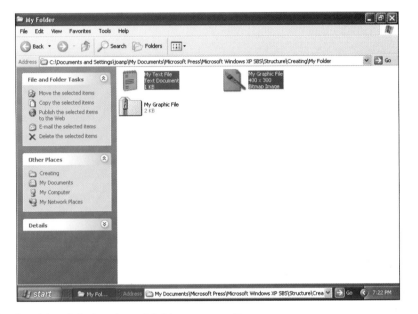

21 Double-click the zipped folder to open it.

You can see your files inside.

22 On the toolbar, click the **Up** button two times to return to the *My Documents \Microsoft Press\Microsoft Windows XP SBS\Structure\Creating* folder.

Up

23 Click the **My Folder** folder to select it.

Tip If you want to save your text file or graphic file, skip step 24.

24 On the **File and Folder Tasks** menu, click **Delete this folder**, and click **Yes** when you are prompted to confirm the deletion of the folder and its contents.

25 Click the window's **Close** button to close it.

Working with Files and Folders on Multiple Computers

If you regularly work on more than one computer, you probably need a simple way of moving files back and forth between computers. You can use *Briefcase* to help avoid the confusion of having different versions of the same file in different places. You can store files in Briefcase, carry Briefcase to another computer, and then carry Briefcase back to your main computer, where Briefcase will synchronize the working version with the originals. To use Briefcase:

1   Right-click the desktop, or right-click an empty area of the right pane in Windows Explorer.

2   On the shortcut menu, point to **New**, and then click **Briefcase**.

A new folder named *New Briefcase* is created.

3   Right-click the briefcase icon, click **Rename** on the shortcut menu, and give the briefcase any name you want.

4   Double-click the briefcase icon to open it in Windows Explorer. (If you see an information window, read the information, and click **Finish**.)

5   Drag your files into the briefcase.

A copy of each file is created inside the briefcase. The copy is linked to the original file, and the location of the original file is displayed, along with its status (whether the original and the copy are synchronized).

6   Move the briefcase folder to a floppy disk or other portable storage medium, or copy the briefcase folder to another computer over the network or via a direct cable connection.

7   Work on the original files or the files inside the briefcase.

8   After you make changes, insert the disk containing the briefcase into your main computer, or reconnect your laptop computer to your main computer, and click **Update All** on the **Briefcase** menu to bring your files up to date.

Moving and Renaming Files and Folders

When you have accumulated enough files that you need to organize them in some way, you can easily make copies of existing files and folders, move files and folders from one location to another, and rename files and folders. The organization methods of copying, pasting, moving, and renaming are the same for both files and folders.

In this exercise, you will make copies of files and folders using four different methods and then move files between folders using two different methods.

BE SURE TO log on to Windows and display the Address toolbar on the taskbar before beginning this exercise.

> **Tip** If the Address toolbar is not open on the taskbar, open it by right-clicking the task-bar, pointing to **Toolbars** on the shortcut menu, and clicking **Address**. Then resize the toolbar by dragging the dotted line to the left. The taskbar must be unlocked for you to be able to resize the Address toolbar.

USE the *Folder 1* and *Folder 2* folders and the *My Graphic File* image in the practice file folder for this topic. These practice files are located in the *My Documents\Microsoft Press\Microsoft Windows XP SBS\Structure\Organizing* folder.

Follow these steps:

1 On the taskbar, click in the **Address** box, and type My Documents\Microsoft Press\Microsoft Windows XP SBS\Structure\Organizing.

2 Press **ENTER** or click the **Go** button.

The *My Documents\Microsoft Press\Microsoft Windows XP SBS\Structure \Organizing* folder opens in Windows Explorer. The folder contains two subfolders named *Folder 1* and *Folder 2*. Folder 1 contains a file called *My Graphic File*. Folder 2 is currently empty.

3 Click the **Views** button, and make sure that **Tiles** is selected.

Views

4 Click **Folder 1** to select it. On the **File and Folder Tasks** menu, click **Copy this folder**.

The **Copy Items** dialog box appears:

5 In the dialog box, browse to the *My Documents\Microsoft Press\Microsoft Windows XP SBS\Structure\Organizing* folder, and then click **Copy**.

Windows creates a copy of the folder, called *Copy of Folder 1*.

6 Right-click the new folder, and click **Rename** on the shortcut menu.

The folder name is selected for editing.

7 Type **Folder** 3, and press **ENTER**.

The folder is renamed.

8 Double-click **Folder 3** to open it.

Folder 3 opens in Filmstrip view. The folder contains a file called *My Graphic File*.

9 Now you'll create a copy of this file. Right-click the file, and click **Copy** on the short-cut menu.

10 Right-click an empty area at the bottom of the right pane, and click **Paste** on the shortcut menu.

Troubleshooting In Filmstrip view, you manipulate the files shown at the bottom of the window rather than the preview file at the top of the window.

Windows creates a copy of the file, called *Copy of My Graphic File*.

11 To create a second copy by using a different method, on the **Edit** menu, click **Paste**.

Windows creates a copy with the name *Copy (2) of My Graphic File*:

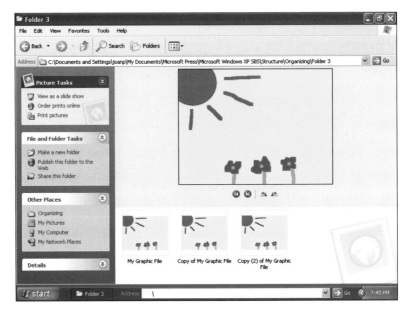

12 To create a third copy by using a different method, on the toolbar, click the **Up** button to return to the *My Documents\Microsoft Press\Microsoft Windows XP SBS \Structure\Organizing* folder.

Up

13 Double-click **Folder 2** to open it, and press **CTRL+V**, the keyboard shortcut for the **Paste** command, to paste the copy in that folder.

Windows creates a copy of the file. Because it is the first copy in this location, it is named *My Graphic File* without a copy number.

Tip *Keyboard shortcuts* provide a quick way of carrying out actions from the keyboard instead of using the mouse. If a command has a keyboard shortcut, the shortcut appears next to the command on its menu. For a list of keyboard shortcuts, search the Help file for *Windows keyboard shortcuts overview*.

14 On the toolbar, click the **Back** button two times to return to Folder 3.

15 Click **Copy (2) of My Graphic File** to select it.

16 On the **File and Folder Tasks** menu, click **Move this file**.

The **Move Items** dialog box appears with the *My Documents\Microsoft Press \Microsoft Windows XP SBS\Structure\Organizing* folder highlighted:

![Move Items dialog box showing folder tree with Connecting, Personalizing, Playing, Solving, Structure expanded to show Creating, Information, Organizing. Buttons: Make New Folder, Move, Cancel.]

17 Click **Organizing**, click **Folder 2**, and then click **Move** to move the file to Folder 2. When prompted to confirm the move, click Yes.

The file disappears from Folder 3.

18 Click the **Up** button, and then double-click **Folder 2** to open it.

The file is now in this folder.

Folders **19** On the toolbar, click the **Folders** button to change to Folders view.

The left pane displays the hierarchical structure of your computer, expanded to show the current folder:

20 Drag **Copy (2) of My Graphic File** from the right pane, and drop it in Folder 1 in the left pane. Click **Yes** when prompted to confirm the move.

The file disappears from Folder 2.

21 In the left pane, click **Folder 1** to open it.

The file is now in this folder.

Close

22 Click the window's **Close** button to close it.

143

Finding Files

new for
WindowsXP

Search
Companion

You can search for all types of objects, including files, printers, and computers, using a feature of Windows XP called *Search Companion*. You can search for files on your own computer, on other computers on your network, or even on the entire Internet. You can search for computers on your organization's network, and you can also search for people on your network or on the Internet.

Search Companion is user-friendly and comes equipped with a guide, in the form of an animated screen character. The default character is Rover the dog, but you can change the character to Merlin the wizard, Courtney the tour guide, or Earl the surfer. If you want, you can remove the character entirely.

Included in Search Companion is *Indexing Service*, which indexes the files on your computer while your computer is idle, improving search speed. (Indexing creates a database of file names and contents so that Search Companion can search the database instead of having to search the files themselves.)

In this exercise, you will search for a text file called *Find this file* on your computer, turn on Indexing Service to speed up future searches, and change the Search Companion animated screen character.

BE SURE TO log on to Windows before beginning this exercise.
USE the *Find this file* text file in the practice file folder for this topic. This practice file is located in the *My Documents\Microsoft Press\Microsoft Windows XP SBS\Structure\Searching* folder.

Follow these steps:

Search

1 On the **Start** menu, click **Search**.

The **Search Results** window opens, with Search Companion displayed on the left side:

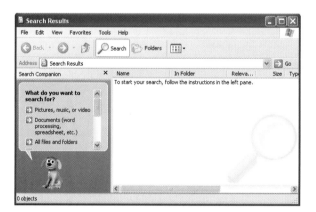

Maximize

2 Click the window's **Maximize** button so that you can see all the options at once.

3 In the list of search options, click **All files and folders**.

Search Companion's next page prompts you to enter identifying characteristics, called *search criteria*, for the file or folder you are searching for:

4   In the **A word or phrase in the file** box, type **Windows XP Step by Step**.

Tip   In searches, the asterisk (*) is a *wildcard* that represents any number of characters (including zero). The question mark (?) is a wildcard that represents one character. For example, enter *.txt* to search for any text file; enter *s*.txt* to search for any text file with a file name that begins with the letter *s*; and enter *s??.txt* to search for any text file that has a three-letter file name beginning with the letter *s*.

5   In the **Look in** box, make sure that **Local Hard Drives** is selected in the drop-down list, and then click **Search**.

Search Companion searches your computer for all files containing the search phrase and displays a list of the files in the right pane. The search might take some time, but entering a specific phrase helps to narrow the results.

When the search is complete, Search Companion's next page asks whether your desired file was found. It should now be easy to spot the file you're looking for, Find This File.

6   In the left pane, click **Yes, but make future searches faster**.

7   On the next page, click **Yes, enable Indexing Service**, and then click **OK**.

There is no apparent change when you turn on Indexing Service, but from that point on, it will run continuously on your computer.

8   Click the Rover character to open this page:

9   Just for fun, click **Do a trick** a few times to see how talented Rover is.

10   When you're done, click **Choose a different animated character**.

11   On the selection page, click **Next** to cycle through the available options, and when you find a character you like, click **OK**.

Rover wanders off, and your selected character takes his place.

Tip   If having Indexing Service turned on seems to slow down your computer, you can turn it off by clicking **Search** on the **Start** menu, then **Change preferences**, then **Without Indexing Service**, and then **No, do not enable Indexing Service**. Then click **OK**.

12   Click the **Close** button in the Search Companion title bar to close the pane.

Close

Accessing Your Entire Network

Windows Explorer gives you access not only to drives and resources on your own computer, but also to drives and resources across your entire network and the Internet through the My Network Places folder.

To browse to another computer or resource on your network, open Windows Explorer in either Tasks view or Folders view, and click **My Network Places**.

If you want to access a particular network drive or resource on a regular basis—for example, if you regularly connect to a specific server—you can *map* the drive in Windows Explorer to make it more easily available. When you map a drive, you assign it a *local* drive letter so you can easily browse to it. You can also instruct Windows to reconnect to that drive every time you log on.

To map a drive in Windows Explorer:

1 Open Windows Explorer in Tasks view or Folders view.

2 On the **Tools** menu, click **Map Network Drive**.

3 Specify the drive letter you would like to use for this drive.

4 Browse to the folder, specify your connection options, and click **Finish**.

Key Points

■ Windows XP displays graphic representations of the files and folders on your computer. Different file types are represented by different graphic icons, so you can more easily differentiate between them.

■ Certain data such as file size and author is stored with each file. You can view and change this data in Windows Explorer.

■ You can use Windows Search Companion to locate a file or folder on your computer using whatever information you have about that item. You can locate specific files based on words or phrase contained therein.

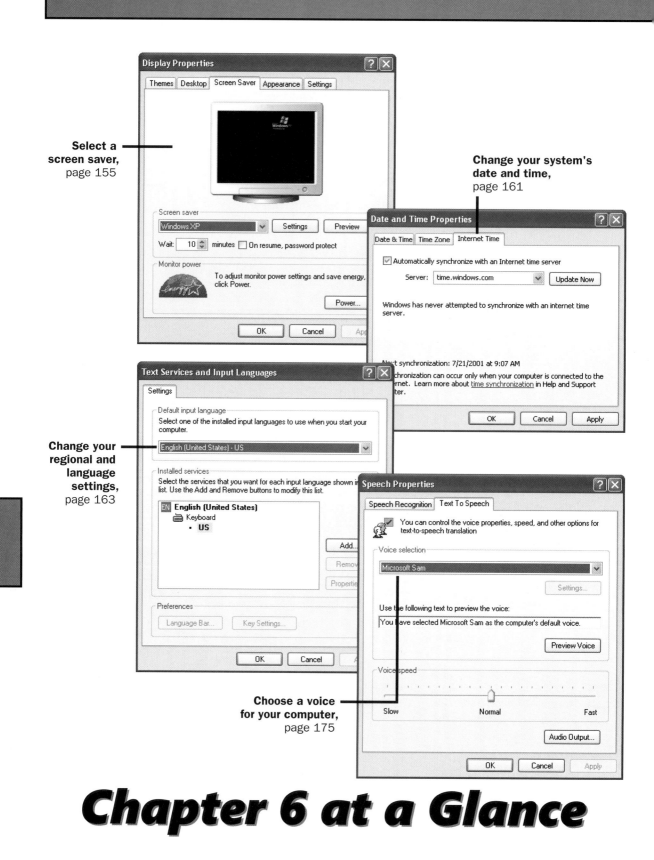

Select a screen saver, page 155

Change your system's date and time, page 161

Change your regional and language settings, page 163

Choose a voice for your computer, page 175

Chapter 6 at a Glance

6 Personalizing Windows XP

In this chapter you will learn to:

✔ Change the look of your working environment.

✔ Change your system's date, time, regional, and language settings.

✔ Make Windows XP easier to see and use.

✔ Train your computer to recognize your voice.

✔ Choose a voice for your computer.

The way programs look on your computer screen and the way you use them are determined to a large extent by the Microsoft Windows XP user interface. Some elements of the interface, such as the graphics, fonts, and colors, are cosmetic. Other aspects, such as how much you can see on the screen, how the computer handles numeric values, and which language it uses, affect the way you work. In this chapter, you will learn how to personalize your computer to fit the way you work.

Until recently, the only way most people could communicate with their computers was by typing and clicking the mouse buttons. With Windows XP, talking to your computer is no longer science fiction. You can train your computer to recognize your voice so you can input information by talking. You can also choose the voice you'd like to hear when the computer talks to you!

For some people, talking to the computer might be a way of working around physical limitations. Many special devices are available to people with disabilities to give them full access to the capabilities of their computers. Microsoft is at the forefront of efforts to make technology more accessible and works closely with other companies and organizations to ensure that its technology fully supports accessibility devices. Windows XP includes options and special programs that you can use to better see, hear, and control your computer.

See Also Do you need only a quick refresher on the topics in this chapter? See the Quick Reference entries on pages xxxii–xxxiv.

 Important Before you can use the practice files in this chapter, you need to install them from the book's companion CD to their default location. See "Using the Book's CD-ROM" on page xv for more information.

Changing the Look and Feel of Windows

new for
WindowsXP

Theme
Improvements

You can easily change the look of the Windows interface by applying a different *theme*. Each theme includes a desktop background color or picture; a color scheme that affects title bars and labels; specific fonts that are used on title bars, labels, and buttons; icons that graphically represent common programs; sounds that are associated with specific actions; and other elements. Previous versions of Windows came with a long list of available themes, and additional themes could be downloaded from the Internet. Windows XP has simplified the theme-selection process by offering only two basic themes—Windows XP and Windows Classic—and making all the other themes available online.

In this exercise, you will switch between the Windows XP and Windows Classic themes. If you want, you can explore the online options on your own at a later time.

BE SURE TO log on to Windows before beginning this exercise.
OPEN Control Panel.

Follow these steps:

1 In the Control Panel window, click the **Appearance and Themes** icon.

The Appearance and Themes window opens:

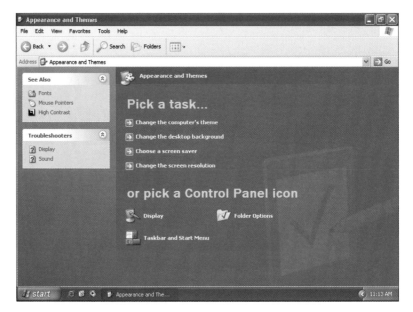

2 Click the **Change the computer's theme** task.

The **Display Properties** dialog box appears, with the **Themes** tab selected.

A preview of the current theme is displayed in the Sample window.

3 Click the down arrow to the right of the **Theme** box, and click **Windows Classic** in the drop-down list.

The Sample window changes to reflect your selection:

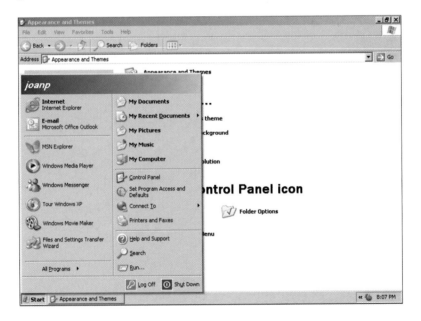

4   Click **OK** to close the dialog box and apply your settings.

The **Appearance and Themes** dialog box appears again, now with a white background. The taskbar and **Start** menu have also changed:

Close

5 Click the window's **Close** button to return to the desktop.

The classic desktop looks quite boring compared to the Windows XP desktop!

6 Repeat steps 1 through 3 to return to the **Themes** tab of the **Display Properties** dialog box.

7 Click the down arrow to the right of the **Theme** box, and click **Windows XP** in the drop-down list.

8 Click **OK** to close the dialog box and return to the Appearance and Themes window, which now has the Windows XP look and feel.

CLOSE the Appearance and Themes window.

Applying a Custom Desktop Background

The default desktop background for Windows XP Professional is an outdoor scene, with the Windows XP logo and version in the lower right corner. If this background doesn't appeal to you, you can easily change it. Your choice of background usually reflects your personal taste—what you'd like to see when your program windows are minimized or closed. Some people prefer simple backgrounds that don't interfere with their desktop icons, and others like photos of family members, pets, or favorite places.

Windows XP comes with over 30 desktop backgrounds to choose from. Some of them are photographs; others are geometric patterns. If you prefer, you can opt for a plain background and then set its color. You can also choose a photograph of your own.

In this exercise, you will first switch to a plain, colored background, choose a background photograph, and then return to the default background.

OPEN Control Panel, and then click the Appearance and Themes icon.

Follow these steps:

1 In the Appearance and Themes window, click the **Change the desktop background** task.

The **Display Properties** dialog box appears with the **Desktop** tab selected:

A preview of the current desktop background is displayed at the top of the dialog box.

The **Background** box contains a list of background options.

Tip   You can quickly open the **Display Properties** dialog box by right-clicking an empty area of the desktop and clicking **Properties** on the shortcut menu.

2   Use the Up Arrow and Down Arrow keys to scroll through the list of available backgrounds.

As you select each background, it is displayed on the preview screen at the top of the dialog box.

3   In the **Background** box, click **None**.

The preview screen now displays a plain, colored background.

4   Click the down arrow to the right of the **Color** box, and click the purple square in the drop-down list.

Your choice is reflected on the preview screen.

5   Click **Apply** to apply your background selection.

Minimize

6 Click the Appearance and Themes window's **Minimize** button so that you can see your new background behind the dialog box, like this:

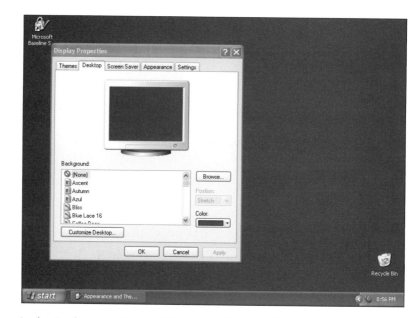

7 In the **Background** box, click **Azul**, and then click **Apply**.

The selected background is visible behind the dialog box, like this:

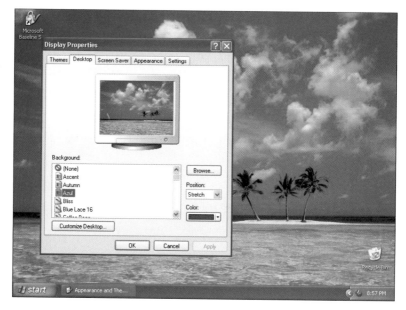

8 Click **OK** to close the **Display Properties** dialog box.

9 Now you will return the desktop to its default state. Right-click a blank area of the desktop, and click **Properties** on the shortcut menu.

10 Click the **Desktop** tab.

11 In the **Background** box, click **Bliss**.

12 Click the down arrow to the right of the **Color** drop-down list, click **Other**, and then click the smoky blue that is in the third square down in the fifth column in the **Basic colors** area.

13 Click **OK** to close the **Color** dialog box and save your changes.

14 Click **OK** to close the **Display Properties** dialog box.

CLOSE the Appearance and Themes window.

Selecting a Screen Saver

new for
WindowsXP

My Pictures
Screen Saver

Screen savers are static or moving images that are displayed on your computer after some period of inactivity. The original concept behind screen savers was that they prevented your computer's monitor from being permanently "imprinted" with a specific pattern when it was left on for too long without changing. Modern monitors are not as susceptible to this kind of damage, but it is still a good idea to use a screen saver or to have your monitor automatically use power-saver mode after a given period with no activity.

Using a screen saver is also an excellent way to protect your computer from prying eyes when you are away from your desk. To further protect your data, you can require that your password be entered to unlock the screen saver after it is set in motion.

Windows XP comes with 10 animated screen savers. The default Windows XP screen saver is a Windows XP logo that moves around on a black background. You can download other animated screen savers from the Internet. Alternately, you can instruct Windows XP to display images from a specific folder as your screen saver.

Tip To quickly locate additional screen savers visit *search.microsoft.com*, type **screen savers** in the **Search Microsoft.com for** box, and then click the **Go** button.

In this exercise, you will select a screen saver that consists of a slideshow of photographs.

USE the image files in the practice file folder for this topic. These practice files are located in the *My Documents\Microsoft Press\Microsoft Windows XP SBS\Personalizing\ScreenSaver* folder.

Tip If you have a folder of your own favorite photos on your computer, feel free to use the photos in that folder instead.

OPEN Control Panel, and then click the Appearance and Themes icon.

Follow these steps:

1   In the Appearance and Themes window, click the **Choose a screen saver** task.

The **Display Properties** dialog box appears with the **Screen Saver** tab selected:

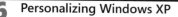

2   Click the down arrow to the right of the **Screen saver** box.

3   In the drop-down list, click **My Pictures Slideshow**.

The preview screen displays a slideshow of the pictures in your My Pictures folder, if there are any pictures there.

4   Click the **Settings** button.

The **My Pictures Screen Saver Options** dialog box appears:

5 Click **Browse**.

The **Browse for Folder** dialog box appears.

6 Browse to the *My Documents\Microsoft Press\Microsoft Windows XP SBS*
Personalizing\ScreenSaver folder, and click **OK**.

7 Click **OK** to close the **My Pictures Screen Saver Options** dialog box, and then click
Preview on the **Screen Saver** tab to see what your slideshow will look like as a
screen saver.

Notice the variety of transitional effects used between photos. (Don't move the
mouse or the preview will stop.)

8 Move the mouse or press any key on the keyboard to finish previewing the slideshow.

Tip To use a password to return to your regular desktop in Windows XP Professional, select the **On resume, password protect** check box on the **Screen Saver** tab.

9 Click **OK** to close the dialog box and apply your settings.

CLOSE the Appearance and Themes window.
BE SURE TO repeat the exercise to revert to the original *Windows XP* screen saver if you want.

Changing Specific Interface Elements

In addition to making major changes to your theme and background, you can also make finer adjustments to various parts of your working environment, such as the following:

■ Choose Windows XP–style or Windows Classic–style windows and buttons.

■ Choose from 3 Windows XP color schemes or 22 Windows Classic color schemes.

■ Choose normal, large, or extra large display fonts.

■ Stipulate a fade or scroll transition effect for menus and ScreenTips.

■ Smooth the edges of screen fonts using standard or ClearType technology.

■ Use large icons.

■ Show shadows under menus.

■ Show the contents of a window while you are dragging it.

■ Hide keyboard shortcuts on menus.

All these options can be set on the Appearance tab of the Display Properties dialog box.

Changing Your Monitor Settings

When you purchase a computer monitor, one of the things you consider is its size or display area, which is measured like a television screen: diagonally in inches. After the monitor is set up, you are more likely to be concerned about its resolution or *screen area*, which is measured in *pixels* and is expressed as *pixels wide* by *pixels high*.

When personal computers first became popular, most computer monitors were capable of displaying a screen area of only 640 pixels wide by 480 pixels high (known as 640 × 480). Now most computer monitors can also display at 800 × 600 pixels and 1024 × 768 pixels, and some can display a screen area of 1600 × 1200 pixels (or perhaps by the time this book is published, even higher). In effect, as the screen resolution increases, the size of the pixels decreases, and a larger screen area can be shown in the same display area.

Most computer users have a choice of at least two different screen resolutions. Some people prefer to work at 640 × 480 because everything on their screen appears larger; others prefer to fit more information on their screen with a 1024 × 768 (or higher) display. Recent statistics indicate that approximately 1 percent of Internet users have their screen resolution set to 640 × 480, and approximately 38 percent have a screen resolution of 800 × 600. The fastest-growing segment of the market, approximately 60 percent of Internet users, have a screen resolution of 1024 × 768 or greater.

In this exercise, you will change your screen area to the maximum and minimum sizes supported by your computer.

Troubleshooting   Screen resolution capabilities are partly dependent on your specific monitor. The settings shown or specified in this exercise might not be available on your computer.

OPEN Control Panel, and then click the Appearance and Themes icon.

Follow these steps:

1   In the Appearance and Themes window, click the **Change the screen resolution** task.

The **Display Properties** dialog box appears with the **Settings** tab selected:

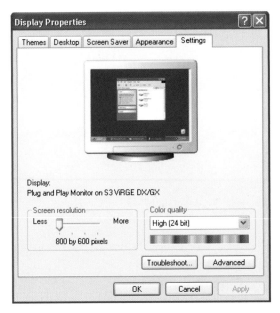

2   Point to the marker on the **Screen resolution** slider, hold down the mouse button, and drag the marker all the way to the right to change to the maximum resolution.

The change is reflected on the preview screen.

Tip   As you move the resolution slider to the right, the color quality setting might change. Often the maximum resolution will not support the highest color quality.

3   Click **Apply**.

Your screen resolution changes. The **Monitor Settings** dialog box appears, prompting you to indicate whether you like the change:

You have 15 seconds to make your decision. If you click **Yes**, the resolution is retained; if you click **No** or don't click either button, the resolution returns to its previous setting.

4 Click **Yes**.

The dialog box closes, and your screen is at its maximum resolution:

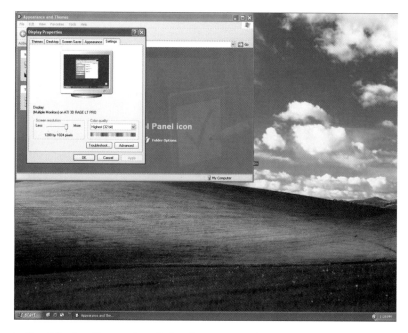

5 In the **Display Properties** dialog box, move the **Screen resolution** slider all the way to the left to change to the minimum resolution.

The change is reflected on the preview screen.

6 Click **OK**, and then if prompted, click **Yes** in the **Monitor Settings** dialog box to complete the change.

CLOSE the Appearance and Themes window.
BE SURE TO repeat the exercise to select your preferred screen resolution if you want.

Changing Your System's Date and Time

By default, Windows XP displays the *system time* in the notification area at the right end of the taskbar. When you point to the time, the *system date* is displayed as a ScreenTip. The system time controls a number of behind-the-scenes settings and is also used by Windows and your programs to maintain an accurate record of happenings on your computer.

Tip If you prefer to not display the time, right-click a blank area of the taskbar, click **Properties** on the shortcut menu, and clear the **Show the clock** check box in the **Taskbar and Start Menu Properties** dialog box.

new for
WindowsXP

Internet Time
Synchronization

You can set the system date, system time, and time zone manually, or if your computer is connected to a network domain, you can use a *time server* to synchronize your computer clock automatically. If your computer is not connected to a network domain, you can synchronize your system time with an Internet-based time server. If you have a continuous Internet connection, you can program your computer to be synchronized automatically once a week.

In this exercise, you will manually reset your system time and then connect to an Internet time server for an automatic update.

Troubleshooting Many corporate and organizational *firewalls*, and some personal firewalls, prevent your computer from connecting to time-synchronization services. If you have a personal firewall and cannot access an Internet time server, read your firewall documentation for information about unblocking network time protocol (NTP) or switch to the *Microsoft Windows Firewall*.

BE SURE TO have an active Internet connection available before beginning this exercise.

Troubleshooting If your computer is part of a network domain, you will not be able to complete steps 8 through 12.

Follow these steps:

1 Close any open programs to display the Windows desktop.

Your taskbar looks something like this:

> start   🔲 🔲 🔲   4:53 PM

The current system time is displayed in the notification area.

2 Position the mouse pointer over the clock.

The current system date is displayed as a ScreenTip.

3 Right-click the notification area, and then click **Adjust Date/Time** on the shortcut menu.

161

The **Date and Time Properties** dialog box appears:

Your current system date is displayed on a calendar on the left. Your current system time is displayed in both analog and digital formats on the right, and both clocks are changing once a second. Your current time zone is displayed at the bottom of the tab.

4 Drag the mouse pointer over the hour setting displayed in the digital clock to select it, and then use the spinner (the up and down arrows) to the right of the clock to change the hour.

The analog clock reflects your change, and both clocks stop advancing.

5 Repeat step 4 for the minutes setting, and for the AM/PM setting.

6 Click **OK** to close the dialog box and update your settings.

The clock on the taskbar changes to reflect your new time setting.

7 Double-click the clock on the taskbar.

The **Date and Time Properties** dialog box appears.

8 Click the **Internet Time** tab, which looks like this:

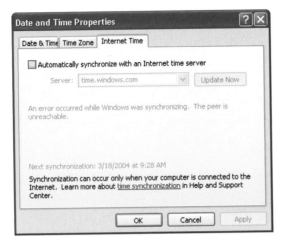

If the contents of the tab are dimmed, the Internet Time Synchronization feature is not currently available.

9   If Internet Time Synchronization is not available, manually reset the time on the **Date & Time** tab, and then skip to step 13.

10   Select the **Automatically synchronize with an Internet time server** check box.

11   Select a server in the drop-down list, and then click **Update Now**.

Your computer connects to the selected time server via the Internet, and updates your system time.

12   Click the **Date & Time** tab to see your updated setting.

13   Click **OK** to close the **Date and Time Properties** dialog box.

The clock once again reflects the current time.

Tip   The Internet time servers currently available in the **Server** drop-down list might not update your system time if the system date is incorrect.

Changing Your Regional and Language Settings

International
Options

Different regions express numeric values, such as dates, times, currencies, decimals, and so on, in different formats. Your computer was set by its manufacturer to express these values in keeping with the area in which the computer will probably be used. Most people will never need to change these settings. However, if you are located in a region for which the manufacturer's settings are not correct—or if you move, work with international customers, or want to experiment just for fun—you can change your regional settings. Windows XP includes number, currency, time, date, and language settings for over 90 regions of the world (including 13 different English-speaking regions).

In this exercise, you will change your regional settings to those of Sweden and then restore them to your original settings.

Tip   If you are already working with Swedish settings, substitute another region in this exercise.

BE SURE TO quit any programs and close any open windows before beginning this exercise.
OPEN Control Panel.

Follow these steps:

1   In the Control Panel window, click the **Date, Time, Language, and Regional Options** icon.

The Date, Time, Language, and Regional Options window opens:

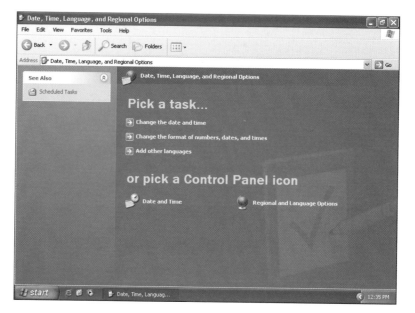

2   Click the **Regional and Language Options** icon.

The **Regional and Language Options** dialog box appears:

Regional and Language Options

Regional Options | Languages | Advanced

Standards and formats

This option affects how some programs format numbers, currencies, dates, and time.

Select an item to match its preferences, or click Customize to choose your own formats:

English (United States) | Customize...

Samples

Number:	123,456,789.00
Currency:	$123,456,789.00
Time:	12:36:47 PM
Short date:	8/26/2001
Long date:	Sunday, August 26, 2001

Location

To help services provide you with local information, such as news and weather, select your present location:

United States

OK | Cancel | Apply

3   In the **Standards and formats** area, click the current region to open the drop-down list.

4   Scroll through the list as necessary and then click **Swedish**.

The settings in the **Samples** area change to reflect the appropriate number, currency, time, and date expressions for the Swedish language.

5   In the **Location** area, click the current region to open the drop-down list, and click **Sweden**.

6   Click the **Languages** tab.

7   In the **Text services and input languages** area, click **Details**.

This **Text Services and Input Languages** dialog box appears:

If you have additional languages installed on your computer, they are listed in your dialog box.

8   Click **Add**.

The **Add Input Language** dialog box opens.

Important   Make a note of your current **Input language** and **Keyboard layout/IME** settings before changing the input language.

9   Click the down arrow to the right of the **Input language** box, and click **Swedish** in the drop-down list.

The keyboard selection changes to match your language selection.

10   Click the down arrow to the right of the **Keyboard layout/IME** box, and click your original setting in the drop-down list to ensure that your keyboard will still work as expected.

11   Click **OK** to close the dialog box.

Swedish is added to your list of installed services and to the **Default input language** drop-down list. Your original language is still selected as the default, as indicated both in the drop-down list and by the bold font in the **Installed services** box.

Note that each language in the **Installed services** box is represented by a specific two-letter combination in a small blue square.

12   Click the down arrow to the right of the **Default input language** box, and click **Swedish** in the drop-down list.

Swedish is now selected as the default, as indicated both in the drop-down list and by the bold font in the **Installed services** box.

13   Click **Apply** to apply your settings and activate the Language bar.

14   In the **Preferences** area, click the **Language Bar** button.

The **Language Bar Settings** dialog box appears:

```
Language Bar Settings                    [?][X]

   ☑ Show the Language bar on the desktop

   ☐ Show the Language bar as transparent when inactive

   ☑ Show additional Language bar icons in the taskbar

   ☑ Show text labels on the Language bar


              [    OK    ]   [  Cancel  ]
```

15   Review the Language bar settings, and then click **Cancel** to close the dialog box.

16   Click the **Advanced** tab to see the additional options, click **OK** to close the **Text Services and Input Languages** dialog box, and click **OK** to close the **Regional and Language Options** dialog box.

The Language bar is displayed at the right end of the taskbar. The clock in the notification area of the taskbar now displays the time in 24-hour format because that is the Swedish time display setting.

17   Position the mouse pointer over the clock.

The day and date are displayed in Swedish.

18   Now you will return to your original regional and language settings. Open the **Regional and Language Options** dialog box by clicking the **Regional and Language Options** icon.

19   On the **Regional Options** tab, select your original language and location settings.

20   On the **Languages** tab, click **Details** to open the **Text Services and Input Languages** dialog box.

21   In the **Installed services** box, click **Swedish**, and then click **Remove**.

22 Click **OK** to close the **Text Services and Input Languages** dialog box, and click **OK** to close the message that Swedish won't be removed until you restart your computer or log off and log on again.

23 Click **OK** to close the **Regional and Language Options** dialog box, and then close the Date, Time, Language, and Regional Options window.

Making Windows XP Easier to See and Use

If you have trouble seeing and using some of the elements of your computer screen, you can adjust many of the features of Windows XP to make those elements clearer or easier to use. For example, you can change the size of the font used in the title bars and menus; make icons larger; change the width of the insertion point and the rate at which it blinks; and make the scroll bars and window borders wider.

Because it can be difficult to undo some of these options after you have set them, this topic briefly describes the Windows XP accessibility tools, but you won't actually change anything. These tools are available when you click **Accessibility Options** in Control Panel and are intended to include a minimum level of functionality for users with special needs. Most users with disabilities will need utility programs with more advanced functionality for daily use.

Windows XP includes these programs to assist people with visual disabilities:

■ The **Accessibility Wizard** leads you through the process of configuring basic accessibility settings.

■ The *Utility Manager* starts, stops, or checks the status of the Accessibility programs. If you have administrator-level access, you can have programs start when Utility Manager starts.

> **Tip** To start the Utility Manager, press **WINDOWS LOGO+U**. You can start Accessibility programs before logging on to your computer by pressing **WINDOWS LOGO+U** at the Welcome to Windows screen.

■ *Microsoft Magnifier* opens a magnification panel in which the screen under the mouse pointer is displayed, magnified up to nine times. You can adjust the size and location of the magnification panel.

■ *Microsoft Narrator* works with Windows setup, the Windows desktop, Control Panel programs, Internet Explorer, *Notepad*, and *WordPad* as a text-to-speech tool. It reads menu commands, dialog box options, and other screen features out loud, telling you what options are available and how to use them. It also reads your keystrokes to you as you type and tells you your location as you move around. You can also choose to have the mouse pointer follow the active item on the screen. Narrator speaks in the voice of a character named *Microsoft Sam*. You have some control over the features of Sam's voice, including speed, volume, and pitch, but Narrator speaks only in English.

■ *SoundSentry* flashes a part of the screen that you specify every time the system's built-in speaker plays a sound.

■ *ShowSounds* instructs programs that usually convey information only by sound to also include visual information, such as displaying text captions or information icons.

If you think any of these tools will help you use your computer more effectively, you can activate them through **Accessibility Options** in Control Panel.

Inputting Text Without Using the Keyboard

The traditional method of entering information into a computer document is by typing it using the keyboard. However, if you have mobility problems, you might find it difficult to use the keyboard to type. Windows XP includes a variety of tools to help, including the following:

■ *On-Screen Keyboard* allows is a way of selecting the full range of keys using your mouse or other device. This keyboard can be used to enter text into any application.

■ *StickyKeys* makes it easier to use the keyboard with one hand by making the **CTRL**, **SHIFT**, and **ALT** keys "stick" down until you press the next key.

■ *FilterKeys* causes Windows to ignore brief or repeated keystrokes, or slows the repeat rate.

■ *ToggleKeys* sounds a tone when you press the **CAPS LOCK**, **NUM LOCK**, or **SCROLL LOCK** keys. A high-pitched sound plays when the keys are switched on, and a low-pitched sound plays when the keys are switched off.

■ *MouseKeys* is a way to use the numeric keypad to control the mouse pointer.

If you have Microsoft Office Handwriting Recognition installed, you have access to other methods of inputting text, including the On Screen Standard Keyboard, an alternative point-and-click keyboard that works only with Office applications; Writing Pad, a handwriting input window where words you write with your mouse or a stylus on a special line are converted to typed words in the current document; Write Anywhere, a handwriting utility you can use to write words across any portion of a document and have them converted to text; and Drawing Pad, a quick way to create a simple drawing and insert it into a Microsoft Office document. Handwriting Recognition can be installed during a custom installation of Office XP or Office 2003. If Office was installed on your computer without the handwriting recognition option, you can use the **Add or Remove Programs** dialog box, which is available through Control Panel, to change the Office installation options.

Training Your Computer to Recognize Your Voice

Not so long ago, if an executive didn't know how to type or how to type fast enough, he or she could dictate letters and memos to a secretary, who would type them. Similarly, if a student had a broken arm and couldn't take notes in class or write out his or her homework assignment, another student would be assigned to do the writing or take dictation.

new for
WindowsXP

Text-to-Speech:
Speech
Recognition

Dictation has naturally evolved into the development of speech recognition software. You can use this technology to dictate to your computer in a normal speaking voice and have your information recorded as text. Although as of this writing Windows XP does not come with its own speech recognition software, if you install the *Microsoft Speech Recognition* feature that comes with Office XP and Office 2003, you can control this feature from within Windows XP.

Tip   The Microsoft Speech Recognition engine can be installed during a custom installation of Office XP or Office 2003. If Office was installed on your computer without the speech recognition option, you can start its installation from within Microsoft Office Word 2002 by starting Word, and on the **Tools** menu, clicking **Speech**.

Each person who uses your computer can create a speech profile so that the Speech Recognition engine recognizes his or her speech pattern accurately. You might also want to create specific speech profiles for different environments. For example, if you are going to talk to your computer both in a relatively noisy work environment and in a relatively quiet home office environment, you would want to create separate profiles to ensure that the ambient noise is handled appropriately. After you've decided which profiles you will need, an easy-to-use wizard guides you through a series of sessions that train the Speech Recognition engine to recognize your particular voice. The accuracy of the Speech Recognition engine increases as you complete more of these training sessions.

Tip   The accuracy of speech recognition is dependent on the quality of your microphone, the way you speak, and the amount of ambient noise. If you are serious about using this technology, invest in a good headset microphone. If you have a fast computer (over 400 MHz), consider using a USB headset.

In this exercise, you will configure the Microsoft Speech Recognition software to recognize your voice, and you will dictate a simple text document.

USE the *Buzzy Bee* document in the practice file folder for this topic. This practice file is located in the *My Documents\Microsoft Press\Microsoft Windows XP SBS\Personalizing\SpeechToText* folder.
BE SURE TO install Word 2003 and have a microphone, speakers, and approximately 45 minutes of uninterrupted time (in a reasonably quiet environment) available before beginning this exercise.
OPEN Control Panel, and then click the Sounds, Speech, and Audio Devices icon.

Follow these steps:

1 In the Sounds, Speech, and Audio Devices window, click the **Speech** icon.

The **Speech Properties** dialog box opens, with the **Speech Recognition** tab selected:

Tip If there is no **Speech Recognition** tab in the **Speech Properties** dialog box, this feature has not been installed. To start its installation, open Word, and on the **Tools** menu, click **Speech**. During installation, you will work through the steps in the **Microphone Wizard**, just as you would do here, to add a new profile. If you are installing Speech Recognition now, skip to step 5 after you start the installation process.

2 In the **Recognition Profiles** area, click **New**.

The **Profile Wizard** opens with your logon information shown.

3 Accept the logon information, or type a profile name (such as *Joan at Home* or *Headset Microphone*) in the **Profile** box.

4 Click **Next**.

The **Microphone Wizard** starts:

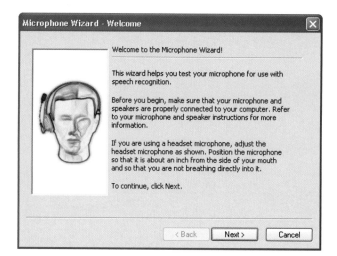

5 Follow the instructions for positioning your microphone, and then click **Next** to move to this **Test Microphone** page:

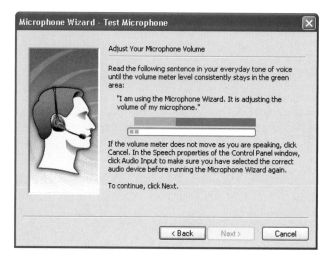

6 Read the sample text aloud in a normal voice.

The volume meter moves in response to your voice; the microphone sensory equipment automatically adjusts to record your voice at the most appropriate level.

7 Click **Next** to move to this **Test Positioning** page:

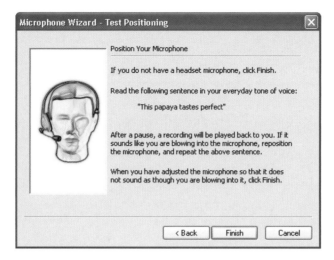

The sample text on this page is designed to test the recording of "spitting" sounds, such as *p*, *s*, and *t*.

8   Read the sample text aloud in a normal voice.

After a short delay, your words are repeated back to you.

9   If the sounds are unclear, adjust the distance of the microphone from your mouth, and repeat the process until you are satisfied with the results.

10   Click **Finish**.

The **Voice Training Wizard** starts.

11   Follow the instructions to complete the vocal exercises.

Remember to speak in a normal tone of voice so that the Speech Recognition Engine can accurately profile your specific speech pattern. This process takes approximately 10 minutes, depending on how fast you speak.

As you work through the training session, you will learn more about the way the Speech Recognition Engine works. As you read the sample text aloud, the **Voice Training Wizard** highlights the words it recognizes. If it doesn't hear the word it is expecting, it stops highlighting and returns to the last recognized pause. You should then stop reading and return to the beginning of the unrecognized text. When you successfully finish reading each page of sample text, the **Voice Training Wizard** moves to the next page.

12   When you finish with the first training session, *Introduction to Microsoft Speech Recognition*, click **Finish** to return to the **Speech Recognition** dialog box.

Your new profile is now selected in the **Recognition Profiles** area.

13   Click **OK** to close the dialog box.

The Language bar opens, making the dictation options available.

14 Click the **Folders** button, browse to the *My Documents\Microsoft Press\Microsoft Windows XP SBS\Personalizing\SpeechToText* folder, and open the *Buzzy Bee* document.

15 If the **Dictation** and **Voice Command** options are not visible on the Language bar, click **Microphone** to display them.

The first time you use the microphone from within Office, the **Office Voice Training Wizard** opens and leads you through a voice training session that is similar to the one you have already completed.

16 On the Language bar, click **Dictation**.

The Speech Message changes to reflect first that Dictation is on and then that it is listening to you.

17 Position the insertion point at the end of the Buzzy Bee document.

18 Read the story paragraph aloud, including the punctuation. Say *comma, period, semicolon, quote,* and so on for the punctuation marks. At the end of the paragraph, say *new paragraph.*

As you read, a highlighted series of dots appears, like an expanding ellipsis. As the Speech Recognition Engine completes its deliberations, it translates each dot into a word. Don't expect your first attempt at speech translation to come out perfectly—it generally requires at least three training sessions to come up with something that is intelligible.

19 On the Language bar, click **Tools**, and then click **Training**.

20 Walk through another training session. When you complete the training session, re-read the story paragraph.

When you compare the two computer-generated paragraphs, the results are much closer to the actual words in the second version.

21 Complete one more training session, and then re-read the story paragraph and compare the results to the first two versions.

The computer should be generating something close to the actual text at this point.

You can see that the speech-recognition capabilities increase as you complete additional training sessions. If you are going to use speech recognition, you might choose to complete further sessions at this point, or as time permits, to ensure the greatest possible accuracy.

CLOSE the document, saving your changes if you want, and then close the Sounds, Speech, and Audio Devices window.

Tip If you installed speech or handwriting recognition and would like to remove one of them, you can do so through **Add or Remove Programs** in **Control Panel**.

Choosing a Voice for Your Computer

new for
WindowsXP

Text-to-Speech:
Speech
Recognition

Software products are available to enable your computer to "read" documents to you. For example, your computer can let you know when you receive a new e-mail message and can read the message to you. These products work with the Windows *text-to-speech (TTS)* software, which can "speak" in a variety of voices and languages. Windows XP comes with three voices: LH Michael, LH Michelle, and Microsoft Sam. (LH is for Lernout & Hauspie, the original creator of the voice translation software.) The default voice is LH Michael.

In this exercise, you will switch to a different voice and adjust the speed of the voice.

OPEN Control Panel, and then click the Sounds, Speech, and Audio Devices icon.

Follow these steps:

1 In the Sounds, Speech, and Audio Devices window, click the **Speech** icon.

2 In the Speech Properties dialog box, click the Text To Speech tab to display these options:

> **Tip** If you don't have Office XP and Speech Recognition installed, you will not have a *Speech Recognition* tab or additional voices.

3 Click **Preview Voice**.

The text in the preview box is read aloud in the default voice.

4 In the **Voice selection** drop-down list, click **LH Michelle**.

The text in the preview box changes to reflect your selection, and the computer reads it aloud in the LH Michelle voice.

5 In the **Voice selection** drop-down list, click **Microsoft Sam**.

The text in the preview box changes to reflect your selection, and the computer reads it aloud in the selected voice.

6 Select the text in the preview box, and type I am Oz, the Great and Terrible. Who are you, and what do you want?.

7 Click **Preview Voice**.

The computer reads your text aloud in the selected voice.

8 Select the voice you prefer to use on your computer.

9 Adjust the voice speed selector to **Fast**, and click **Preview Voice**.

10 Adjust the voice speed selector to **Slow**, and click **Preview Voice**.

11 Adjust the selector, and click **Preview Voice** until you find the speed you like best for this voice.

12 Click **OK** to close the dialog box and save your settings.

CLOSE the Sounds, Speech, and Audio Devices window.

Key Points

- You can easily personalize Windows XP interface elements such as colors, fonts, and the desktop background. You can choose from a number of screen savers that come with Windows XP, download others from the Web, and display your own pictures as a screen saver.

- The size and number of elements that appear on your screen are determined by the screen resolution. You can change the screen resolution to make things appear larger or to view more information at one time.

- The date and time shown on your computer can be automatically updated from an Internet time server. Your computer will display the date and time as well as numbers and currencies in any of over 100 different languages.

- Windows XP includes many alternative input and output options designed to make your computer more accessible.

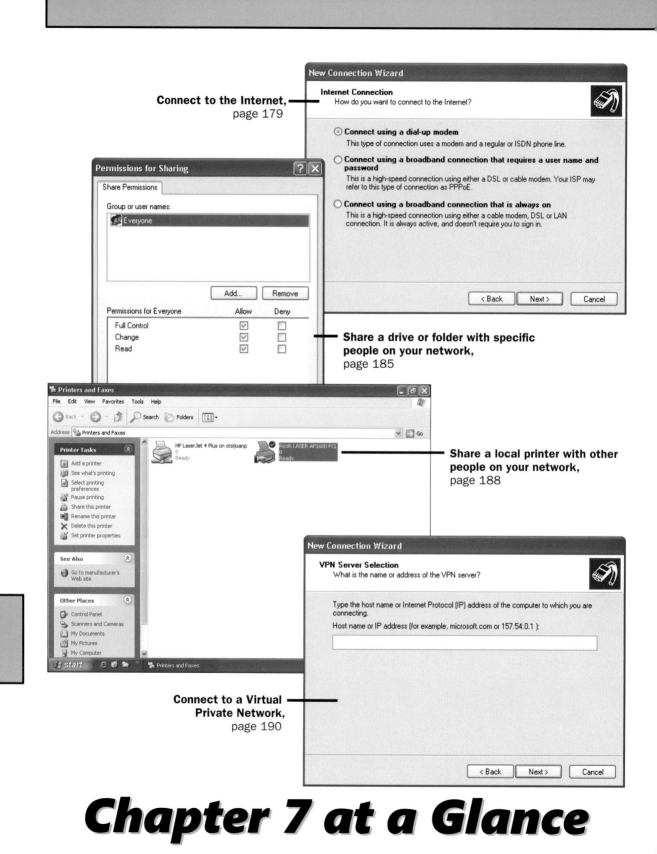

Chapter 7 at a Glance

7 Making Connections

In this chapter you will learn to:

✓ Connect to the Internet through a dial-up or broadband connection.

✓ Understand what's needed to create a network of computers.

✓ Share printers, drives, and folders with other people.

✓ Create a Virtual Private Network connection.

Computers can be connected in a variety of ways that enable them to communicate across a room or across the world. Until recently, computer connections, servers, gateways, and routers were the domain of techies. But connecting computers has become easy enough that almost anyone can take advantage of the convenience and efficiency that can result from sharing the resources of one computer with another.

In this chapter, you will learn about three types of computer connections that can enhance your computing capabilities. First you see how to set up a connection between your computer and the Internet. Then you learn a bit about the Microsoft Windows XP tools available to set up a connection between your computer and one or more other computers, and you explore how to share your computer's resources after the network is established. And finally, you see how these first two types of connections can be combined so you can connect your computer remotely to a network over the Internet.

See Also Do you need only a quick refresher on the topics in this chapter? See the Quick Reference entries on pages xxxiv–xxxvii.

 Important Before you can use the practice files in this chapter, you need to install them from the book's companion CD to their default location. See "Using the Book's CD-ROM" on page xv for more information.

Connecting to the Internet

In the past, many employers thought that giving their employees access to the Internet from their work computers would mean a loss of productivity, because people could receive and send personal e-mail messages or indulge in surreptitious surfing of the Web. These days, more and more employers are coming to the conclusion that Internet access can actually enhance the productivity of people in some jobs, and many provide organization-wide access. If you work for such an employer, Internet access has likely been set up for you. If you don't, and you can't persuade your boss that Internet access would be an advantage, you'll have to be content with setting up access on a computer at home. In fact, Internet access is fast becoming one of the primary reasons for buying a home computer, and setting up access is easier than ever with Windows XP.

New Connection Wizard

As an individual, you cannot connect your computer directly to the Internet; you must access the Internet through a computer or network of computers that acts as a go-between. To connect your computer to this go-between, you might use a *local area network (LAN)*; a high-speed *broadband connection* such as *cable*, *ISDN*, or *DSL*; or a *dial-up connection*. Whichever type of connection you use, the **New Connection Wizard** can help you with the necessary setup work:

■ If you are connecting to the Internet through a LAN, you are actually connecting to a computer on your network that has been set up to provide Internet access.

■ If you have set up a user account with an *Internet service provider (ISP)* to gain access through that company's computers, you can use the **New Connection Wizard** to simplify the connection configuration process.

■ If you are connecting though a dial-up connection, you are making a connection from your computer to another computer using two *modems* and an ordinary telephone line. The remote computer usually belongs to the ISP with whom you have set up your user account.

■ If you are connecting though a dedicated cable or DSL connection—one that doesn't require a user account name or password—you do not need to use the **New Connection Wizard**; no additional configuration should be required.

To create an Internet connection through an ISP, you need to set up a user account. The ISP will then provide the information the wizard will ask for during the connection process, such as:

■ The specific *IP address* or the address of the *DHCP server*

■ *DNS* addresses and domain names

■ *POP3* or *IMAP* settings for incoming e-mail

■ *SMTP* settings for outgoing e-mail

In this exercise you will use the **New Connection Wizard** to connect to the Internet through a broadband or dial-up connection.

BE SURE TO log on to Windows and have your Internet connection information available before beginning this exercise.

Tip   If you are connecting through a dial-up connection, you must have the name and phone number of your ISP, your user account name, and your password. If you are connecting through a password-protected broadband connection, you must have the name of your ISP, your user account name, and your password.

Follow these steps:

1 On the **Start** menu, click **Control Panel**, and then click the **Network and Internet Connections** icon.

The Network and Internet Connections window opens:

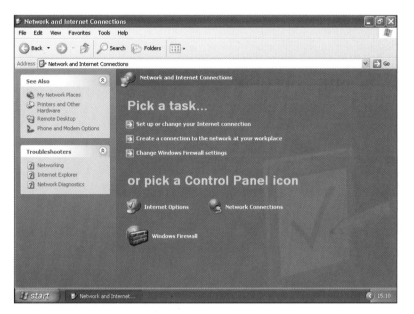

2 Click the **Set up or change your Internet connection** task.

The **Internet Properties** dialog box appears with the **Connections** tab displayed:

3   Click **Setup** to start the **New Connection Wizard**.

Important   The first time you use the **New Connection Wizard**, the **Location Information** dialog box is displayed so that you can enter the local area code and a few other pieces of information that should be common to any connection you create.

4   If the **Location Information** dialog box appears, click **OK**, provide the requested information, and then click **OK** again.

5   Click **Next** to display the wizard's **Network Connection Type** page:

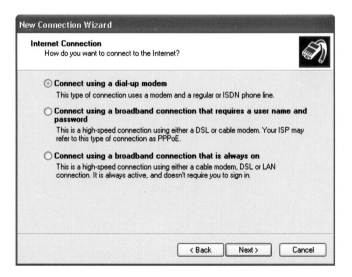

6   Click **Connect to the Internet**, and then click **Next**.

7   On the **Getting Ready** page, click **Set up my connection manually**, and then click **Next** to display the connection options:

8 If you are connecting using a modem and phone line, select the first option, and click **Next**. You will then be prompted for the name and phone number of your ISP, your user account name, and your password.

9 If you are connecting using a password-protected broadband connection, select the second option, and click **Next**. You will then be prompted for the name of your ISP, your user account name, and your password. You must also specify whether to turn on the Internet Connection Firewall for this connection and the name(s) of any other user(s) who has permission to use the connection.

10 If you are connecting using a dedicated, or constant, broadband connection, select the third option, and click **Next**. You will not have to provide any additional information.

11 Click **Finish** to close the wizard and create the connection.

If you created a connection that requires you to sign in to your user account, a shortcut is added to your desktop.

CLOSE the Network and Internet Connections window.

Accessing Your Computer Remotely

new for
WindowsXP

Remote
Desktop

If you travel a lot or often work at home, you don't necessarily have to take all your files and folders with you. Instead, you can work, through your Internet connection, on your own computer using *Remote Desktop*, a new Windows XP feature.

To use Remote Desktop, both the computer you are currently working on and the one you want to access must be running Windows XP. You must have *administrative permissions* on the computer you want to be able to access remotely to turn on Remote Desktop.

To set up your computer so that it can be accessed using Remote Desktop:

1 On the **Start** menu, click **Control Panel**.

2 In the Control Panel window, click the **Performance and Maintenance** icon, and then click the **System** icon.

3 In the **System Properties** dialog box, click the **Remote** tab.

4 In the **Remote Desktop** area, select the **Allow users to connect remotely to this computer** check box.

5 If the **Remote Sessions** message box appears, read the message, and then click **OK** to close it.

6 You are automatically authorized as a remote user of your own computer. If you want to authorize additional remote users, click **Select Remote Users**, add users in the **Remote Desktop Users** dialog box, and then click **OK**.

7   Click **OK** to close the **System Properties** dialog box, and then close the Performance and Maintenance window.

To access your computer from another Windows XP computer through Remote Desktop:

1   On the **Start** menu, point to **All Programs**, point to **Accessories**, point to **Communications**, and then click **Remote Desktop Connection**.

2   If the multi-tabbed dialog box area is not displayed, click **Options** to expand the dialog box.

3   Enter the connection information on the **General** tab.

4   Specify the display information on the **Display** tab.

5   Specify any other pertinent information, and then click **Connect**.

To turn off Remote Desktop access on your computer:

1   On the **Start** menu, click **Control Panel**.

2   In the Control Panel window, click the **Performance and Maintenance** icon, and then click the **System** icon.

3   On the **Remote** tab, clear the **Allow users to connect remotely to this computer** check box.

4   Click **OK** to close the **System Properties** dialog box, and then close the Performance and Maintenance window.

For more information, search for *Remote Desktop* in the Help and Support Center.

Networking Two or More Computers

If you have two or more computers in your office or at home, you can connect them together to form a simple network. You can then share the resources on one computer, such as an Internet connection, a printer, or a scanner, with any other computer on the network. Networking also makes it easy to share files and folders.

Tip   A discussion of how to install the hardware and software necessary to create a network is beyond the scope of this book. For more information, see "Home and Small Office Networking with Windows XP" at *www.microsoft.com/windowsxp/homenetworking/*.

After you physically connect the computers using hardware and cables designed for this purpose, you can use the tools that come with Windows XP to easily set up a simple network:

new for
WindowsXP

Network Setup
Wizard

■   The **Network Setup Wizard** walks you through the process of establishing the necessary software connections between the computers after they are physically connected.

new for
WindowsXP

Internet
Connection
Sharing

■ *Internet Connection Sharing (ICS)* lets all the computers on your network share one Internet connection. After ICS is turned on, you can use programs such as Microsoft Internet Explorer and Microsoft Outlook Express from all the computers on your network as though they were connected directly to the Internet.

new for
WindowsXP

Windows
Firewall

■ A *firewall* is a security system that acts as a protective barrier between a computer and the outside world. *Windows Firewall (previously called Internet Connection Firewall)* is firewall software that provides a secure information pipeline between your network and the outside world, specifying what information can be communicated from your computer or network to the Internet and from the Internet to your network or computer. Windows Firewall is turned on by default in Windows XP Service Pack 2.

new for
WindowsXP

Network
Bridge

■ In the past, special hardware was required to allow communication between segments of a network that used different types of *network adapters*, such as *Ethernet*, home phoneline network adapter (HPNA), wireless, and IEEE 1394. *Network Bridge* connects (bridges) these segments using software. To bridge two or more segments, a single Windows XP computer must contain an adapter card of each type. A single bridge can be used with as many different types of network adapters as the computer is physically able to accommodate.

When these tools are in place, you can take advantage of any resource available on the network, no matter where it is physically located.

Sharing Drives and Folders

Whether you work on your computer in a work or a home environment, you might need to share documents with other people on your network. Rather than sending copies of documents to everyone who might need them, you can place the documents on a *shared drive* or in a *shared folder*.

You can share folders and drives from within Windows Explorer or from the **Computer Management** administrative tool. When you share a drive or a folder on your computer, you allow other people to access the documents that the drive or folder contains whenever they need them (as long as your computer is turned on). The icon of a shared drive or folder has an outstretched hand beneath it.

Tip You can share the entire contents of your hard drive or the contents of a removable storage device such as a Zip drive or USB memory stick.

When you share a drive or a folder, by default any other user on the network can see the contents of the drive or folder, open files, save changes, create new files on the drive or in the folder, and delete files from the drive or folder. You can limit access so that only selected people or groups of people can work with the contents, and you can limit the types of access granted to each person or group.

Tip Windows XP computers that are not connected to a network domain have a Shared Documents folder that contains the Shared Pictures and Shared Music folders. The contents of these shared folders are available to anyone using the computer, meaning that multiple users of the same computer can share files with each other by placing the files in these folders.

In this exercise, you will share a folder on your computer from within Windows Explorer and give access to the shared folder to a specific group of people.

USE the documents in the practice file folder for this topic. These practice files are located in the *My Documents\Microsoft Press\Microsoft Windows XP SBS\Connecting\Sharing* **folder.**

Follow these steps:

1 On the **Start** menu, click **My Documents**.

The My Documents folder opens in Windows Explorer:

2 Browse to and open the *My Documents\Microsoft Press\Microsoft Windows XP SBS \Connecting\Sharing* folder.

The selected folder opens in Windows Explorer:

3   On the **File and Folder Tasks** menu, click **Share this folder**.

The **Sharing Properties** dialog box appears:

4   Select the **Share this folder** option.

The dialog box options become available. The default share name is the folder name.

5   Click **Permissions**.

The **Permissions for Sharing** dialog box appears:

You can add or remove users and change permissions in this dialog box.

6   Click **Cancel** to close the dialog box without making changes.

7   Click **OK** to share the folder.

8   Click the **Up** button to move up one level to the *My Documents\Microsoft Press\Microsoft Windows XP SBS\Connecting* folder.

Up

The hand below the Sharing folder's icon now indicates that the folder is shared.

CLOSE the folder window.

Sharing a Printer

To be able to print from a stand-alone computer, you must have a printer physically connected to one of the computer's ports. When two or more computers are networked, multiple computers can use the same printer.

You can share a printer that is attached to your computer with the entire network or with a select group of people. When you share your printer, you assign it a name. This name might be based on the manufacturer or model of the printer (such as *HP LaserJet*), some special feature (such as *Color*), or perhaps the physical location of the printer (such as *Front Office*). Regardless, simple names work best because they are more likely to be easily identified by everyone who needs to use the printer.

Tip   Some printers suggest their own printer name during the sharing process. You can either accept the suggested name or replace it with one you choose.

In this exercise, you will share a printer that is attached to your computer.

BE SURE TO have a printer attached to and properly installed on your computer before beginning this exercise.

See Also   For more information about installing a printer, refer to "Installing a Local Printer" in Chapter 4, "Working with Hardware, Software, and Middleware."

Important   You do not need to be connected to a network in complete this exercise, but your shared printer will be available to another computer user only when you are.

Follow these steps:

1   On the **Start** menu, click **Printers and Faxes**.

The Printers and Faxes window opens, displaying your installed printers:

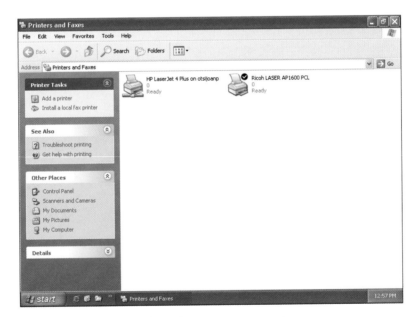

2   In the right pane, click the printer you want to share.

3   On the **Printer Tasks** menu, click **Share this printer**.

The printer's **Properties** dialog box appears with the **Sharing** tab selected.

4   Click **Share this printer**.

5   In the **Share name** box, type a simple name for the printer.

6 Click **OK** to close the dialog box and turn on sharing for the specified printer.

The Printers and Faxes window is displayed again, and the printer's icon now indicates that it is shared:

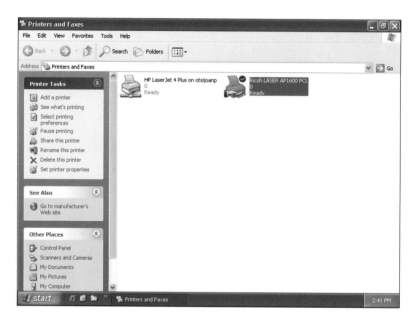

CLOSE the Printers and Faxes window.

Connecting to a Virtual Private Network

Another type of network connection that is becoming increasingly common in the corporate world is a *Virtual Private Network (VPN)* connection. A VPN connection uses the Internet to access a private (corporate or institutional) network, thus extending the private network so that you are virtually, if not physically, part of it.

If your organization has set up a *remote access server*, you can create a VPN connection to your network over the Internet. Using this connection, you have full use of network resources while you are away from the office, which is extremely useful when you are traveling or working from home.

Naturally, the speed of your VPN connection is limited by the speed of your Internet connection. On one hand, if you are using VPN with a dial-up connection, you might find that you run out of patience while waiting for your computer to access common network resources. On the other hand, VPN with a broadband connection can be nearly as good as being there!

In this exercise, you will create a VPN connection over the Internet.

BE SURE TO have the host name or IP address of your organization's remote access server and your user account name and password for your organization's network available before beginning this exercise.

Troubleshooting If you do not have access to a remote access server, you can't complete this exercise.

Follow these steps:

1 On the **Start** menu, click **Control Panel**, and then click the **Network and Internet Connections** icon.

The Network and Internet Connections window opens.

2 Click the **Create a connection to the network at your workplace** task.

The **New Connection Wizard** starts:

3 On the **Network Connection** page, select the **Virtual Private Network connection** option, and then click **Next**.

The **Connection Name** page opens:

4   Type a name for your connection in the **Company Name** box, and click **Next**.

You will usually name the connection after the organization to which you are connecting.

5   If you don't have a full-time Internet connection, the **Public Network** page opens to give you the option of dialing an existing connection before making the VPN connection:

Make your selection, and click **Next**.

Whether or not you have a full-time Internet connection, you now see the **VPN Server Selection** page:

New Connection Wizard

VPN Server Selection
What is the name or address of the VPN server?

Type the host name or Internet Protocol (IP) address of the computer to which you are connecting.

Host name or IP address (for example, microsoft.com or 157.54.0.1):

< Back   Next >   Cancel

6 Type the remote access server's host name or IP address in the box, and click **Next** to display the **Connection Availability** page:

New Connection Wizard

Connection Availability
You can make the new connection available to any user or only to yourself

A connection that is created for your use only is saved in your user account and is not available unless you are logged on.

Create this connection for:

⦿ Anyone's use
○ My use only

< Back   Next >   Cancel

7 Specify whether you want to make the connection available to other users of your computer or keep it to yourself.

8 Click **Next** to display the wizard's last page:

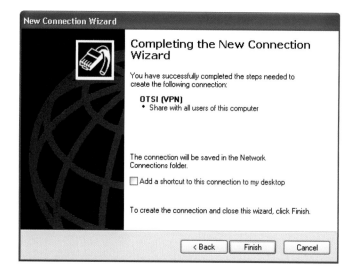

9 Select the **Add a shortcut to this connection to my desktop** check box, and then click **Finish** to create the connection.

10 Click the **Close** button to close the Network and Internet Connections window.

⊠
Close

11 On the desktop, double-click the icon for your new connection.

If you have to start your Internet connection, you are prompted to do so now. You are prompted to enter the user account name and password for the connection:

12 Enter your user account name and password for the network to which you are connecting.

194

13   Select the **Save this user name and password for the following users** check box, and then make sure that the **Me only** option is selected.

14   Click **Connect**.

You connect to the network. The network verifies your user account name and password, and then logs you on.

When you are connected to the network, a network icon appears in the notification area, and you can connect to the same network resources as you could if you were sitting at your desk at work.

15   To close the VPN session, right-click the network icon, and click **Disconnect**.

Key Points

- The Network Connection Wizard walks you through the process of creating a connection from your computer to the Internet or to you business network.

- You can connect over a network to other computers to share documents and resources.

- You can connect over the Internet to a remote computer and interact with it directly as though it were your own desktop.

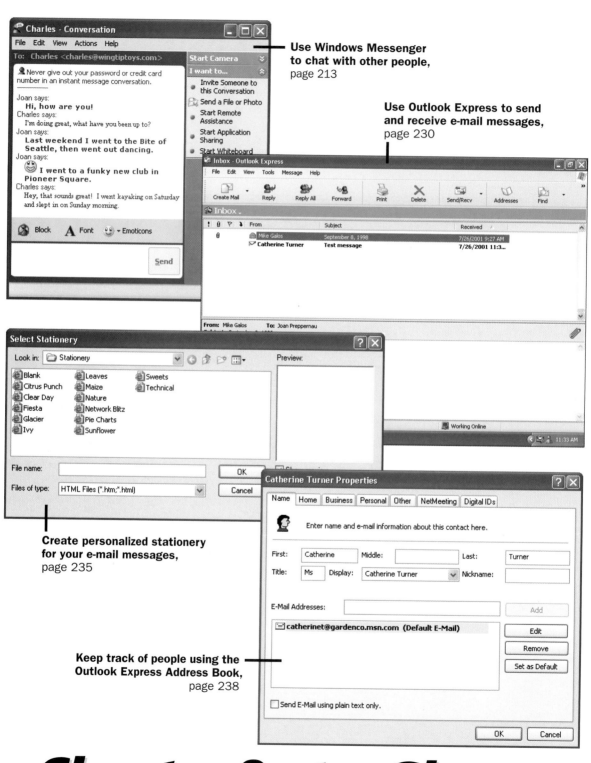

Use Windows Messenger
to chat with other people,
page 213

Use Outlook Express to send
and receive e-mail messages,
page 230

Create personalized stationery
for your e-mail messages,
page 235

Keep track of people using the
Outlook Express Address Book,
page 238

Chapter 8 at a Glance

8 Communicating with Other People

In this chapter you will learn to:

✔ Create a Passport account.

✔ Configure and use Windows Messenger for Internet-based instant messaging.

✔ Configure and use Outlook Express for server-based e-mail.

With computer communications, the world has become a much smaller place. It used to take months for a letter to travel from one side of the world to the other; it now takes seconds for an electronic letter to make the same trip. And with instant messaging, real-time electronic conversations between people who are miles apart are becoming commonly accepted as a comfortable, secure form of communication.

In this chapter, you venture beyond your own computer and communicate with the outside world by using an instant messaging service and an e-mail program.

See Also Do you need only a quick refresher on the topics in this chapter? See the Quick Reference entries on pages xxxvii–xl.

Creating a Passport Account

Microsoft .NET Passport is an Internet-based user account system that includes two classes of service:

■ You can use *.NET Passport* to sign in to a variety of Microsoft and commercial Web sites using a single user account name and password. If you choose to share your user profile information, it can be transmitted directly to .NET Passport–participating sites when you sign in to them, to save you the trouble of re-entering your information every time.

■ You can use *Kids Passport* to protect your children's online privacy by specifying what information your children can share with participating Web sites and what those sites can do with that information. For example, children under 12 years old need a Kids Passport to use Windows Messenger. Kids Passports require the consent of a parent or guardian.

See Also For more information about Kids Passports, visit *kids.passport.com*.

The concept behind .NET Passport is that you have a single user account name and password that you can use all over the Web, instead of having to set up separate accounts with each Web site that requires one. Your personal information and preferences are stored as part of your .NET Passport, so you don't have to re-enter them each time you visit a site. (Sharing your information is optional.) Because your information is stored on a central server, it is available to you whether you connect to the Internet from your own computer or another one.

.NET Passport started out as a Microsoft service, but now more and more companies are using it, including 1-800-FLOWERS, Costco, eBay, Expedia, Godiva, Hilton, and Starbucks. Web sites that use .NET Passport to verify your credentials display the **.NET Passport Sign In** button, which looks like this:

Sign In .net

How personal information is stored and used is a big concern for most online consumers, and .NET Passport has taken strict measures to ensure that your information is secure. Many of the methods that Web sites use to verify your identity do not use advanced security technologies, making it easier for an unauthorized person to access your personal information. .NET Passport, on the other hand, uses powerful Internet security technologies to prevent unauthorized people from accessing your personal sign-in profile. Here's how:

- Even though you can use your .NET Passport on numerous sites, your password is stored only in the secured .NET Passport database. When you sign in, the password you type is shared only with the .NET Passport database to verify your identity. Your password is never shared with any of the .NET Passport participant sites. This reduces the number of avenues hackers can use to gain access to your personal information.

- When you sign in to .NET Passport, your sign-in name and password are sent over the Internet using a secure connection. This means that only .NET Passport is authorized to access the data sent across the connection.

- After you sign in to a participating .NET Passport site and leave the secure connection, the site keeps track of who you are by using a computer-generated key rather than your .NET Passport sign-in name. Participating sites regularly refresh this key to make it difficult for anyone else to pose as you at these sites.

- If you or someone else makes several incorrect attempts at guessing your password during sign in, .NET Passport automatically blocks access to your account for a few minutes. This makes it significantly more difficult for password-cracking programs to try out thousands of common passwords using your sign-in name.

■ Each time you sign in to your .NET Passport account, your session information is stored in a small encrypted text file (called a *cookie*) on your computer. When you sign out of your .NET Passport account, the cookie (and all your personal information) is deleted from the computer, which means that you can safely use your .NET Passport account from any computer, even a public or shared computer.

Your personal information—including your e-mail and mailing addresses—is also protected by strict privacy policies, and you're always in control of which sites have access to it.

.NET Passport
Wizard

So how do you set up a .NET Passport account? If you have an MSN or MSN Hotmail e-mail account, it is already .NET Passport–enabled. If you don't have one of these accounts, the **.NET Passport Wizard** helps you create one or associate your existing e-mail account with the .NET Passport program.

Important   To maintain an active free MSN Hotmail account, you must sign in at least once within the first 10 days and at least once every 60 days thereafter. Using your Passport on any Passport–enabled site counts as signing in.

In this exercise, you will use the .NET Passport Wizard to add an existing e-mail account to your Windows XP user profile.

Troubleshooting   If you don't already have an e-mail account and would like to create an MSN Hotmail account, the wizard will help you create one.

Tip   These steps show you how to set up a .NET Passport account on a computer in a networked environment. The steps for setting up a .NET Passport account on a stand-alone computer are slightly different. If your computer is not on a network domain, you will be able to follow along with the majority of these steps, and the differences should be self-evident.

BE SURE TO log on to Windows and have an active Internet connection available before beginning this exercise.
OPEN Control Panel, and then display the User Accounts window.

Follow these steps:

1   In the User Accounts window, click the **User Accounts** icon.

2   In the **User Accounts** dialog box, click the **Advanced** tab.

3   In the **Passwords and .NET Passports** area, click **.NET Passport Wizard**.

The **.NET Passport Wizard** starts:

4   Click **Next** to display the wizard's next page:

The wizard prompts you to specify an existing e-mail account or to create a new e-mail account.

Troubleshooting   If you don't have an existing e-mail account, select the **No, I would like to open an MSN Hotmail e-mail account** option, click **Next**, and follow the wizard's instructions.

5 Select the **Yes** option and click **Next**.

The e-mail account registration page opens:

6 If you have an MSN or MSN Hotmail e-mail account, select the **Yes** option, click **Next**, enter your e-mail address and password, and then skip to step 14.

7 If you are using an unregistered e-mail account, select the **No, I want to register my e-mail address with Passport now** option, and then click **Next**.

8 On the Register with .NET Passport page, click **Next** to connect to the Microsoft .NET Passport Member Services Web site:

Tip From this point on, you are working on the Web. Because Web sites can and do change, the dialog boxes you see and the interactions between you and the Web site might differ from those described here.

9 Enter your e-mail address where indicated. In the **Password** and **Retype Password** boxes, enter the password you will use to access your .NET Passport account.

Tip To prevent the automatic creation of accounts for malicious purposes, the .NET Passport registration system requires you to enter a string of characters that would not be recognized by a computer program.

10 A picture appears in the **Registration Check** area. Type the letters and numbers you see in the picture into the text box.

Tip The characters are difficult to read. If you mistype them, you will have an opportunity to try again.

11 In the **Review and Sign the Agreements** area, click each of the links to read the legal agreements. If you agree with them, type the e-mail address you are registering in the box, and then click the **I Agree** button. Otherwise, click the **Cancel** button.

If the system detects any problems with your registration, you are prompted to rectify them. When your registration is complete, you see this page:

12 Click the **Continue** button to close the Internet browser window and return to the **.NET Passport Wizard**.

Your e-mail account is now .NET Passport–enabled.

13 With the **Associate my Passport with my Windows user account** check box selected, click **Next**.

Your Windows XP user account is now configured with your .NET Passport:

14 Click **Finish**.

CLOSE the User Accounts dialog box and the Control Panel window.

Creating Strong Passwords

No computer system is ever completely secure. You can help keep your information secure by using a strong password. Here are some tips for creating strong passwords:

- Use a combination of uppercase letters, lowercase letters, numbers, symbols, and punctuation marks.

- Don't use single words—merge two or more words or misspell them.

- Don't choose words or numbers that might be easy to guess, such as your birthday, your spouse's name, or your phone number.

- Change your password at least every three months.

Getting to Know Windows Messenger

Windows Messenger is a nifty electronic communication system. Primarily known for its instant messaging (IM, also know as *chat*) capabilities, Windows Messenger also supports voice and video conversations over your Internet connection. If you have speakers and a microphone installed, you can place phone calls from your computer to another computer, to a telephone, or to a mobile device without paying long-distance charges (other than any incurred by your Internet connection).

Tip Voice conversations require that each participant have a microphone and speakers or a headset. Video conversations require that each participant have an Internet video camera as well as audio equipment.

Windows Messenger utilizes the Windows XP Remote Assistance technology to make it easy to ask for help when you're experiencing computer difficulties. You can share programs with other Windows XP users, including a special whiteboard application that everyone can use to contribute to a common whiteboard interface.

In addition to these standard features, Windows Messenger versions 4.6 and later support add-ins that you use to see how many e-mail messages are waiting in your Inbox (and alert you when you receive new messages), send text messages to mobile phones and pagers, join special public chat rooms, publish a public profile, and view daily messages in the Windows Messenger window.

Windows Messenger maintains and displays a special list of contacts that includes each contact's online status. You can add new contacts to your list (and they can add you to their lists) using their .NET Passport–enabled e-mail addresses. However, you can't interact with a new contact or see his or her current online status unless he or she has expressly granted you permission. Granting permission is a one-time interaction, but you can revoke a contact's permission to see your online status or to contact you at any time.

Instant messaging and e-mail are in many ways similar, but they have a few significant differences. An instant message can be initiated only when both the sender and receiver are online and signed in to Windows Messenger. Unless you specifically save a Windows Messenger session, the contents of the discussion are gone after you close the discussion window, and they can't be retrieved for later reference.

In addition to text and *emoticons*, your instant messages can include attachments such as files, photos, and Web pages. Up to four people can participate in a Windows Messenger conversation at any time.

Setting Up Windows Messenger

To use Windows Messenger, you must have already set up a .NET Passport account (or a Kids Passport account for children under 12). MSN Internet Access accounts and MSN Hotmail accounts are already part of the .NET Passport system, so if you have one of these accounts, you can use Windows Messenger.

When you use Windows Messenger, the people you communicate with see your *display name* in their contact lists. When you select your display name, keep in mind that the people with whom you exchange instant messages might have lots of names in their contact lists. If your display name does not clearly identify who you are, they might not be sure who they are chatting with. For example, a display name of *J* might be for Jan, Jeff, Jim, Joan, or Joe. A display name of *Joan* might be for Joan Jones or Joan Smith. Also keep in mind that all your instant-message buddies will see your display name, so keep it respectable!

Another way to establish a distinct online presence and imbue it with your own personality is to jazz up the appearance of your messages. You can specify the name, size, style, and color of the font in which your messages appear to differentiate them from those of other conversation partners. You can also select a user account picture to appear next to the conversation area.

You can tailor your Windows Messenger sessions in a variety of ways:

- You can make your home, work, and mobile phone numbers available to other Windows Messenger users so they can call you or send electronic messages to your mobile phone. Do this only if you want your phone numbers to be available to all your current and future Windows Messenger contacts.

- By default, Windows Messenger starts automatically when you log on to your computer. (You can disable this feature if you find it distracting.)

- You can specify how long you can be away from your computer before Windows Messenger shows your status as Away. The default is five minutes.

- Windows Messenger can display pop-up messages or play sounds to alert you to new chat messages, new e-mail messages, or the arrival of one of your contacts online.

- You can choose who can see your online status and who has permission to send you messages. When another Windows Messenger user adds you to his or her contact list, you receive an instant message the next time you sign in, asking if you would like to allow that person to see your online status. Whenever you're online, you can see a list of the people who have added you to their contact list and either allow them to see you or block them from seeing you.

Protecting Children's Privacy

In November 1998, the U.S. Congress passed the Children's Online Privacy Protection Act (COPPA), which requires that operators of U.S.-based online services or Web sites obtain parental consent prior to the collection, use, disclosure, or display of the personal information of children under the age of 13. COPPA went into effect on April 21, 2000, and is governed by regulations established by the Federal Trade Commission.

More information about COPPA, including parents' pages, kids' pages, and public service announcements, is available at *www.ftc.gov/kidzprivacy/*.

In this exercise, you will start Windows Messenger and configure some of your options.

BE SURE TO log on to Windows and have an active Internet connection and a .NET Passport account available before beginning this exercise.

Troubleshooting   This exercise provides steps for users who have not used Windows Messenger before and who have not configured Windows XP to start Windows Messenger automatically when the computer starts.

Tip   If you regularly use a Passport service such as Windows Messenger, you might want to automatically sign in to your Passport account each time you log on to the computer, rather than signing in manually.

Follow these steps:

1   On the **Start** menu, point to **All Programs**, and then click **Windows Messenger**.

Windows Messenger signs you in:

Windows Messenger monitors the status of your e-mail account.

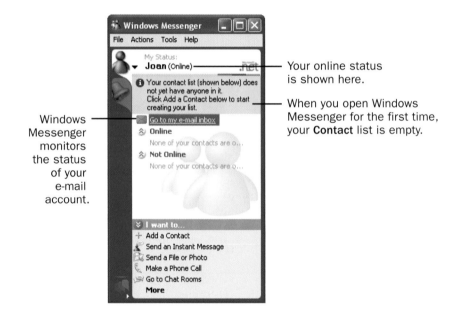

Your online status is shown here.

When you open Windows Messenger for the first time, your **Contact** list is empty.

2   On the **Tools** menu, click **Options**.

The **Options** dialog box appears with your personal information displayed:

3 In the **My .NET Messenger Service Display Name** area, type the name you want other Windows Messenger users to see when you are online To reduce spam, Microsoft recommends that you not use your e-mail address as your display name.

Troubleshooting If you registered your own e-mail address, you will be required to verify that it belongs to you before you can change your user display name. To verify the address, open the e-mail message you received from Passport Member Services with a subject "Please Verify Your .NET Passport E-mail Address," and click the link in the message to verify that you received it.

4 Click the **Change Font** button to open this **Change My Message Font** dialog box:

5 Make the following selections:

- Scroll down in the **Font** box, and click **Verdana**.

- In the **Font style** list, click **Bold**.

- In the **Font size** list, click **8**.

- In the **Color** drop-down list, click **Purple**.

The **Sample** box changes to display each of your selections.

6 Click **OK** to close the dialog box and save your changes.

7 Click each of the tabs in turn to examine your other options, providing any information or changing any options you want.

8 When you are done, click **OK** to close the dialog box.

If you changed any sign-in information, a message box reminds you that those changes won't take effect until the next time you sign in.

9 Click **OK** to close the message box.

10 Click the **Close** button to close Windows Messenger.

Close

11 If a message box appears, telling you that the service will continue to run in the background, click anywhere in the box.

Both the message box and the dialog box close.

The **Windows Messenger** icon is displayed in the notification area of the taskbar. It remains there as long as you are signed in and changes to reflect your online status.

Windows
Messenger

12 Click (don't double-click) the **Windows Messenger** icon on the taskbar, and click **Exit** on the shortcut menu to close the program.

Adding Contacts to Windows Messenger

As long as you know someone's e-mail address or .NET Passport name, you can easily add that person to your contact list. If you don't have a person's contact information but he or she is enrolled in the MSN Member Directory, you can look up his or her contact information online as part of the process.

When you add someone to your contact list, Windows Messenger notifies that person with a message like this:

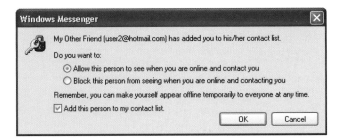

New contacts can allow you to see their status or not, and they can choose whether to add you to their own contact list.

Until new contacts agree to allow you to see them, they are listed as *Offline*. If they choose to block your access, you won't know it; they simply won't ever be listed as *Online*. After contacts agree to allow you to see their status, they appear as either *Online* or *Offline*, depending on whether or not they are logged on to their account. You cannot add a contact who doesn't have a .NET Passport–enabled account to your contact list, but you can have Windows Messenger send e-mail to the contact with instructions on how to obtain a .NET Passport account. When a contact is listed as *Offline*, you cannot send him or her an instant message, but you can still send e-mail messages to that contact through your .NET Passport–enabled e-mail account.

The following icons indicate the status of your Windows Messenger contacts:

Icon	Status	Icon	Status
👤	Online	👤	Offline
👤	Busy/On The Phone	👤	Away/Be Right Back/Out To Lunch

Tip   For further information, refer to "Changing Your Windows Messenger Status," later in this chapter.

In this exercise, you will add people to your Windows Messenger contact list using their e-mail addresses.

BE SURE TO have an active Internet connection available, start Windows Messenger, and know the IM address of at least one other person before beginning this exercise.

Tip   You can create a free MSN Hotmail or .NET Passport account to practice with if you don't have another person's account handy.

Follow these steps:

1   If you did not select the Windows Messenger automatic logon option, sign in now using your .NET Passport account.

Windows Messenger starts, displaying your name, e-mail account status, and contact list:

2   In the **I want to** list, click **Add a Contact**.

The **Add a Contact Wizard** starts:

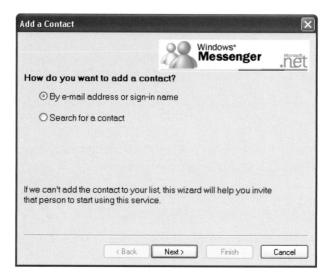

3   Select the **By e-mail address or sign-in name** option, and click **Next**.

4   Type your contact's IM address in the box (if you don't know anyone else's address, use someone@microsoft.com), and then click **Next**.

When the contact has successfully been added, you see a confirmation message like this one:

If you have already created Windows Messenger contact groups, you can add the new contact to a group by selecting the group in the drop-down list.

See Also   For more information about creating contact groups, refer to "Sorting Contacts into Groups" later in this chapter.

---

5   If you would like to add additional contacts to your contact list, click **Next** and do so; otherwise click **Finish** to close the wizard.

The contact is added to your list with a status of *Offline*. After the contact agrees to allow you access, his or her actual status is displayed:

Tip   To delete a contact from your contact list, select the contact's name, press **DELETE**, and then click **Yes** in the message box.

6   On the **File** menu, click **Close**.

The window closes, but Windows Messenger is still active and appears as an icon in the notification area of the taskbar.

7   Click the **Windows Messenger** icon on the taskbar, and then click **Exit** on the shortcut menu to close the program.

Windows
Messenger

Sorting Contacts into Groups

By default, your Windows Messenger contacts are shown in alphabetical order, grouped by online status. Online contacts are listed first (even if they are away or busy) followed by offline contacts. This makes it easy for you to quickly see who is online.

When you have more than a screenful of IM contacts, it can be difficult to keep track of all of them, especially if your contacts choose display names that are not intuitive (such as "the obsessive compulsive one"). To make it easier to keep track, you can sort your contacts into groups, such as Family, Friends, and Colleagues. You can display the groups in whatever order you want, and collapse or expand each group. The group name is followed by an indicator of the number of online and total contacts in that group.

To create a group and add contacts to it:

1   In the **I want to** list at the bottom of the Windows Messenger window, click **Add a Group**.

The new group is created and the group name is editable.

2   Type the name you want for the group, and then press **ENTER**.

You can change the group name at any time by right-clicking it and then clicking **Rename Group** on the shortcut menu.

3   Drag each contact you want to add to the group. The group text color changes when it is selected so you can easily differentiate between groups.

When you add a contact to a group, it still appears in the **All Contacts** list.

Sending and Receiving Instant Messages

Chatting by sending and receiving instant messages is a great way to exchange information with co-workers and friends without making inconvenient telephone calls or crowding inboxes with e-mail messages. You start the conversation with one person, and you can then add more people.

Instant message conversations are held in a conversation window that you can resize by dragging its frame. Unless you explicitly save it, the text in the conversation window is lost when you close the window.

In this exercise, you will send and receive instant messages with one or more online contacts.

BE SURE TO have an active Internet connection available, start Windows Messenger, and configure at least two online contacts before beginning this exercise.

Follow these steps:

1 If you did not select the Windows Messenger automatic logon option, sign in now using your .NET Passport account.

Windows Messenger starts, displaying your name, e-mail account status, and contact list.

2 Double-click the name of the online contact you want to chat with.

A conversation window opens:

The conversation is displayed in the top box.

You write your messages in the bottom box.

At this point, your contact hasn't received any indication that you are going to send a message.

3 Type a message in the input box, and click **Send** or press **ENTER**.

The message is displayed in the conversation area. A conversation window opens on your contact's computer so that he or she can reply to you.

Tip For information about customizing your message font, refer to "Setting Up Windows Messenger" earlier in this chapter.

The status of your conversation is shown in the status bar at the bottom of the conversation window. The status bar tells you when your contact is typing a response. When your contact clicks the **Send** button, the response appears in the conversation area on both your screens. You can continue this conversation for as long as you like, and you don't need to receive a response to continue your side of the conversation:

4   To add another contact to your conversation, click **Invite Someone to this Conver-sation** on the **I want to** menu, select the contact in the **Add Someone to this Con-versation** dialog box, and click **OK**.

A notification appears in the conversation area that a new person has been added to the conversation. The next time you send a message, a conversation window will open on the new person's computer, and he or she can join in.

Multiple people can chat within the conversation, and anyone can leave at any time. Comings and goings are recorded in the conversation window like this:

Tip   New participants cannot see any part of the conversation that happened before they joined.

Close

5   When you no longer want to participate in the conversation, click the conversation box's **Close** button to leave the conversation.

6   Click Windows Messenger's **Close** button to close the conversation window.

The program is still running and is represented by its icon in the notification area of the taskbar.

Expressing Emotions Online

One frequent complaint about electronic communications is that emotions and intent are not always clear in typewritten messages—which can lead to miscommunication between co-workers and friends. One way to clarify emotions and intent is with *emoticons*. Emoticons are graphic images that are created by typing a series of keyboard characters. These character combinations are used in electronic messages to express a sentiment.

The first emoticons represented emotions (hence the name). Recent technology has enabled the development of another series of emoticons: playful symbols representing people and things that make an amusing (if sometimes unnecessary) addition to electronic communications.

Emotions are represented by these character combinations:

Symbol	Meaning	Character combination	Symbol	Meaning	Character combination
	Angel	(A) or (a)		Party	<:o)
	Angry	:-@ or :@		Sad	:-(or :(
	Confused	:-S or :s		Sarcastic	^o)
	Crying	:'(		Sealed lips	:-#
	Devil	(6)		Sick	+o(
	Disappointed	:-| or :|		Secret-telling	:-*

Symbol	Meaning	Character combination	Symbol	Meaning	Character combination
	Embarrassed	:-$ or :$		Sleepy	|-)
	Eye-rolling	8-)		Smile	:-) or :
	Growling	8o|		Surprised	:-O or :o
	Hot	(H) or (h)		Thinking	*-)
	I don't know	:^)		Tongue out	:-P or :p
	Nerd	8-|		Wink	;-) or ;)
	Open-mouthed	:- D or:d			

People, symbols, and things are created by typing these character combinations in a program that supports emoticons:

Symbol	Meaning	Character combination	Symbol	Meaning	Character combination
	Airplane	(ap)		Martini glass	(D) or (d)
	Auto	(au)		Mobile phone	(mp)
	Beer mug	(B) or (b)		Money	(mo)
	Birthday cake	(^)		MSN Messenger	(M) or (m)
	Black sheep	(bah)		Musical note	(8)
	Bowl	(||)		Pizza	(pi)

Symbol	Meaning	Character combination	Symbol	Meaning	Character combination
	Boy	(Z) or (z)		Plate	(pl)
	Broken heart	(U) or (u)		Red heart	(L) or (l)
	Camera	(P) or (p)		Red lips	(K) or (k)
	Cat face	(@)		Red rose	(F) or (f)
	Clock	(O) or (o)		Right hug	(})
	Coffee cup	(C) or (c)		Sleeping half-moon	(S)
	Computer	(co)		Snail	(sn)
	Dog face	(&)		Soccer ball	(so)
	E-mail	(E) or (e)		Star	(*)
	Filmstrip	(~)		Stormy cloud	(st)
	Gift with a bow	(G) or (g)		Telephone receiver	(T) or (t)
	Girl	(X) or (x)		Thumbs down	(N) or (n)
	Island with a palm tree	(ip)		Thumbs up	(Y) or (y)
	Left hug	({)		Umbrella	(um)
	Light bulb	(I) or (i)		Vampire bat	:-[or :[
	Lightning	(li)		Wilted rose	(W) or (w)

If you don't want the character combinations to be displayed as emoticons in your instant messages, do either of the following in Windows Messenger:

- On the **Tools** menu, click **Options**. On the **Personal** tab of the **Options** dialog box, clear the **Show graphics (emoticons) in instant messages** check box, and then click **OK**.

- On the **View** menu of a message window, click **Enable Emoticons** to clear the check box.

If you don't want to type the character combinations, click the **Emoticons** button in a message window to display a drop-down list of 34 common emoticons. Click any emoticon to insert it in the message box.

Changing Your Windows Messenger Status

By default, your Windows Messenger status is set to *Offline* when you are not logged on, *Online* while you are working on your computer, and *Away* when you are inactive (not typing on your computer or using the mouse) for five minutes or more. You can change the inactive time setting, and you can choose from a variety of alternate settings that provide a bit more description to your Windows Messenger contacts.

Contacts can send you instant messages while you are Online, Away, or Busy. While you are Away or Busy, an alert at the top of the message window notifies them that you might not respond due to your status. If a contact tries to send you an instant message while you are Offline, an e-mail window opens so that they can send you an e-mail message instead.

The following notification tray icons indicate your Windows Messenger status:

Icon	Status	Icon	Status
	Not Signed In		Away/Be Right Back/Out To Lunch
	Signing In		Busy/On The Phone
	Online		Offline

If, for example, you receive an important phone call and want to indicate to your Windows Messenger contacts that you are unable to IM at this time, you could set your status to *On The Phone*.

In this exercise, you will change the length of inactive time that triggers the Away setting, and then experiment with different ways to change your online status.

BE SURE TO have an active Internet connection available before beginning this exercise.
OPEN the Windows Messenger program window.

Follow these steps:

1   On the **Tools** menu, click **Options**, and then click the **Preferences** tab:

Look at the Windows Messenger icon in the notification tray. Note that it currently shows you as Online.

2   In the **Show me as "Away" when I'm inactive for** box, type **30**, and then click **OK**.

You can now remain inactive for longer without your Windows Messenger buddies thinking that you're not around.

3   In the **My Status** area at the top of the Windows Messenger window, click your display name, and click **Be Right Back**.

The Windows Messenger icons in the **My Status** area and the notification tray change to reflect your new status. This status change is also visible to your Windows Messenger contacts.

4   On the **File** menu, point to **My Status**.

A list of status options opens:

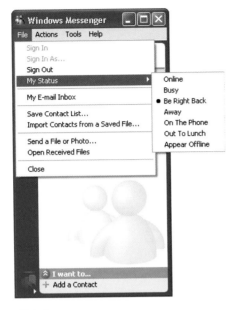

5   Click **Busy**.

The Windows Messenger icons change again.

6   In the notification tray, right-click the **Windows Messenger** icon. Point to **My Status** on the shortcut menu, and then click **Appear Offline**.

The Windows Messenger icon changes again.

CLOSE the conversation window and quit Windows Messenger.

Updating Windows Messenger

Windows XP includes Windows Messenger version 4.0. Windows XP SP2 includes Windows Messenger version 4.7. When a version of Windows Messenger newer than the version installed on your computer is available, the program notifies you the next time you are signed in and prompts you to upgrade to the newer version. If you don't want to upgrade at that time, you can install the latest version at any time from the .NET Messenger Service Web site at *www.microsoft.com/windows/messenger/*.

After upgrading your Windows Messenger installation, sign in using your .NET Passport account, and all your contacts will be available as usual.

Setting Up Outlook Express

Microsoft Outlook Express is an e-mail program that ships with Windows XP. With Outlook Express, you can quickly and easily connect to your existing e-mail server to send and receive e-mail messages and track your contacts. You can download e-mail from your server and work either *online* or *offline*. If you work offline, you can direct Outlook Express to connect to your server to send and receive e-mail messages at regular intervals. You can also block junk mail senders or other people or companies from whom you do not want to receive e-mail messages.

Outlook Express includes an *Address Book* in which you can keep track of information about your friends, family members, co-workers, customers, and anyone else you come in contact with. You can track multiple e-mail addresses, home and work contact details, family information, NetMeeting contact information, and even digital IDs. You can also create groups of contacts so that you can send e-mail to multiple people using only one address. You can export your contact list from the Address Book as a Microsoft Exchange Personal Address Book file or as a text-delimited file that can then be imported into Microsoft Office Excel, Microsoft Office Access, and a variety of other programs.

Tip If you have configured Windows Messenger, the Address Book also displays your Windows Messenger contacts and their online status.

You can format your e-mail messages almost any way you like—using backgrounds, fonts, and colors—and you can create a personalized signature to automatically finish off each of your e-mail messages with a professional touch. You can send electronic business cards (*vCards*) to new contacts to give them all your contact information. If your contact uses Microsoft Office Outlook or Outlook Express, he or she can drop your vCard into his or her own electronic address book. If your contact information changes, you can send updated vCards to all your contacts.

An in-depth discussion about e-mail technology is beyond the scope of this book, but this topic discusses some of the basic concepts to ensure that you understand how to work with Outlook Express.

Most business people today have e-mail accounts at work. Many people also have separate e-mail accounts that they use for personal e-mail, either through their Internet service provider (ISP) or through a Web-based e-mail program such as MSN Hotmail. With Outlook Express, you can connect to each of your e-mail accounts through the same interface. You can also connect to *newsgroups* and *Internet directory services*, including BigFoot, VeriSign, and WhoWhere.

E-mail administration is managed through one or more *e-mail servers*—computers that manage your *mailbox* and send, receive, and distribute e-mail messages. E-mail servers operate under specific rules set by the server administrator. These rules govern the size of individual e-mail messages that can be sent and received, as well as the amount of space available for your individual mailbox. Incoming messages are handled by a server running one of three *protocols*: *Hypertext Transfer Protocol (HTTP)*, *Internet Message Access Protocol (IMAP)*, or *Post Office Protocol 3 (POP3)*. Each of these protocols has a different set of rules for handling e-mail messages; your network administrator or ISP will be able to tell you which protocol your server uses. Outgoing messages are handled by a server running *Simple Mail Transfer Protocol (SMTP)*.

Tip   E-mail servers can do their jobs because every mailbox has a unique *e-mail address*. This address has two parts—the *alias* and the *domain*—separated by an *at* symbol (@). For example, the e-mail address *someone@microsoft.com* represents a user named *someone* who has an e-mail account on the *microsoft.com* domain (in other words, the person works at Microsoft). Business e-mail aliases generally consist of a person's first and last name or initials. The domain name that follows is also where you'll find that business's Web site—simply replace the alias and the @ symbol with *www* and a period, and you have the URL. Exceptions are ISP and Web-based e-mail accounts, where the domain name leads to the service provider's home page.

Within your mailbox, your e-mail is stored in a series of folders. The folder structure varies depending on your e-mail program. Outlook Express includes these folders:

- *Inbox.*   Your new messages are delivered to this folder.

- *Outbox.*   Messages that you have sent, but that have not yet been delivered to the e-mail server, are held in this folder. If you are working offline, messages are held here until the next time you connect to the server.

- *Sent Items.*   After you send a message to someone, a copy of it is stored in this folder. Depending on your e-mail program, you might have to stipulate that you want to save your sent messages.

- *Deleted Items.*   Deleted messages are stored here until you purge the folder. This is the Outlook Express equivalent of the Windows Recycle Bin.

- *Drafts.*   While you are preparing your message but before it has been sent, a copy of the message is saved periodically in the Drafts folder. If your e-mail program suddenly closes, or if you want to close the message and send it later, you can open the most recent version from this folder.

In addition to these standard folders, you can create your own folders in which you can organize your e-mail messages as you like. For example, you might create a folder for each project you're working on and then move messages to the appropriate folders as they arrive. Folders help to keep your Inbox less cluttered and make it easier to find specific messages later.

When you're using Outlook Express, you can choose whether you want to see all your e-mail folders and whether you want to *synchronize* your Outlook Express folders with the folders on your e-mail server. When you synchronize your folders, Outlook Express compares the folder on your computer to the folder on the server and updates both folders to the current status, downloading new messages to your computer and removing messages that have been deleted from either version.

In this exercise, you will configure Outlook Express to send and receive e-mail messages using your existing e-mail account.

BE SURE TO have an active network or Internet connection available and have your e-mail account name and password, the name and type of your incoming e-mail server, and the name of your outgoing e-mail server available before beginning this exercise.

Follow these steps:

1   On the **Start** menu, point to **All Programs**, and then click **Outlook Express**.

Outlook Express starts. If this is the first time you've started Outlook Express, the **Internet Connection Wizard** starts:

2   If the **Internet Connection Wizard** doesn't automatically start, click **Accounts** on the **Tools** menu, and in the **Internet Accounts** dialog box, click the **Add** button, and then click **Mail**.

Tip   If you see a message asking whether you want Outlook Express to be your default e-mail client, click **Yes** or **No** according to your preferences.

3 Enter your name as you want it to appear to recipients of e-mail messages from you, and then click **Next** to display the wizard's second page:

Internet Connection Wizard

Internet E-mail Address

Your e-mail address is the address other people use to send e-mail messages to you.

E-mail address: [   ]

For example: someone@microsoft.com

< Back   Next >   Cancel

4 Enter the e-mail address you want displayed to recipients of your messages, and click **Next** to move to the third page:

Internet Connection Wizard

E-mail Server Names

My incoming mail server is a [POP3 ▼] server.

Incoming mail (POP3, IMAP or HTTP) server:
[   ]

An SMTP server is the server that is used for your outgoing e-mail.

Outgoing mail (SMTP) server:
[   ]

< Back   Next >   Cancel

5   Type the names of your incoming and outgoing mail servers in the boxes. Then select the type of server that handles your incoming mail from the drop-down list, and click **Next**.

The **Internet Mail Logon** page is displayed, where the wizard prompts you for your e-mail account name and password:

If you clear the **Remember password** check box, Outlook Express will prompt you for your password each time you start the program.

6   Click **Next**, click **Finish** to close the wizard and then click **Close** to close the **Internet Accounts** dialog box.

Troubleshooting   If you are configuring Outlook Express for an IMAP server, you will also need to complete steps 7 through 12. The remaining exercises in this chapter show an IMAP account. If you have a POP3 or HTTP account and have any problems with steps 13 through 19, contact your system administrator or ISP.

7   Outlook Express prompts you to download the list of folders from your mail server. Click **Yes**.

Outlook Express downloads a list of folders and then displays the folders that are available for your account:

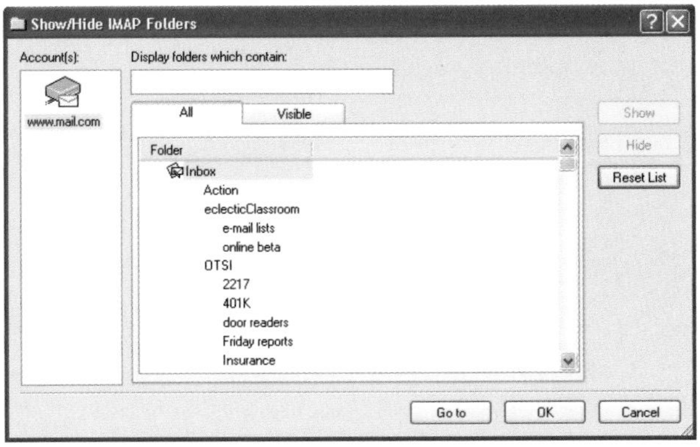

8 Double-click the folders you want to display.

An icon appears next to each folder you double-click to indicate that the contents of the folder will be downloaded.

9 Click **OK** to download the selected folders to your computer.

The account and folders are now displayed in your **Folders** list.

10 Click the account name to display the synchronization options:

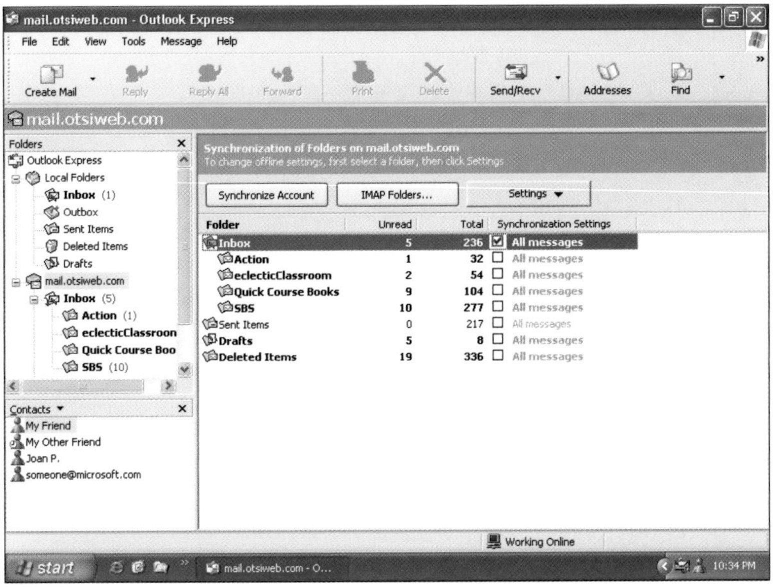

11 Select the check boxes of the folders you would like to synchronize, and then click **Synchronize Account**.

E-mail messages from the selected folders are downloaded to your computer.

E-mail messages from folders that you did not select for synchronization will be downloaded the first time you select that folder for viewing.

12   In the **Folders** list, click **Outlook Express**.

Outlook Express now looks something like this:

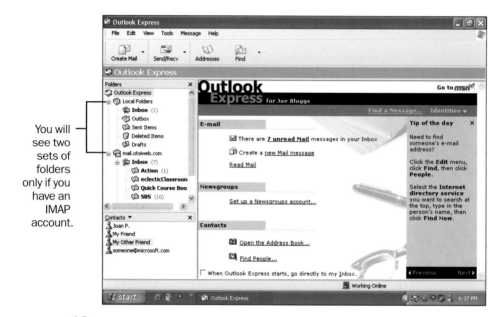

You will
see two
sets of
folders
only if you
have an
IMAP
account.

13   In the **Folders** list, click **Inbox** to open your local Inbox.

14   On the **View** menu, click **Layout**.

The **Window Layout Properties** dialog box appears:

15   To enlarge your work area, clear the **Contacts** and **Folder List** check boxes.

16 Check that the **Preview Pane** options are selected as shown, and click **OK**.

Your Inbox now looks something like this:

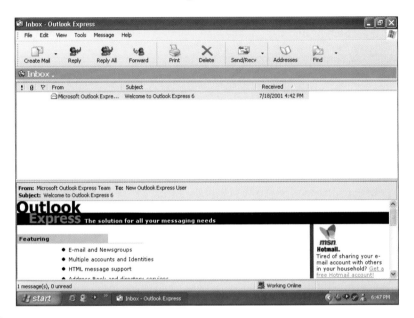

17 In the preview pane, use the scroll bar to scroll through the contents of the welcome message.

18 In the Inbox, double-click the message to open it in its own window.

Initially, the message opens in a small window:

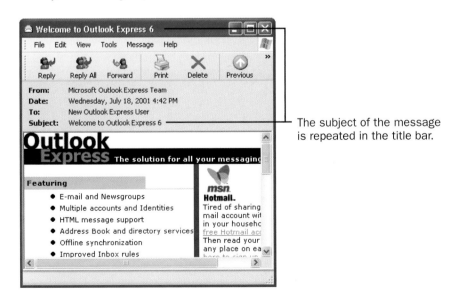

The subject of the message is repeated in the title bar.

229

19   Click the message's **Maximize** button.

Maximize

The message expands to fill the screen.

CLOSE the message, and quit Outlook Express.

Connecting to Newsgroups Through Outlook Express

Newsgroups are moderated or unmoderated "message boards" on which people communicate about a specific subject. You can find a newsgroup for just about any topic you can think of, from Windows XP to American Eskimo dogs and from maternity to medical treatments. If people are talking about it, there are probably people talking about it in a newsgroup.

You can add newsgroups to Outlook Express in the same way that you add e-mail accounts: On the **Tools** menu, click **Accounts**, and then click the **News** tab. Click the **Add** button, click **News**, and then follow the simple instructions.

A variety of newsgroups are available for Windows XP. To see a current list of newsgroups, visit *www.microsoft.com/windowsxp/expertzone/newsgroups/*. For step-by-step instructions on configuring Outlook Express for a newsgroup, click the **Windows XP Newsgroup Setup Instructions** link on that site.

Sending and Receiving E-Mail Messages

Although an in-depth tutorial on Outlook Express is beyond the scope of this book, it is certainly worth investigating the main capabilities of the program on your own. With Outlook Express, you can send and receive professional-looking e-mail messages with most of the features that are available in larger programs such as Microsoft Office Outlook. For example, you can use *stationery*, customize fonts, create personal *signatures*, request *read receipts*, and check the spelling of your messages. You can send fancy messages in *Hypertext Markup Language (HTML)* or simple messages in plain-text format. You can also send and receive files that are sent with messages as *attachments*.

Tip   With an IMAP account, until you select a message you have received, Outlook Express downloads only the message *header*. As a result, you can't see whether an e-mail message has an attachment until you select that e-mail message for viewing.

Each e-mail message that is displayed in Outlook Express is represented by an icon indicating the type of message and its priority and status. The most common icons include:

Category	Icon	Represents	Icon	Represents
Unread messages	✉	Standard unopened message	✉	Digitally signed
	✉	Encrypted	✉	Digitally signed and encrypted
Read messages	✉	Standard opened message	✉	Replied to
	✉	Digitally signed	✉	Forwarded
	✉	Encrypted	✉	Digitally signed and encrypted
Extra designations	📎	Attachment	!	High priority
	⚑	Flagged for further action	↓	Low priority

A complete list of icons is available in the Outlook Express Help file.

In this exercise, you will send, receive, reply to, and delete e-mail messages.

BE SURE TO have an active network or Internet connection available and set up Outlook Express as your default e-mail program before beginning this exercise.

Follow these steps:

1   On the **Start** menu, click **E-mail**.

   Tip   If Outlook Express is not the default e-mail program, click **Start**, point to **All Programs**, and then click **Outlook Express**.

Outlook Express opens, looking something like this:

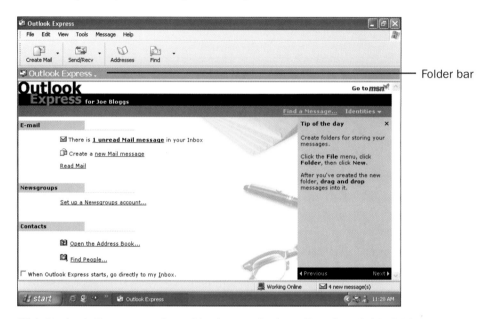

Folder bar

2   Click **Outlook Express** on the Folder bar to display a list of available folders:

Click push pin to keep open

Outlook Express
Local Folders
    Inbox ————————————————— This is your local Inbox.
    Outbox
    Sent Items
    Deleted Items
    Drafts
mail.otsiweb.com
    Inbox (1) ———————————— For IMAP accounts, this is
        Action (1)   the Inbox associated with
        eclecticClassroom (2)   your e-mail account on the
        Quick Course Books (9)   server.
        SBS (10)
    Sent Items
    Drafts (5)
    Deleted Items (6)

3   Click the **Inbox** folder for your e-mail account.

The **Folder List** closes.

4 On the toolbar, click the **Create Mail** button.

A New Message form opens with a blank background.

5 In the **To** box, type your own e-mail address (the one you used to configure this account).

6 In the **Subject** box, type Test message.

As you type, the text of the subject line is repeated in the title bar.

7 In the body of the message, type This is a test of sending a new e-mail message.

Your message is displayed in the font that is selected and shown above the body of the message, which is the default for all messages.

8 On the message form's toolbar, click the **Send** button.

Outlook Express sends the new message and then receives it in your Inbox:

Messages displayed in bold haven't been read yet. —

File Edit View Tools Message Help	

Create Mail   Reply   Reply All   Forward   Print   Delete   Send/Recv   Addresses   Find

Inbox

!	0	▽	From	Subject	Received
	0		Mike Galos	September 8, 1998	7/26/2001 9:27 AM
			Catherine Turner	Test message	7/26/2001 11:3...

From: Mike Galos   To: Joan Preppernau
Subject: September 8, 1998

Are we on for lunch?

Mike

2 message(s), 1 unread   Working Online

start   Inbox - Outlook Express   11:33 AM

Tip To check for new e-mail, click the **Send/Recv** button on the toolbar.

9 Double-click the message to open it.

10 On the message window's toolbar, click the **Reply** button.

Tip   Always check to see if anyone else appears on the **To** line or on the **Cc** line of the e-mail messages you receive. If you want your reply to be sent to everyone who received the original message, on the message window's toolbar, click the **Reply All** button instead of the **Reply** button.

A new e-mail message form opens, set up so that you can respond to the message you received. The sender of the original message has been entered in the **To** line, and the original subject is preceded by *RE:* on the **Subject** line to indicate that this is a response.

11   In the message body, type This is a test of replying to an e-mail message.

12   Click the **Send** button.

Outlook Express sends your reply and then receives it in your Inbox.

13   Click the original e-mail message to select it, hold down **CTRL**, and click the reply e-mail message to add it to the selection.

14   On the toolbar, click the **Delete** button.

The e-mail messages are deleted from the Inbox. With IMAP accounts, the messages are still visible, but have been "crossed out" to indicate that they have been deleted.

15   If you have an IMAP account, click the double arrows at the right end of the toolbar to display all the options, and then click the **Purge** button.

The deleted e-mail messages are removed from your Inbox.

CLOSE Outlook Express.

Important   Most computer viruses are transmitted as e-mail attachments that aren't dangerous to your computer until they are run. Some virus attachments must be opened to start, and others can activate themselves in the e-mail preview window. If you receive an e-mail message with an attachment from an unknown (or clearly bogus) source, right-click the message in the Inbox and click **Delete** on the shortcut menu to move it to the Deleted Items folder without opening or previewing it. Certain e-mail viruses redistribute themselves to everyone in the recipient's address book without any outward sign. If you receive an e-mail message with an attachment from a known source, but the attachment is unexpected or gives you reason for concern (perhaps it has a strange name or file name extension), it is safest to reply to the message and request further information.

Creating E-Mail Stationery

An e-mail *stationery theme*, or template, includes background colors or pictures, fonts, and margin settings. By default, the stationery theme applied to messages is a blank background, but Outlook Express comes with 14 stationery themes from which you can choose. Many more themes are available online.

If you don't like any of the available themes, you can create your own using the **Stationery Setup Wizard**. You can create a new theme based on the current one, or you can create one of your own design.

In this exercise, you will create a simple stationery theme using the **Stationery Setup Wizard**.

BE SURE TO set up Outlook Express as your default e-mail program before beginning this exercise.

Follow these steps:

1 On the **Start** menu, click **E-mail**.

Outlook Express opens.

2 On the toolbar, click the down arrow to the right of the **Create Mail** button to display the stationery drop-down menu.

3 On the stationery menu, click **Select Stationery**.

The **Select Stationery** dialog box appears, showing the currently installed stationery options:

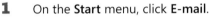

4 Click the **Create New** button.

The **Stationery Setup Wizard** starts.

5   Click **Next** to move to the wizard's **Background** page:

6   Clear the **Picture** check box, and select the **Color** check box.

7   Click the down arrow to the right of the **Color** box, and click **Purple** in the drop-down list.

Your color choice is displayed in the **Preview** area.

8   Click **Next** to move to the **Font** page:

■   Click the down arrow to the right of the **Font** box, and click **Verdana** in the drop-down list.

■   Click the down arrow to the right of the **Color** box, and click **White** in the drop-down list.

■ Select the **Bold** check box.

Your choices are displayed in the **Preview** area.

9 Click **Next** to move to the **Margins** page.

The **Preview** area displays your background and font selections:

Stationery Setup Wizard ⊠

Margins
Enter the margin width you want for this stationery.

Left Margin: [0] ⇕ pixels

Top Margin: [0] ⇕ pixels

Preview:

[< Back] [Next >] [Cancel]

10 Make the following changes:

■ Click the up arrow to the right of the **Left Margin** spinner once to set it to 25 pixels.

■ Click the up arrow to the right of the **Top Margin** spinner once to set it to 25 pixels.

11 Click **Next** to move to the **Complete** page:

Stationery Setup Wizard ⊠

Complete
Your Stationery is complete. Enter a name and click finish to save your creation.

Preview:

Name: [   ]

(e.g. My Stationery)

[< Back] [Finish] [Cancel]

12 In the **Name** box, type My Stationery, and then click **Finish**.

Your new stationery is created, and the file is saved on your computer. (It is visible in the Select Stationery window.)

13 Click **OK** to open a new message form that uses your new stationery theme.

The purple background is immediately visible.

14 Click in the message body, and type This is my custom stationery.

Your message is displayed in bold, white, Verdana font.

Close

15 Click the message form's **Close** button to close the message without sending it.

16 When you are prompted to save the message, click **No**.

17 On the toolbar, click the down arrow to the right of the **Create Mail** button to display the stationery drop-down menu.

Your custom stationery is now available on this menu.

CLOSE Outlook Express.

Adding Contacts to Your Address Book

Outlook Express incorporates an Address Book that you can use to add contacts to your **Contacts** list—and if you want, it will add contact information for you! With the *Address Book*, you can:

- Store e-mail addresses, street addresses, phone numbers, and personal information about contacts or groups of contacts that are important to you.

- Find people and businesses through *Internet directory services*, Web-based search engines that give you access to directory information from around the world.

- Create groups of contacts for mailing lists. You might want a group for each project you're working on, a group for external vendors, a group for family members, or any other type of group you want to e-mail collectively.

- Share contacts with other people who use your computer.

- Import information from and export information to other address books, including those from Microsoft Exchange, Netscape Communicator, Eudora Light, Eudora Pro, or any other program that exports comma-separated text files.

- Send and receive electronic business cards that contain contact information in a format that can easily be merged into other people's contact databases.

- Print your Address Book information in a variety of formats so that you can carry it with you when you don't have access to your computer or handheld electronic organizer.

By default, Outlook Express adds your Windows Messenger contacts to your Address Book, and adds e-mail contacts to the Address Book whenever you reply to them. This means that you can pretty much populate your address book without trying. It's also easy to add new contacts manually.

In this exercise, you will add three new contacts to your Address Book and then create a group of contacts.

BE SURE TO set up Outlook Express as your default e-mail program before beginning this exercise.

Follow these steps:

1 On the **Start** menu, click **E-Mail**.

Outlook Express starts.

2 On the toolbar, click **Addresses**.

The Address Book opens:

3 Click the Address Book's **Maximize** button so you can see its contents.

Maximize

4 On the Address Book's toolbar, click the **New** button, and then click **New Contact** on the drop-down menu.

New

A contact form appears.

5 Create the contact by typing the following:

■ In the **First** box, type Catherine.

Tip As you type the name, it is repeated in the title bar of the dialog box and in the **Display** box.

239

■ In the **Last** box, type Turner.

■ In the **Title** box, type Ms.

■ In the **E-Mail Addresses** box, type catherinet@gardenco.msn.com.

■ Click the **Add** button.

The e-mail address is added and is designated as the default address, like this:

6 Click the **Business** tab, and then do the following:

■ In the **Company** box, type The Garden Company.

■ In the **Street Address** box, type 1234 Oak Street.

■ In the **City** box, type Seattle.

■ In the **State/Province** box, type WA.

■ In the **Zip Code** box, type 10101.

Tip If this were a real address, you could click **View Map** to locate the address on an Expedia map.

■ In the **Web Page** box, type http://www.gardenco.msn.com.

Tip If this URL were real, you could click **Go** to open the Web page in your default browser.

- In the **Job Title** box, type **Owner**.

- In the **Phone** box, type **(206) 555-0100**.

- In the **Fax** box, type **(206) 555-0101**.

7 Click the **Home**, **Personal**, **Other**, **NetMeeting**, and **Digital IDs** tabs, and review the options available there.

8 Click **OK** to add Catherine Turner to your Address Book.

9 Position the mouse pointer over Catherine's Address Book entry.

Her contact information is displayed as a ScreenTip.

10 Repeat steps 5 through 9 to create an Address Book entry for Mr. Mike Galos. Mike's e-mail address is *mike@gardenco.msn.com*. Mike is the manager of The Garden Company, and he has the same business contact information as Catherine Turner.

Tip Mike Galos, Catherine Turner, Kim Yoshida, and The Garden Company are fictional identities created for the Step by Step series.

11 On the Address Book's toolbar, click the **New** button, and then click **New Group** on the drop-down menu.

A contact form appears:

Properties [?] [X]

Group | Group Details

Type a name for your group, and then add members. After creating the group, you can add or remove members at any time.

Group Name: [_____] 0 Member(s)

You can add to a group in three ways: select someone from your address book, add a new contact for the group and your address book, or add someone to the group but not to your address book.

Group Members:

[Select Members]
[New Contact]
[Remove]
[Properties]

Name: [_____]
E-Mail: [_____] [Add]

[OK] [Cancel]

12 In the **Group Name** box, type **Work**.

13   Click **Select Members**.

The **Select Group Members** dialog box appears:

Your current contacts are listed here.

Group members will be listed here.

14   Click **Catherine Turner**, and then click **Select**.

Catherine is moved to the **Members** list.

15   Click **Mike Galos**, and then click **Select**.

Mike is moved to the **Members** list.

Tip   To locate people through an Internet directory service, click **Find** and then select a directory service from the **Look in** drop-down list.

16   Click **OK** to close the **Select Group Members** dialog box.

The **Work Properties** dialog box now lists two members.

17   Click the **New Contact** button to add a new group member who doesn't yet exist in the address book.

A contact form appears.

18   Repeat steps 5 through 9 to add Ms. Kim Yoshida. Kim's e-mail address is kim@gardenco.msn.com. Kim is the purchasing manager at The Garden Company and has the same business contact information as Catherine and Mike.

Tip   To add a contact to the group, but not to your address book, enter his or her name and e-mail address at the bottom of the **Group** tab, and click **Add**.

19 After you have entered Kim's information, click **OK** to close the **Kim Yoshida Properties** dialog box.

Kim is automatically added to the Work group.

20 Click **OK** to close the **Work Properties** dialog box.

Your three contacts are listed in the right pane of the Address Book, and the Work group is shown in the left pane.

21 In the Address Book, select the **Work** group, and then click **Delete**.

22 Click **Yes** when asked to confirm the deletion.

23 Select and delete each of the contacts you created in this exercise.

CLOSE the Address Book, and then quit Outlook Express.

Key Points

■   Windows XP includes the tools you need to communicate with others: Windows Messenger for instant messaging and Outlook Express for e-mail.

■   By attaching your .NET Passport or.NET Passport–enabled account to your Windows XP user account, your contact list is available to you in Windows Messenger and Outlook Express.

■   You can easily personalize your IM and e-mail communications to reflect your unique personality.

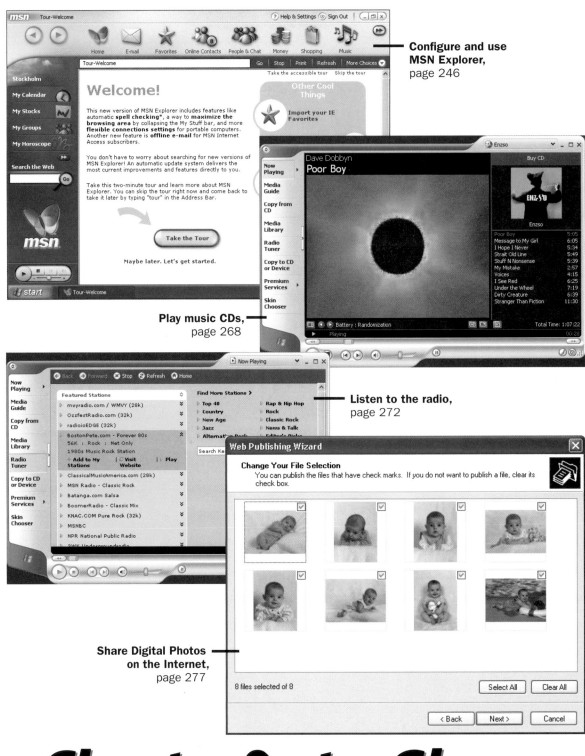

**Configure and use
MSN Explorer,**
page 246

Play music CDs,
page 268

Listen to the radio,
page 272

**Share Digital Photos
on the Internet,**
page 277

Chapter 9 at a Glance

9 Having Fun with Windows XP

In this chapter you will learn to:

✔ Play games on your computer or over the Internet.

✔ Configure and use MSN Explorer.

✔ Allow or restrict the viewing of objectionable Internet content.

✔ Use Windows Media Player to listen to music or watch a movie.

✔ Personalize Windows Media Player.

✔ Create your own music playlist.

✔ Share digital photos on the Internet.

Microsoft Windows XP comes with more leisure-time options than any previous version of Windows. In addition to the traditional solitaire-style games that came with earlier versions of Windows, you now have access to multi-player games on the Internet. A number of exciting new software programs are also included with Windows XP that make it easy to play or create audio compact discs (CDs), play digital video discs (DVDs), create your own movies, and manage your photograph collections.

In this chapter, you explore a few of the Windows XP entertainment options. If you use Windows XP on your computer at work, playing games might not be appropriate; however, some of the topics in this chapter, such as working with digital photographs, might give you just the information you need to jazz up an important document or presentation.

See Also   Do you need only a quick refresher on the topics in this chapter? See the Quick Reference entries on pages xl–xliii.

 Important   Before you can use the practice files in this chapter, you need to install them from the book's companion CD to their default location. See "Using the Book's CD-ROM" on page xv for more information.

Playing Games

Computer games have been around almost as long as computers. Windows XP comes with all the standard favorites and more. If you like card games, you can choose from FreeCell, Solitaire, Spider Solitaire, and Hearts. All are installed on your computer's hard disk, and are played alone. If cards aren't your strong suit, you can play Minesweeper or

Pinball. Minesweeper is a one-person game, but Pinball can be played with up to four players on one computer.

With Windows XP and an Internet connection, you now have more gaming options than ever. Windows XP includes links to Internet Backgammon, Internet Checkers, Internet Hearts, Internet Reversi, and Internet Spades. You can play these games against other players around the world by joining the MSN Gaming Zone at *zone.msn.com*.

You access all the games that come with Windows XP from the **Games** menu. On the **Start** menu, point to **All Programs**, and then click **Games**. Instructions for playing each game are available from that game's **Help** menu.

Of course, you aren't limited to the games that come with Windows XP. You can install other gaming software, or if you have Internet access, you can play hundreds of solo and multi-player computer games through any of the many popular gaming sites, including:

- Games.com (*play.games.com*)

- Gamesville (*www.gamesville.com*)

- MSN Gaming Zone (*zone.msn.com*)

- Pogo.com (*www.pogo.com*)

Using MSN Explorer

new for
WindowsXP

MSN Explorer

Included with Windows XP is *MSN Explorer*, an all-in-one package that has all the tools you need to work effectively on the Web. MSN Explorer integrates several popular MSN services, including:

- MSN Calendar, where you can keep track of appointments, tasks, and reminders. MSN Explorer can send a reminder to you through e-mail, MSN Messenger, or your cell phone.

- MSN Communities, where you can interact online with others who share common interests. You can join an existing community or start your own.

- MSN Custom Web Sites, which makes it easy to create your own Web site to share photos and files with other people around the world.

- MSN eShop, where you can research products, compare prices, and make online purchases from hundreds of retailers.

- MSN Hotmail, which you can use to send and receive e-mail messages for free.

- MSN Messenger Service, which you can use to send instant messages and files to your friends who are online, or even converse with them over the Internet, using a microphone.

- MSN MoneyCentral, where you can track your accounts and pay your bills online.

■ MSN Music, which you use to find online radio stations that suit your taste, based on favorite songs, artists, albums, or just your general mood.

MSN Explorer also integrates with Windows Media Player, so you can listen to music or watch a video while you're surfing the Web or sending e-mail.

When you sign in to MSN Explorer, you are automatically signed in to the other password-protected MSN services , so you don't have to retype your password when moving between them.

Important   Don't confuse *MSN Explorer* with *MSN Internet Access*. The *Microsoft Network (MSN)* spans a number of services including all those just listed. MSN is also an ISP through which you can configure a local dial-up account from almost any location in the world. Along with your Internet access, you can also get an MSN e-mail address (*someone@msn.com*) that is part of the Passport program.

MSN Explorer is available in specialized versions. Currently available versions (in multiple languages where indicated) include:

International MSN Explorer Versions			
Australia	Germany	Malaysia	Singapore
Austria	Greece	Mexico	South Africa
Belgium (Dutch and French versions)	Hong Kong SAR	Netherlands	Spain
Brazil	Hungary	New Zealand	Sweden
Canada (English and French versions)	India	Norway	Switzerland (French and German versions)
Czech Republic	Italy	People's Republic of China	Taiwan
Denmark	Japan	Poland	Turkey
Finland	Korea	Portugal	United Kingdom
France	Latin America	Russia	United States (English and Spanish versions)

Regional installations of MSN Explorer are available in a variety of languages from *explorer.msn.com/intl.asp*. If you want to send the program to a friend, you can order individual installation CDs from the MSN Explorer Web site at *explorer.msn.com/install.htm*. All versions of MSN Explorer include a special automatic update feature that ensures that your software stays up to date.

Each installation of MSN Explorer supports up to nine users by maintaining a separate profile for each one. As a result, you can store your personal information, including favorite Web pages, e-mail contacts, and instant messaging contacts, without having to worry that the information will be accessed or changed by someone else. When you're away from your computer, you can have MSN Explorer deliver information to your Web-enabled cellular phone or other handheld device.

In this exercise, you will walk through the initial installation of MSN Explorer and then configure an MSN Explorer user account for yourself.

BE SURE TO have an active Internet connection or a properly installed modem and phone line connection available before beginning this exercise. If you do not have an ISP or e-mail address, you can sign up for one during this exercise.

Important The steps illustrated in this exercise are for a computer with a full-time broadband connection. If you are using a different Internet access method, you might have to vary the steps slightly based on the on-screen instructions, but you will still be able to follow along with the exercise.

Follow these steps:

1 On the **Start** menu, point to **All Programs**, and then click **MSN Explorer**.

2 If prompted to confirm that you want to open MSN Explorer, click **Yes**.

The Welcome page opens:

3 Click **Continue**.

The next page prompts you to enter your geographic location.

4 In the drop-down list, click your location, or the closest location within your time zone.

5 Click **Continue**.

6 If you are prompted to select a customized international version of MSN Explorer, click the most appropriate country or region, and then click **OK**.

Your selection governs the language in which MSN Explorer is displayed, as well as the links available to you.

The next page includes the option of signing up for MSN Internet Access:

7 Select the appropriate option, and then click **Continue**:

- If you don't currently have an ISP or an e-mail address, select the **Yes, I would like to sign up for MSN Internet Access and get a new MSN e-mail address** option.

- If you don't have an ISP but you do have either a Hotmail or MSN e-mail address, select the **Yes, I would like to sign up for MSN Internet Access but keep my existing e-mail address** option.

- If you have an ISP or are using a broadband connection, select the **No, I already have Internet Access** option.

8 If you chose to sign up for MSN Internet Access, follow the prompts to complete the process, and then rejoin this exercise.

9 If you already have Internet access, the next page asks if you already have an MSN Internet Access dial-up account. Select the appropriate option, click **Continue**, and follow the prompts. You are prompted to specify a Hotmail or MSN e-mail address, or create a new one, and agree to the MSN Terms of Use.

10 Sign in to MSN Explorer with your MSN or Hotmail account when prompted to do so.

When the sign-in process is complete, MSN Explorer starts:

11 Browse through the site to see all the great tools that are available to you.

12 When you are finished, click **Sign Out** in the window's title bar to sign out of MSN Explorer and return to the welcome screen.

MSN Explorer prompts you to save your logon information.

13 If you want to enable automatic logon to all Passport-enabled sites, click **Yes** (otherwise, click **No**).

14 Click the **Close** button to close the MSN Explorer welcome screen.

Close

To sign in to MSN Explorer in the future, on the **Start** menu, point to **All Programs**, and then click **MSN Explorer**. You will automatically be signed in to the entire suite of services.

Troubleshooting   MSN Explorer uses *cookies* to sign you in to the Web sites that provide its services. If you have chosen not to allow cookies to be placed on your computer, the MSN Explorer services will not be available. MSN Explorer checks the settings on your computer during the setup process, and if necessary, prompts you to change your security settings to allow cookies.

Maintaining Your Privacy

The MSN Explorer registration process requires you to supply a certain amount of personal information, including your name and address, occupation, and geographic location. This information might be supplied through your Passport, or you might be asked to enter it.

In addition to the information that you actively provide, MSN Explorer gathers anonymous statistical data, including how often you log on, how long it takes for your browser to display the home page, and how long you spend using the service. This data is gathered only for technical quality-control purposes and does not include any information that identifies you personally.

MSN Explorer tracks your favorite Web sites in a Favorites list that is available to you from anywhere in the world when you sign in to MSN Explorer. Your Favorites list is not shared with or available to anyone other than you (or another person to whom you have given your user account name and password).

If you experience an error while using MSN Explorer, you will be asked to send data to MSN to help them determine the cause of the error so that they can correct it in future software versions. If you choose to send this data, you can review it before sending it. Information that identifies you personally might be included in this data, but Microsoft's policy is that any such information is deleted before it gets to the person who reviews the error.

Microsoft and MSN are licensees of the TRUSTe Privacy Program, which means that every Microsoft or MSN Web site contains a link to a privacy statement that must inform you of the following:

- The types of personal, identifying information that are collected from you through the Web site

- The name of the organization that is collecting the information

- How the information is used

- With whom the information might be shared

- Your choices regarding collection, use, and distribution of the information

- The kind of security procedures that are in place to protect against the loss, misuse, or alteration of your information

- How you can correct inaccuracies in the information

For more information about TRUSTe, you can visit *www.truste.org*. If you have concerns about the protection of your personal information while using MSN Explorer, you can send an e-mail message to *MSNPrivacy@msn.com*.

Allowing and Restricting Objectionable Content

In addition to the basic options you can configure for your Web-browsing experience, Internet Explorer includes settings that protect your privacy and offer peace of mind regarding the types of content that can be viewed on your computer.

Internet Explorer 6 includes a feature called Content Advisor, which controls the types of content that can be displayed in the Internet Explorer Web browser. Content Advisor monitors Web sites in accordance with the Internet Content Rating Association, an independent company that catalogs Web sites within four rating categories:

- *Language.* Choose to allow inoffensive slang but not profanity, mild expletives, or mild terms for bodily functions; moderate expletives, non-sexual terms, and anatomical references; strong vulgar language, obscene gestures, and epithets; or extreme "hate speech," discriminatory language, crude language, and explicit sexual references.

- *Nudity.* Choose not to allow nudity, revealing attire, partial nudity, frontal nudity, or the provocative display of frontal nudity.

- *Sex.* Choose not to allow portrayal of sexual activity, passionate kissing, clothed sexual touching, non-explicit sexual touching, or explicit sexual activity.

- *Violence.* Choose not to allow aggressive, natural, or accidental violence; fighting in which creatures are injured or killed and damage to realistic objects; injuring or killing of humans or non-threatening creatures; injuring or killing of humans with blood and gore; or wanton and gratuitous violence.

Tip In a network setting, your network administrator can enable Content Advisor settings across the entire network.

Web sites are voluntarily submitted for rating by their authors and owners. You can block unrated sites by specifying that you want to allow only rated sites.

Tip For more information about the Internet Content Rating Association, visit *www.icra.org.*

In this exercise, you will configure the Content Advisor settings.

BE SURE TO have an active Internet connection available before beginning this exercise.
START Internet Explorer.

Important The steps illustrated in this exercise are for a computer with a full-time broadband connection. If you are using a different Internet access method, you might have to vary the steps slightly based on the on-screen instructions, but you will still be able to follow along with the exercise.

Follow these steps:

1   On the Internet Explorer **Tools** menu, click **Internet Options**, and then click the **Content** tab:

2   In the **Content Advisor** area, click the **Enable** button.

The **Content Advisor** dialog box appears:

3 Click each of the categories, and adjust the slider to specify what users are allowed to see within each category.

4 Click the **Approved Sites**, **General**, and **Advanced** tabs to see your other options, and then click the **OK** button.

If this is the first time you have used the Content Advisor, you are prompted to create a supervisor password that protects access to these settings:

Create Supervisor Password

To prevent unauthorized users from changing Content Advisor settings, provide a password.

Content Advisor settings can be changed or turned on or off only by people who know the password.

Password:

Confirm password:

Provide a hint to help you remember your password. Set the hint so that others cannot use it to easily guess your password.

Hint:

OK   Cancel

5 Enter a password in the **Create Supervisor Password** dialog box, and then click **OK**.

This message box informs you that Content Advisor is enabled:

Content Advisor

Content Advisor has been enabled. If you want to change the rating levels or other settings later, click Settings.

To ensure that recently viewed sites cannot be viewed if they do not meet your criteria, please close any Internet Explorer windows, and then open a new one.

OK

Close

6 Click the **OK** button once to close the message box and again to close the dialog box, and then click Internet Explorer's **Close** button to close the window and quit the program.

The Content Advisor settings are applied to all windows opened after this point. If you try to open a site that does not meet your stipulated criteria, you will see a dialog box such as this one:

You must enter the supervisor password to access sites that don't meet your criteria.

7 To disable Content Advisor, start Internet Explorer, open the **Internet Options** dialog box, and click the **Disable** button on the **Content** tab. Enter the supervisor password when prompted, and then click **OK**.

Introducing Windows Media Player

Many people enjoy playing music or videos on their computers, either while they're working or during their leisure time. With recent advances in disk drive technology, you can now enjoy all the comforts of an entertainment center on your desktop computer or your laptop.

Tip Many new laptops will play CDs without even being booted up. If you travel often and are in the market for a new laptop, you might consider adding this capability to your wish list.

Windows
Media Player

Windows XP comes with Microsoft Windows Media Player for Windows XP. Windows XP Service Pack 2 installs Windows Media Player 9 Series, which includes over 120 new features. You can use Windows Media Player to play, copy, and catalog audio and video files from your computer, from CDs or DVDs, or from the Web. But that's really just the tip of the iceberg; this latest version of Windows Media Player has loads of exciting new features. In this topic, we'll investigate some of these features.

Tip For extensive descriptions of all the new Windows Media Player 9 Series features, including demonstrations and comparisons, visit *www.microsoft.com/windows /windowsmedia/9series/player.aspx*.

Windows Media Player 9 Series offers the following options for playing music:

- Smart Jukebox. Your media files are automatically organized in folders.

- Advanced Tag Editor. Available album information is downloaded from the Internet and displayed when you play songs on your computer. You can edit the information and add comments of your own.

- Ratings. Rate the songs in your collection on a scale of 1 to 5, or have Windows Media Player rate them for you based on frequency of play.

- Windows Media Audio 9 Series format. Windows Media Audio (WMA) is the default audio compression format for saving music from a CD or other source to your computer. Using Variable Bit Rate audio and new compression technology, WMA compression results in smaller files and higher quality. This means that you can store more music in less space. WMA files can be played on all the major PC playback programs as well as on over 70 types of portable devices. On devices with 5.1 capable sound cards and speakers (six-speaker systems), WMA 9 Pro supports multi-channel surround sound audio.

See Also   For more information about experiencing multi-channel surround sound music with Windows Media Player, refer to "Are You Ready for 5.1 Audio on Your PC?" on the Microsoft Web site at *www.microsoft.com/windowsXP/windowsmediaplayer/51audio.asp*.

- Expanded MP3 support. If you prefer to stick with the MP3 format, Windows Media Player still gives you all the support you could want. You can play and organize MP3 files, and transfer them to your portable device. You can install a third-party MP3 Creation Pack plug-in that enables Windows Media Player to compress music into the MP3 format. But here's the cool part—you can enhance your MP3 files with your own custom lyrics and album art. When you're playing MP3s in Windows Media Player, you can specify a *visualization* (graphic representation of the music) and *skin* (Windows Media Player user interface) to go with each song to truly personalize your MP3 experience.

- High-performance CD burning technology. If you have a *CD-RW* drive that supports Windows XP, you can compile and create your own CDs through the Windows Media interface or directly from your My Music folder. Windows XP supports CD burning at the full speed of your drive, so creating a CD is as fast as it is easy!

- Auto Volume Leveling. When you burn a CD with songs from multiple albums, Windows Media Player equalizes the volume of the selected tracks so your home recordings sound more professional.

Troubleshooting   If you are working within a networked organization, your IT department might have created a customized version of Windows Media Player that limits the available features. The ability to restrict Windows Media Player within network environments is a new feature, designed to help companies utilize the features they need without risking that employees might be distracted by some of the more entertainment-oriented options.

Windows Media Player 9 Series includes the following options for watching DVDs (on a computer with a DVD-ROM drive) and video clips:

- DVD video playback. You can watch DVDs and take advantage of all the extras. The DVD controls are visible when you move the mouse but disappear when it is inactive, so they're immediately accessible but never in the way.

- Internet-based DVD information retrieval. If you have an active Internet connection, each time you play a DVD, you can download information about the DVD from the Internet and store it on your computer so it is accessible even when you're offline. Available information includes ratings information, chapter titles, cast listings, and director credits.

- Enhanced DVD navigation. DVD chapters are displayed by title rather than by number, which makes it easier to find a particular scene.

Windows Media Player 9 Series offers the following options for working with all types of media files:

- Intelligent Media Management. After you organize your media files into Windows Media *playlists* (individual *tracks* that you have selected and arranged), the Media Library keeps track of them even if you move them between playlists or onto your hard disk.

See Also   For more information, refer to "Creating a Music Playlist" later in this chapter.

- Programmable auto-play options. When you insert various types of media into your computer, you can select your preferred method of playing or viewing that type of media. For instance, you can choose to always play audio CDs and DVDs, but display the directory content of storage media (such as SanDisk cartridges). You can set a default auto-play option for each type of media or make a selection for each individual item.

- Customizable file names. File naming information is transferred along with the files when you copy media files to your PC. You can choose which parts of the file information you want to see and how you want to see them.

Tip   Want more? You can download the latest Windows Media Player 9 Series add-ons from *www.wmplugins.com*. This Web site gives you access to plug-ins, skins, visualizations, toys, and utilities from Microsoft and other companies.

Tip   Microsoft occasionally updates Windows Media Player, and as this book went to press, Microsoft was testing the next generation of Windows Media Player. Microsoft planned Windows Media Player 10 to include a sleek new design; the ability to download, rent, or stream music and video from a choice of online stores; support for a wide selection of devices, including current portable music players and new Portable Media Center devices; and an improved all-in-one Smart Jukebox. You can download the latest version of WMP from *http://www.microsoft.com/windowsmedia*.

Setting Your Windows Media Player Options

The first time you start Windows Media Player 9 Series, you are prompted to set the Windows Media Player privacy and file type options.

In this exercise, you will set your Windows Media Player 9 Series options and create a desktop shortcut.

BE SURE TO have an active Internet connection before beginning this exercise.

Follow these steps:

1   On the **Start** menu, point to **All Programs**, and then click **Windows Media Player**.

Troubleshooting   If Windows Media Player starts, your options have already been set and you do not need to complete this exercise.

2   On the first page of the setup wizard, click **Next** to display the Privacy Option settings:

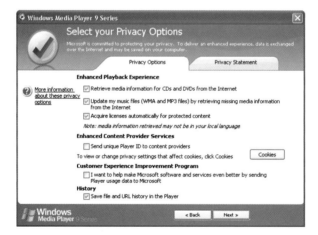

The default settings are suitable for most users.

3 Read through the options, and if you would like to make any changes, select or clear the pertinent check boxes. If you want to view the Microsoft privacy statements, click the **Privacy Statement** tab. When you are satisfied with your privacy options, click **Next**:

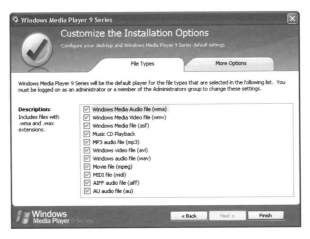

4 Windows Media Player 9 Series is the default player for all file types selected in this list. If you do not want certain file types to open in Windows Media Player, clear those check boxes. Then click the **More Options** tab:

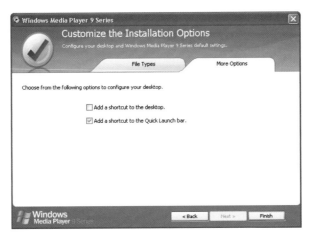

5 Select the **Add a shortcut to the desktop** check box, and then click the **Finish** button.

The Windows Media Player window opens to the Media Guide:

A variety of content cycles through the Media Guide.

Troubleshooting   If you don't have an active Internet connection, the Media Guide content will not appear.

6   If you are not continuing on to the next exercise, click the **Close** button to close Windows Media Player.

✖
Close

Using Windows Media Player

You can display Windows Media Player in either of two modes: *full mode*, which displays information about the media you're using in a television-like format, including a video display screen, taskbar, and menu bar; and *skin mode*, which is smaller and looks like a stylized remote control. It is easy to switch between modes.

Tip   Some people prefer skin mode when listening to music, because full mode's video display can be a bit distracting.

In full mode, Windows Media Player displays a taskbar, a video display area, and a list of all the audio tracks on the currently selected source. (You can choose from a drop-down list that includes the currently inserted CD and any media files stored on your computer.) You can also toggle a traditional Windows menu on and off. The taskbar, which is located on the left side of the window, includes the following options:

■   Now Playing includes a video display area and a playlist (which you can toggle on and off) of your currently available media files.

■   Media Guide, which is hosted on the Windows Media Web site, includes information about and links to various entertainment options on the Internet, including music download sites, video download sites, radio stations, movie discussion sites, entertainment news, and a wide variety of Webcams around the world.

- Copy from CD is a feature you use to copy audio files from a CD to your computer so that you can replay the songs without having the actual CD inserted in the disk drive.

- Media Library is your personal catalog of audio and video files and favorite radio stations. Audio files are cataloged by album, artist, and genre; video files are cataloged by author. Your media playlists are also displayed here.

- Radio Tuner is an element of the Windows Media Web site through which you can link to a variety of radio stations worldwide. You can choose from featured stations or search for a particular station, station format, or location. You can add a station to your My Stations list, visit a station's Web site, connect to a station through its Web site, or just listen to it live.

- Copy to CD or Device is a feature you use to copy audio and video files from the Media Library to a *portable device*, such as a Pocket PC or storage card, or to a CD if you have a CD-RW drive installed on your computer. You can also copy licensed files that you downloaded from the Internet or that you copied from CDs to your portable device.

- Premium Services links you to movie, music, news, sports, and entertainment subscription services. Most of these offer free trials.

- Skin Chooser is a feature that you use to choose from 20 available skins (or more if you have an Internet connection) to tailor the appearance of Windows Media Player to your own taste. Available skins range from high-tech to goofy, with something to appeal to pretty much any gender, age group, or musical taste.

- Play DVD plays DVD movies and downloads information about your DVDs onto your computer. This selection is available only if you have a DVD-ROM drive and a DVD decoder installed on your computer.

Displaying Audio Visualizations

When you are listening to music or radio programs, a visual representation, called a *visualization*, of the audio is displayed on the screen where video would usually be displayed. The visualization moves in time with the music. Windows XP SP2 comes with eight visualization categories—Alchemy, Ambience, Bars and Waves, Battery, Particle, Plenoptic, Spikes, and Musical Colors. Most categories contain multiple visualizations, so you have dozens of options from which to choose. You can download additional visualizations from the Windows Media Web site. Alternately, you can display the album art, which Windows Media Player downloads from the Internet.

In this exercise, you will explore the available Windows Media Player audio display options using a sample song that comes with Windows Media Player. The same options are available to you when you listen to any type of audio file in Windows Media Player.

BE SURE TO have your computer set up with a sound card and speakers or headphones, and have an active Internet connection before beginning this exercise.

Follow these steps:

Windows
Media Player

1 If Windows Media Player is not open, on the Windows XP desktop, double-click the **Windows Media Player** shortcut.

Troubleshooting   If you don't have a Windows Media Player shortcut, on the **Start** menu, point to **All Programs**, and then click **Windows Media Player**.

The Windows Media Player window opens to the Media Guide.

Autohide
menu bar

2 If a Windows menu bar is displayed at the top of the Windows Media Player window, click the **Autohide menu bar** button.

3 On the taskbar at the left, click **Now Playing** to display the current playlist:

Taskbar   Display area   Music selector

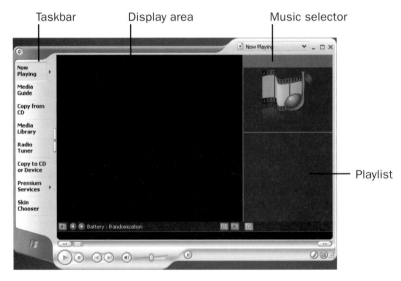

Playlist

4 Click the music selector in the upper-right corner of the media player, click **Sample Playlist** in the drop-down list to display a list of available audio tracks, and start a song:

Current view

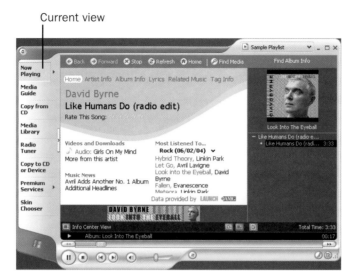

The song plays in Info Center view. Song and album information and related links are available.

5 While the song is playing, to the left of the current view name, click the **Select Now Playing options** button. On the shortcut menu that appears, point to **Visualizations**, point to **Ambience**, and then click **Warp**.

Select Now Playing options

The *Warp* visualization appears in the display area:

6 To display a different type of visualization, click the **Select Now Playing options** button, point to **Visualizations**, point to **Musical Colors**, and then click **CutOut**.

7 To close the playlist and enlarge the display area, click the **Maximize the Video and Visualization pane** button:

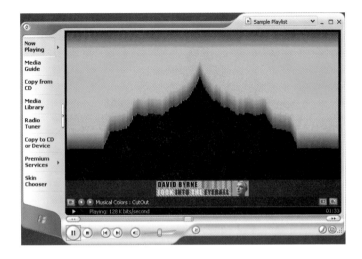
Maximize the Video and Visualization pane

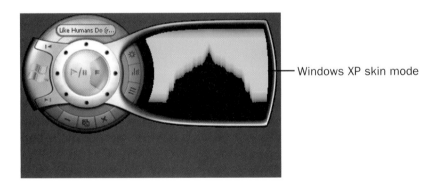

View full screen

Tip To further enlarge the display area, click the **View full screen** button. Then to maximize the display area, click the **Hide playlist** button.

Hide playlist

8 In the lower-right corner, click the **Switch to skin mode** button.

Switch to skin mode

A smaller, stylized version of the Windows Media Player appears:

Windows XP skin mode

The basic audio controls are all available in skin mode. This is a convenient interface to use while listening to audio on your computer.

See Also For more information about skin mode, refer to "Personalizing Windows Media Player" later in this chapter.

Return to Full Mode

9 Move the mouse pointer over the various skin mode controls to see the ScreenTip descriptions of each. Then click the **Return to Full Mode** button.

Next
visualization

10 Click the **Next visualization** button to move to the next of the Musical Colors options, *Rolling Fire*. Then use the methods you've learned to look through the available options, settling on your favorite.

CLOSE the Windows Media Player window.

Watching DVD Movies

Most DVD movies come complete with software that you install on your computer so that you can watch the DVD and use any included interactive content, such as Web links and video games. With Windows Media Player, you can centralize all your media files in one program and play DVDs as easily as you play CDs.

Windows Media Player has all the functionality of a regular DVD player: You can watch movies, fast forward, reverse, move between movie segments, and access all the special features included on your DVD. When you are online, you can also download information about each disc from the Windows Media online database.

To play a DVD, you must have a DVD-ROM drive and a Windows XP-compatible DVD decoder installed on your computer. If you don't have a DVD-ROM drive installed, or if your DVD decoder is not compatible with Windows XP, the **Play DVD** option will not be visible in Windows Media Player. If you upgrade to Windows XP, you will probably need to upgrade your DVD decoder as well. Windows XP–compatible DVD decoders are available from many DVD solution providers, including the following:

■ CyberLink Corporation (PowerDVD): *www.gocyberlink.com/english/products/power-dvd/winxp_plugin.asp*

■ InterVideo, Inc. (WinDVD): *www.intervideo.com/products/custom/ms/windowsxp/upgrade.jsp*

■ MGI Software Corporation (SoftDVD Max): *www.mgisoft.com/products/dvd/updates.html*

■ Sonic Solutions (CinePlayer): *www.cineplayer.com/decoder/*

For more information about Windows Media Player DVD support, refer to *www.microsoft.com/windows/windowsmedia/windowsxp/dvdplay.aspx*.

To watch a DVD movie with Windows Media Player:

1 Insert the DVD into the DVD-ROM drive.

2 Start Windows Media Player, if it doesn't start automatically.

The chapters and titles on the DVD are displayed.

3 Click **Play DVD** to play the entire movie sequentially, or click a specific chapter or title and click **Play DVD** to play only that segment.

Making Movies

new for
WindowsXP

Windows
Movie Maker

One of the new programs that come with Windows XP is Windows Movie Maker, a tool that you use to *capture* audio and video source material. After the source material is captured, you can use Windows Movie Maker to edit and arrange your *clips* to create movies. With Windows Movie Maker, you can download video clips from your digital video camera or import video clips from other sources, and then edit them to create your own movie. You can add music and narration to your video and even insert still photos or title slides. When your movie masterpiece is complete, you can burn it to a CD, send it through e-mail, or publish it on the Web.

To start Windows Movie Maker, on the **Start** menu, point to **All Programs**, point to **Accessories**, and then click **Windows Movie Maker**. For more information about the program, visit *www.microsoft.com/windowsxp/moviemaker/*, or start Windows Movie Maker and then consult its Help file.

Personalizing Windows Media Player

The default skin for Windows Media Player is a gray, black, and blue box that bears some resemblance to a space-age television or radio. More than twenty skins are available from within Windows, and many more can be downloaded from the Internet. If your computer is using the Windows XP theme, the Windows Media Player is by default clad in the Windows XP skin.

In this exercise, you will personalize the look and feel of Windows Media Player by changing the skin.

Change Player
color

Tip To make a simpler change to the Windows Media Player interface in full mode, click the **Change Player color** button. Each time you click the button, the player color scheme changes (over 20 color schemes are available). This change does not affect the appearance of the player in skin mode.

BE SURE TO set your Windows Media Player options before beginning this exercise.

Follow these steps:

1   Start Windows Media Player.

2   On the taskbar, click **Skin Chooser**.

   Tip You must be in full mode to access the taskbar.

   The Skin Chooser window opens, with the current skin selected on the left and the corresponding skin mode displayed on the right:

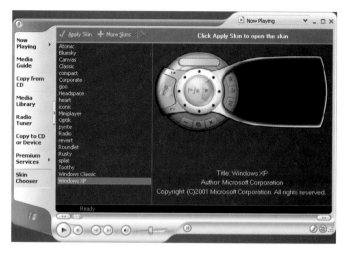

3 In the skin list, click **Atomic**. Then press the **DOWN ARROW** key to preview each of the remaining skin options.

Tip   Clicking **More Skins** opens the Windows Media Web site, where you can select from a variety of other skins.

4 Click your favorite skin, and then click **Apply Skin**.

Windows Media Player changes to reflect your selection and switches to skin mode. For example, the *iconic* skin looks like this:

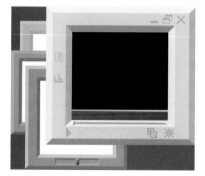

Some skins have alternate views. For example, the *iconic* skin looks like this in small view:

Tip   Move the mouse pointer over the buttons on the skin you select to learn what features are available for that skin.

5   Click the **Return to Full Mode** button to switch the interface to that mode.

Return to Full
Mode

Troubleshooting   The appearance of the **Return to Full Mode** button changes to match the skin, but the icon is the same for all skins.

6   If you want to change back to the standard skin, click **Windows XP in the list of available skins**, and then click **Apply Skin**.

Tip   If you don't change the skin back to the default, your screen will not match the graphics shown throughout the rest of this chapter. However, the step-by-step instructions will still apply.

CLOSE the Windows Media Player window.

Listening to Music from CDs

Windows Media Player gives you virtually unlimited access to radio stations around the world and also plays CDs and audio clips of various types. You can play audio clips in an order you specify or shuffle the available clips to create a random mix. You can also create a compilation of your favorite songs on your computer, or if you have a CD-RW drive installed, on a CD.

When you insert a music CD into your CD-ROM drive, Windows prompts you to specify whether you want to play the CD, view the files on the CD, or copy files from the CD. If you select the Play option, Windows Media Player starts in whatever mode it was in when last closed, displaying the most recently selected visualization option.

You can copy songs from a CD to your hard disk and play them from there. By default, Windows Media Player protects the files so that they can't be played on any other computer, to ensure that you don't inadvertently violate any copyrights.

In this exercise, you will use Windows Media Player to play songs from one of your own music CDs. You will then copy song tracks from the CD to your hard disk.

BE SURE TO have your computer set up with a sound card and speakers or headphones, and have a music CD available before beginning this exercise.

Follow these steps:

1   Ensure that Windows Media Player is not currently running.

2   Insert a music CD into your CD-ROM drive.

3   If the **Audio CD** dialog box prompts you to select an action, click **Play Audio CD using Windows Media Player**, and then click **OK**.

Tip   If you would like to bypass the Audio CD dialog box and automatically play music CDs in the future, select the **Always do the selected action** check box.

The Windows Media Player window opens, and the first song on the CD starts playing. The artist and song title are displayed above the visualization pane. The album cover and track list are displayed in the playlist at the right:

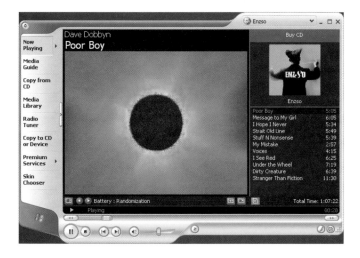

Tip   If Windows Media Player opens in skin mode, click the **Return to Full Mode** button to display the interface shown in the graphic.

Troubleshooting   If your computer is not online when you insert the CD, the album, artist, and individual tracks are not identified by name, only by track number. If the CD is by a well-known artist, the next time you go online and open Windows Media Player, the CD's information is updated from an online database and stored on your computer, and from that point on, the information is available offline. For artists who are not in the online database, you can add track information yourself, and it will be stored on your computer.

Left unattended, the CD plays from beginning to end, and then stops.

Troubleshooting   Some audio CDs contain interactive content, such as games or videos, that is displayed while the CD is playing in your CD-ROM or DVD-ROM drive. If you are connected to the Internet while playing the CD, a special Web page related to the album might open. This display might affect the performance of Windows Media Player, and the audio track might sound a bit jerky while your computer is working on other tasks associated with the interactive content.

4   In the playlist, double-click any other track to play it.

Tip   If the playlist is not displayed, on the **View** menu, point to **Now Playing Options**, and then click **Show Playlist**.

5   On the taskbar, click **Copy from CD**.

Windows Media Player displays the CD contents, with all the audio tracks selected:

✓		Title	Length	Copy Status	Artist			Composer
		Enzso - Enzso		○ Copy Music	🔍 Find Album Info		◎ View Album Info	
✓	1	Poor Boy	5:05		Dave Dobbyn			Tim Finn
✓	2	Message to My Girl	6:05		Neil Finn			Neil Finn
✓	3	I Hope I Never	5:34		Annie Crummer			Tim Finn
✓	4	Strait Old Line	5:49		Neil Finn			Neil Finn
✓	5	Stuff N Nonsense	5:39		Neil Finn			Tim Finn
✓	6	My Mistake	2:57		Dave Dobbyn			Eddie Rayner; Tim Finn
✓	7	Voices	4:15		Neil Finn			Neil Finn
✓	8	I See Red	6:25		Tim Finn			Tim Finn
✓	9	Under the Wheel	7:19		Sam Hunt			Phil Judd; Tim Finn
✓	10	Dirty Creature	6:39		Tim Finn			Neil Finn; Nigel Griggs;
✓	11	Stranger Than Fiction	11:30		Neil Finn; Samantha Hunt; Tim Finn			Phil Judd; Tim Finn

11 track(s) checked to copy to C:\Documents and Settings\joanp\My Documents\My Music

Important   Your display will reflect the music CD you are using for this exercise and will look different from the graphics shown here.

6   Clear the check box above the list of tracks to deselect them all, and then select the check boxes of two individual tracks to select them.

7   With the two check boxes selected, click the **Copy Music** button.

Tip   If you are connected to the Internet, you can click **Find Album Info** to display information from the Windows Media Web site about the album and artist, and you can click **Get Album Info** to display or update the list of track names.

The Copy Options dialog box appears. The first screen includes the option to turn off the automatic copyright protection of your copied CD files:

Copy Options (1 of 2)   ✕

Windows Media Player enables you to protect the music you copy from CDs from unlicensed distribution and unlicensed sharing.

Select one of the following options:

🎵 ○ Add copy protection to your music
Music copied from CDs can be played on this computer and on compatible secure devices.

🎵 ○ Do not add copy protection to your music
Music copied from CDs can be played on any computer or on any device.

☐ I understand that music copied from CDs is protected by law, including US and International copyright laws, and that I am solely responsible for the appropriate use of the content that I have copied.

< Back   Next >   Help

8 Select the **Add copy protection to your music** option, select the **I understand** check box, and then click **Next**.

The second screen of the **Copy Options** dialog box lets you control the format in which audio files are copied:

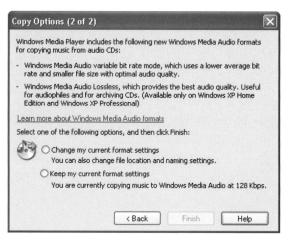

9 Select the **Keep my current format settings** option, and then click **Finish**.

As each of the selected tracks is copied to your hard disk, its copy status changes from *Pending* to *Copying* (with percent copied) to *Copied to Library*.

10 When both files have been copied, click **Media Library** on the taskbar.

Tip The first time you open the Media Library, you are prompted to search your computer for media files. Any files that are found are added to your library. You can repeat the search at any time to update your listings.

The Media Library opens:

Your recently copied album is selected, and the copied files are shown in the file list on the right.

11 Browse through the Media Library to see how it is laid out.

12 To play one of the songs you just copied directly from your computer, double-click it.

CLOSE the Windows Media Player window when you finish listening to the song.

Tip When you close Windows Media Player after acquiring licensed content, a message box prompts you to back up your licenses. You can click **Yes** to back up the licenses, or clear the **Prompt me** check box to prevent the message box from appearing. To manually back up your licenses, display the Windows Media Player menu bar, and on the **Tools** menu, click **License Management**.

Surfing the Radio Waves

Thanks to the Internet, you are no longer limited to listening to canned music; nor do you have to miss your favorite radio programs when you're away from home. Many radio stations now broadcast their content over the Web, which means that you can tune in from just about anywhere, if you have an active Internet connection, a sound card, and speakers or headphones. You can search for and select a station by genre, keyword (such as the call letters of a station or the name of a city), or ZIP Code.

You can listen to Internet radio stations from within Windows Media Player or in your Internet browser. To access the Windows Media radio tuner from within your Internet browser rather than Windows Media Player, go to *windowsmedia.com/radiotuner/*.

In this exercise, you will locate and listen to a radio station over the Internet.

BE SURE TO have your computer set up with a sound card and speakers or headphones, and have an active Internet connection before beginning this exercise.

Follow these steps:

1 Start Windows Media Player.

2 On the taskbar, click **Radio Tuner**.

The Radio Tuner opens:

A list of featured radio stations, links to other stations by genre, and a keyword search box are displayed in the video pane.

3 In the **Featured Stations** list, click through the radio stations until you find one that has a **Play** button:

Station-specific options

Play button

For each station, a description and its options appear. Some stations can be played from Windows Media Player, others require that you link to their Web site to play them.

4 Click the **Play** link to hear the station.

The radio station's Web site opens in a new window, in case you want to check it out. Windows Media Player displays the Now Playing screen, with accompanying video.

Troubleshooting   When Windows Media Player accesses the Internet, you might see a security alert prompting you to specify whether you want to allow the program to recive unsolicited information from external sources. This is a feature of Windows XP Service Pack 2. When a Security Alert message box appears, select your preferred option, and then click **OK**.

5   If the station's Web site opens in the foreground, click the **Windows Media Player** taskbar button to bring it to the front.

Stop

6   To disconnect from the radio station, click the **Stop** button.

7   On the taskbar, click **Radio Tuner**, and in the Radio Tuner, click **Find More Stations**:

8   In the **Browse by Genre** drop-down list, click **Classic Rock**.

The Search Results list displays the available Classic Rock radio stations.

9   Select and delete the text in the **Search** box, and then type Eagles.

10   Click the **Search** button.

Search

The Search Results list displays the radio stations that include music by the Eagles on their playlists:

Tip   To search for radio stations that meet multiple search criteria, click the **Use Advanced Search** link.

11   Click a radio station, and then click **Play** to hear that station.

Information about the station is displayed at the bottom of the Radio Tuner.

CLOSE the Windows Media Player window, and then close any open windows displaying radio station Web sites.

Creating a Music Playlist

If you often copy audio files to your hard disk, you can quickly accumulate hundreds of songs, and scrolling through folders looking for the next song you would like to listen to can be annoying. In Windows XP you can solve this problem by creating playlists. A playlist is a list of digital media files, such as songs, video clips, and links to radio stations. You can think of it as a virtual CD that is limited in size only by the storage capacity of your hard disk. You can treat a playlist as a collection, playing it, copying it, or burning it to a CD-ROM as a unit.

Tip   The songs in this exercise are from the music CD *Shakedown* by Leslie Eliel, who has kindly given permission for several tracks from the CD to be used on this book's CD-ROM.

In this exercise, you will create your own playlist from audio files on your hard disk.

BE SURE TO have your computer set up with a sound card and speakers or headphones before beginning this exercise.

Follow these steps:

1   On the **Start** menu, click **My Documents**.

2   In Windows Explorer, browse to the *My Documents\Microsoft Press\Microsoft Windows XP SBS\Playing\Playlist* folder.

3   Right-click **The Cowgirl Song**, and click **Add to Playlist** on the shortcut menu that appears.

Windows Media Player starts, and the **Add to Playlist** dialog box appears:

4   Click the **New** button, and then type **Leslie Eliel**, which is the name of the singer/songwriter who provided the practice files, and press **ENTER**.

The new playlist is created and selected.

5   Click **OK**.

The dialog box closes.

6   On the Windows Media Player taskbar, click **Media Library**. If necessary, click to the left of the scroll bar at the bottom of the left pane to display the library contents:

You can see that *The Cowgirl Song* has been added to the Leslie Eliel playlist.

7   Click the **Add to Media Library** button, and then click **Add File or Playlist** on the drop-down menu.

8   In the **Open** dialog box, browse to the My Documents\Microsoft Press\Microsoft Windows XP SBS\Playing\Playlist\ folder, and double-click **Time To Be Planting Again**.

The song has now been added to your media library, and it is accessible through any of the categories in the All Music list: by artist, album, or genre.

9   Expand the **Genre** list and click **Contemporary Folk**.

Leslie's two songs are listed in the right pane.

10   Right-click **Time To Be Planting Again** and then on the shortcut menu, click **Add to Playlist**.

11   In the **Add to Playlist** dialog box, click **Leslie Eliel**, and then click **OK**.

12   Double-click the **Leslie Eliel** playlist to play through the playlist.

When the first song is finished, the second song plays.

CLOSE the Windows Media Player window when you finish.

Sharing Digital Photos

If you have a digital camera, you can use Windows XP to easily download photographs to your computer. When you connect a Plug and Play camera to your computer (usually through a USB cable), Windows XP recognizes it and starts the **Scanner and Camera Wizard** to install it. If your camera isn't Plug and Play, you can manually start the wizard by clicking the **Scanners and Cameras** icon in the Printers and Other Hardware category of Control Panel. You can install drivers for as many cameras as you want. After a camera profile is installed, you simply connect it to your computer's input port, and the **Scanner and Camera Wizard** starts and guides you through the process of downloading files.

Tip If your digital camera stores photos on some kind of removable memory media, you can transfer those photos to your computer using an appropriate adapter.

After you download the photos, you can copy them to your My Pictures folder, or to any other folder to which you have assigned picture properties, so that all the picture-folder options are available. For example, you can view all your photos as a slide show, or you can have Windows display your photos as a personalized background for your desktop.

Tip You can assign picture properties to a folder by right-clicking the folder, clicking the **Customize** tab, and then selecting the **Pictures** or **Photo Album** template in the drop-down list of templates.

You can also take advantage of the following new Windows XP photo-processing options:

new for WindowsXP

Photo Printing Wizard

- The **Photo Printing Wizard** walks you through the process of formatting and printing photos. After you start the wizard, you can select one or more of the photo files in the current folder for printing. The wizard then prompts you to select an appropriate printer and type of paper.

new for WindowsXP

Online Print Ordering Wizard

- The **Online Print Ordering Wizard** helps you order prints of your photos over the Internet. You select a printing company, specify the size and number of prints you want, and then provide billing and shipping information. The wizard transmits your photos and information to the printing company, which then processes your order and sends you the prints. This is a great way to get prints of your digital photos without investing in a photo printer, and without even leaving your home!

If you are working on a network, you can save your photos in a folder on your network, and if you have Internet access, you can publish your photos on the Web so that they are available for family and friends to view.

If you don't already have a Web site, you can publish your photos to an MSN Group. MSN Groups are free Web sites created and managed by anyone who wants to do so, and hosted by Microsoft. You can share news, documents, photos, lists, appointments, and many other types of information on an MSN Group Web site.

In this exercise, you will publish photos from your hard disk to the Internet.

USE the photographs in the practice file folder for this topic. These practice files are located in the *My Documents\Microsoft Press\Microsoft Windows XP SBS\Playing\Photos* folder.
BE SURE TO have an active Internet connection beginning this exercise.

Follow these steps:

1   On the **Start** menu, click **My Documents**.

2   In Windows Explorer, browse to the *My Documents\Microsoft Press\Microsoft Windows XP SBS\Playing\Photos* folder.

The folder contains eight photo files.

3   On the **File and Folder Tasks** menu, click **Publish this folder to the Web**.

Troubleshooting   When you select any of the photos, the **Publish this folder to the Web** command disappears from the **File and Folder Tasks** menu. If this happens, click the **Up** button on the Windows Explorer toolbar, and then double-click the **Photos** folder to re-open it with the command available.

The **Web Publishing Wizard** starts.

4   Click **Next** to continue to the wizard's **Change Your File Selection** page:

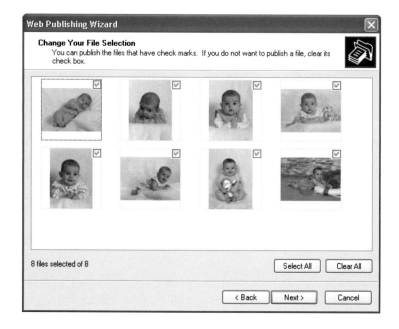

All the photos contained in the folder are displayed on this page. You can select or clear each photo's check box to indicate whether you want to publish it, or you can select or clear all the check boxes using the buttons at the bottom of the page.

5   Leave all the files selected, and click **Next**.

6   On the **Where do you want to publish these files?** page, click **MSN Groups**, and then click **Next**.

7   On the **Select where you want your files stored** page, click **Create a new MSN Group to share your files**, and then click **Next**.

You are asked to specify whether you want other people to be able to view your files or whether they are for your private viewing only.

8   Select the **Shared** option, and then click **Next** to move to the **Create your new group** page:

```
┌────────────────────────────────────────────────────────┐
│ Web Publishing Wizard                              [X]  │
│                                                         │
│   Create your new group                                 │
│     Your files will be stored in this group.            │
│                                                         │
│   ┌──────────────────────────────────────────────────┐ │
│   │                                                    │ │
│   │   Enter a name for your new group                  │ │
│   │   ┌──────────────────────────────────────┐         │ │
│   │   │                                      │         │ │
│   │   └──────────────────────────────────────┘         │ │
│   │                                                    │ │
│   │   Enter your e-mail address                        │ │
│   │   ┌──────────────────────────────────────┐         │ │
│   │   │                                      │         │ │
│   │   └──────────────────────────────────────┘         │ │
│   │                                                    │ │
│   │   I have read and accepted the Code of Conduct     │ │
│   │     ○ Yes                                          │ │
│   │     ○ No                                           │ │
│   │                                                    │ │
│   │                                                    │ │
│   │   (i)  A group is a place on the Web where you can │ │
│   │        share pictures, files, and interests with   │ │
│   │        others.  ©2003 Microsoft Corporation. All   │ │
│   │        rights reserved.                            │ │
│   └──────────────────────────────────────────────────┘ │
│                                                         │
│              [ < Back ]  [ Next > ]  [ Cancel ]         │
└────────────────────────────────────────────────────────┘
```

9   Type a name for your MSN Group (choose something fairly distinctive) and enter your e-mail address. Read the Code of Conduct, select the **Yes** option, and then click **Next**.

Tip   If you have registered your .NET Passport account on this computer, your e-mail address might already be entered for you.

You are prompted to further define your group:

10 In the text box, describe the purpose of your new MSN Group.

For the purposes of this exercise, you can leave the text box blank. If you want people to be able to find your shared group by searching online, you should enter a good description containing common search terms that someone looking for a group like yours might use.

11 Choose a home page language for your MSN Group from the drop-down list, or accept the default if it is correct.

12 If you want to include your MSN Group in the online Group Directory, select the **Yes** option; otherwise accept the default **No** option. Then click **Next**.

Troubleshooting If your group name is already in use by someone else, you will be prompted to specify a different name.

Your group location is specified:

You can write down the URL that begins with *http://www.msnusers.com* or add the site to your Favorites folder and send the link from there.

13 Accept the default **Yes** option to add the URL to your Favorites list, and click **Next**.

The upload folders for your group are specified:

14 If you want to change the names of either or both of the upload folders, click the **Change** button, click the **Or create a new folder** link, type a name for your new folder in the text box, and click the **Done** button twice to return to the upload folder page.

15 Accept the default folder names, and click **Next**.

The wizard offers the option of resizing all your photos to a uniform size:

16 The original photos are relatively small, so accept the **Small** option and click **Next**.

The practice files are published to your MSN Group.

17 When the upload is complete, click the **Next** button.

18 On the last page of the wizard, with the **Open this site when I click Finish** check box selected, click the **Finish** button.

Your MSN Group page opens in your default browser:

You are logged on to your new MSN Group as the manager. You can view the photos you just published or try out some of the management tools included on the right side of the page.

19 Scroll through your MSN Group page to see what it has to offer.

20 To look at the photos you uploaded, click **Pictures** on the menu at the left side of the screen.

CLOSE your Internet browser and Windows Explorer.

Key Points

■ More than just a business system, Windows XP also includes games and entertainment options to enhance your online and offline free time.

■ Windows XP incorporates safeguards that shield computer users from objectionable Internet content. What you see is up to you: You can specify the level of protection you want for yourself and for other computer users.

■ You can listen to music from CDs, from the Internet, or from your computer's hard disk by using Windows Media Player. When you are connected to the Internet, extra information about your media selections is downloaded and saved on your local computer.

■ The Web Publishing Wizard is a simple, free way to share your photos with friends around the world.

Network Diagnostics

Network Diagnostics scans your system to gather information about your hardware, software, and network connections.

Tell me about Network Diagnostics

→ Scan your system
→ Set scanning options

Show Saved Files | Save to file...

Internet Service
☐ Default Outlook Express Mail   Not Configured
☐ Default Outlook Express News   Not Configured
☐ Internet Explorer Web Proxy   Not Configured
Computer Information
⊞ Computer System   XP-PRO
⊞ Operating System   Microsoft Windows XP Professional
⊞ Version   5.1.2600
Modems and Network Adapters
☐ Modems
⊞ Network Adapters
⊞ DNS Servers
⊞ Default Gateways
⊞ DHCP Servers
⊞ IP Address
⊞ WINS Servers
⊞ Network Clients

Diagnose operating system problems, page 288

Disk Cleanup for (C:)

Disk Cleanup | More Options

You can use Disk Cleanup to free up to 837,839 KB of disk space on (C:).

Files to delete:
☑ 🗀 Downloaded Program Files   0 KB
☑ 🔒 Temporary Internet Files   770 KB
☐ 📄 Office Setup Files   287,342 K
☐ 🗑 Recycle Bin   9,741 KB
☐ 📄 Setup Log Files   687 KB

Total amount of disk space you gain: 770 KB

Description

Downloaded Program Files are ActiveX controls and Java applets downloaded automatically from the Internet when you view certain

Clean up your hard disk, page 293

Windows XP Newsgroups - Microsoft Internet Explorer

File Edit View Favorites Tools Help

Back → × ⌂ 🔍 Search ☆ Favorites ⌚ ⌂ 💾 🗖 ▪ ▪

Address http://www.microsoft.com/windowsxp/expertzone/newsgroups/reader.mspx?dg=microsoft.public.windowsxp.photos Go Links »

Microsoft.com Home | Site Map

Windowsxp

Search Microsoft.com for: Go

Windows XP Newsgroups
Windows XP General
Windows XP Tablet PC Edition
Windows XP Media Center Edition

Discussions in Windows XP Photos

Search Type a question in Windows XP Photos

❓ New | Expand All Page: 1 Go

sort threads for newest threads | r

⊞ Force full image file names in XP (1)   4/27
                                                            4/27
    ...d *.psd and *.tiff (1)   4/26
                                                            4/26
    (4)   4/26

💠 Internet

2:53 PM

Join a Windows newsgroup, page 307

Help and Support Center

Back → ⌂ 📖 Index ☆ Favorites ⌚ History Support ✓ Options

Search → ❓ Help and Support Center
Set search options Windows XP Professional

Support

☐ Ask a friend to help
☐ Get help from Microsoft
☐ Go to a Windows Web site forum

⭐ Add to Favorites 🔄 Change View 🖨 Print... 📋 Locate in Contents

Microsoft Online Assisted Support Sign Out

Pick a product support option

Click one of the support options available for Windows XP Professional Edition:

No-Charge Support
◉ No-charge Support

Paid Support
○ Personal Support: General computing issues, including installation and "how-to" questions ($35.00 US per incident)
○ Professional Support: Business environment issues, including development and networking ($99.00 US per incident)

Contract Support
○ Software Assurance license - for servers only (Software Assurance Access ID required)
○ Open License Value (OLV), 5-Pack, Premier, and other contracts (Access ID required)

→ Post your question to a Community Newsgroup

See Also

☐ About Support
☐ My Computer Information
☐ Advanced System Information
☐ System Configuration Utility

🏁 start   ❓ Help and Support Ce...   4:27 PM

Get remote assistance from a friend or colleague, page 299

Chapter 10 at a Glance

10 Solving Problems

In this chapter you will learn to:

- ✔ Update your operating system manually or automatically.
- ✔ Diagnose operating system problems.
- ✔ Clean up and defragment your hard disk.
- ✔ Get answers and help from a variety of sources.
- ✔ Back up and restore files, folders, or your entire operating system.

Microsoft Windows XP is the most advanced Windows operating system to date. Its user-friendly interface, with menus that change depending on where you are or what you are doing, means that your time can be spent working or playing rather than trying to figure out how to use your computer. However, the fact that Windows XP is easy to use doesn't mean that you won't ever experience a problem while using your Windows XP computer. One of the first things you learn about skiing is how to recover safely and gracefully from a fall; this is also a good thing to learn in computing.

As a Windows XP user, you can get help in a variety of ways. In this chapter, you will learn not only how to get help after a problem has occurred, but also how to keep your system up to date so that problems do not occur in the first place.

See Also Do you need only a quick refresher on the topics in this chapter? See the Quick Reference entries on pages xliii–xlvii.

Important Before you can use the practice files in this chapter, you need to install them from the book's companion CD to their default location. See "Using the Book's CD-ROM" on page xv for more information.

Keeping Your Computer up to Date

Microsoft Windows Update is an Internet-based service that scans your computer and recommends or installs any updates that are available for your operating system, your software programs, or your hardware. Quite apart from knowing that you have the "latest and greatest," Windows Update ensures that your computer is equipped with security "patches" as they become necessary and available. You can access the Windows Update site at *windowsupdate.microsoft.com* or through either the Control Panel window or the Help and Support Center.

See Also For further information about manually updating your operating system, refer to "Updating and Safeguarding Your Computer System" in Chapter 1, "Getting Started with Windows XP."

During the update process, Windows Update collects the version numbers of your operating system, Web browser, and other installed software, as well as the Plug and Play ID numbers of the hardware devices that are connected to your computer, and then compiles a list of updates that are available for your system. Some updates are classified as critical and are selected for installation by default. (If you do not want to install an update that is marked as critical, you can remove it from your list of selections.) Other updates are optional and are not selected. Windows Update displays a list of the updates and their descriptions and then installs only those you select. When the update process is complete, the version and ID information that was collected from your computer is discarded.

If you don't want to bear the responsibility of remembering to manually update your system, or if you want to be sure you have updates as soon as they become available, you can instruct Windows XP to automatically update your system through the Windows Update site. You can choose to have Windows XP install updates automatically, download updates and notify you when they are ready to be installed, or you can choose to be notified before the updates are downloaded.

See Also For further information about preventive maintenance, refer to "Analyzing Your Computer's Security" in Chapter 3, "Managing Computer Security."

Windows XP prompts you to turn on Automatic Updates the first time you start your computer after installing Windows XP Service Pack 2. If you have not selected an automatic update option, Windows XP displays a security icon in the notification area and prompts you to update your operating system from time to time by displaying a message near the notification area. Clicking the icon or message opens the **Automatic Updates Wizard**, which leads you through a short process to select your preferred update option. You can change your selected update option at any time through Control Panel or the Help and Support Center.

In this exercise, you will instruct Windows Update to automatically install available software and hardware updates on your computer at the beginning of each week.

BE SURE TO log on to Windows before beginning this exercise.
OPEN Control Panel.

Follow these steps:

1 In the Control Panel window, click the **Performance and Maintenance** icon.

2 In the Performance and Maintenance window, click the **System** icon.

3   In the **System Properties** dialog box, click the **Automatic Updates** tab to display these options:

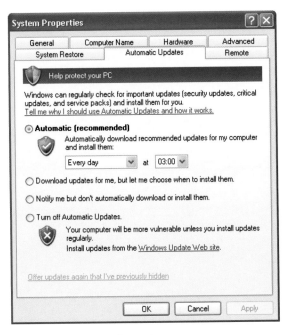

4   Select the **Automatic** option.

The option might already be selected by default.

Tip   If you prefer to have more control over the update process but still enjoy the benefit of automatic updates, select the **Download updates for me, but let me choose when to install them** option. If you select this option, Windows XP downloads available updates to your computer and displays a security icon in the notification area. Click the icon to review and approve or reject the installation of each update.

5   Click the down arrow to the right of the day box, and then click **Every Monday** in the drop-down list.

6   Click the down arrow to the right of the time box, and then click **9:00 AM** in the drop-down list.

7   Click **OK** to close the dialog box and save your changes.

CLOSE the Performance and Maintenance window.

Diagnosing System Problems

When your computer crashes, it's a pretty obvious problem. But if it just seems to be slower than usual, it can be hard to figure out what's wrong. Windows XP comes with a variety of tools that you can use to find out what's happening with your computer, including:

- *My Computer Information*, which you can use to find out what programs and hardware are installed on your computer and how much memory is available. You can also review diagnostic information such as the operating system and the speed of your processor.

- *Network Diagnostics*, which you can use to gather information about your computer to help you troubleshoot network-related problems.

- *Advanced System Information*, which links you to specialized information that a technical support person might need in order to solve a particularly difficult problem.

All these tools are available through the Help and Support Center.

In this exercise, you will gather diagnostic information about your computer.

BE SURE TO log on to Windows before beginning this exercise.

Follow these steps:

1 On the **Start** menu, click **Help and Support**.

The Help and Support Center window opens.

See Also For more information about the Help and Support center, refer to "Helping Yourself" later in this chapter.

---

2 In the Help and Support Center, click **Use Tools to view your computer information and diagnose problems**.

The Help and Support Center displays this **Tools** menu:

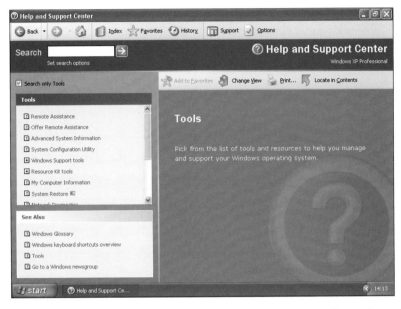

3 On the **Tools** menu in the left pane, click **My Computer Information**.

The My Computer Information tool opens in the right pane of the Help and Support Center. Five options are available:

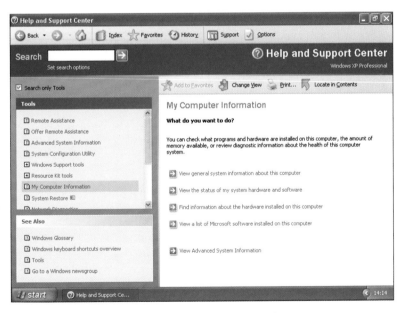

4 Click **View general system information about this computer**.

Windows XP polls your computer for general information and generates a report displaying this type of information:

My Computer Information - General
Refresh screen

Specifications		Processor	
System Manufacturer		**Intel Pentium II processor**	
System Model:	System Name	Version:	x86 Family 6 Model 5 Stepping 2
BIOS Version:	Award Software, Inc. ASUS P2B ACPI BIOS Revision 1012	Speed:	350 MHz

Operating System		General Computer Info	
Microsoft Windows XP Professional		System Name:	XP-PRO
Version:	5.1.2600	Domain:	otsihq.local
Service Pack:	2.0	Time Zone:	Pacific Daylight Time
Location:	C:\WINDOWS	Connection:	Workstation
PID:	55274-006-4501997-22743	Proxy Server:	None
Hot Fix:	KB838909	IP Address:	192.168.2.39 192.168.1.57
		IPX Address:	Not Enabled

Memory (RAM)	
Capacity:	256 MB

Local Disk
Total Capacity: 9.53 GB
Sum of Hard Disks: (C:)
Used: 4.17 GB Free: 5.36 GB

Tip To display the report in its own window as shown here, click the **Change View** toolbar button.

5 When you finish looking at the report, click the **Back** button on the toolbar.

6 Click **View the status of my system hardware and software**.

Windows XP generates a report displaying this type of information:

My Computer Information - Status
Refresh screen

Obsolete Application and Device Drivers			
App/Device	**Driver File Name**	**Manufacturer**	**Help**
None			

System Software		
System Software	**Date Created**	**Help**
Microsoft Windows XP Professional	Monday, December 29, 2003 12:00:00 AM	Windows Update
BIOS	Friday, March 03, 2000 12:00:00 AM	View Help Topic

Hardware			
Component	**Status**	**Update**	**Help**
Video Card	Supported	Not Required	Troubleshooter
Network Card	Supported	Not Required	Troubleshooter
Sound Card	null	null	null
USB Controller	Supported	Not Required	Troubleshooter

Hard Disk		
Disk Partition	**Usage**	**Help**
Local Disk (C:)	44% (Low)	More Info

7 When you finish looking at the report, click the **Back** button.

8 Click **Find information about the hardware installed on this computer**.

Windows XP generates a report displaying this type of information:

My Computer Information - Hardware
Refresh screen

Local Disk (non-partitioned) ST310212A
(C:) Capacity - 9.53 GB
Used: 4.17 GB
Free: 5.36 GB

Local Disk (non-partitioned) M-Sys DiskOnKey USB Device
(E:) Capacity - 62.18 MB
Used: 27.91 MB
Free: 34.26 MB

Display
Type: Plug and Play Monitor
Color: True Color (32 Bit)
Resolution: 800 x 600
Screen Saver: Active

Video Card
Model: S3 Graphics Inc. Savage4
Driver: s3sav4m.sys
Monday, December 29, 2003
Supported

Sound Card
Not Installed

Modem
Not Installed

Network Card
Model: Intel(R) PRO/100+ PCI Adapter - Packet

USB Controller

9 When you finish looking at the report, click the **Back** button.

10 Click **View a list of Microsoft software installed on this computer**.

Tip The name of this link is somewhat misleading, because the report includes all the software that runs automatically when you start your computer, and non-Microsoft software is not excluded from that list.

Windows XP polls your computer for software information and generates a report like this one:

My Computer Information - Software
Refresh screen

Software

Microsoft Registered Software	Product Identification (PID)
Windows	55274-006-4501997-22743
Office	73931-721-0397943-57307
Office	

Startup Program Group

Software	Install Date
IDW Logging Tool	Friday, March 19, 2004
ctfmon.exe	Friday, March 19, 2004
HyperSnap-DX 4	Unknown

Windows Watson Crash Information

Date - Time	Description
None	

11 When you finish looking at the report, scroll down the **Tools** menu and click **Network Diagnostics**.

The Network Diagnostics tool opens in the right pane of the Help and Support Center. These two options are available:

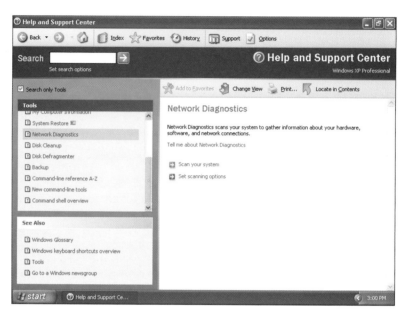

12 Click **Set scanning options**.

A list of options replaces the command.

13 Select all the check boxes, and then click **Scan your system**.

Windows XP gathers information about your hardware, software, and network connections, and then generates a report:

Tip   To save your settings for reuse the next time you scan your system, click **Save Options**.

CLOSE the Help and Support Center when you finish looking at the report.

Command-Line Operations

Advanced (or old-fashioned) users can use the *command shell*, a non-graphical program through which you can communicate directly with the operating system. Windows XP includes a complete command-line reference and a number of new *command-line tools*, which are available through the Help and Support Center.

For more information about the command-line tools, search for *command-line reference* in the Help and Support Center.

Cleaning Up Your Hard Disk

Every time you open a file, access a Web page, install a program, or download a file, a temporary file is created on your computer. Most of these files are deleted automatically when they are no longer needed. However, poorly behaved programs sometimes don't clean up after themselves, resulting in megabytes of unnecessary files on your hard disk.

Other types of unused files can also clutter up your hard disk. A common culprit is the Recycle Bin—by default, deleted files are stored in the Recycle Bin until you empty it.

Tip   To delete a file without temporarily storing it in the Recycle Bin, press **SHIFT+ DELETE** instead of **DELETE**. To always bypass the Recycle Bin, right-click the Recycle Bin, click **Properties**, select the **Do not move files to the Recycle Bin** check box, and click **OK**.

You can use *Disk Cleanup* to free up space on your hard disk by removing downloaded program files, temporary files, and offline files; compressing old files; and emptying the Recycle Bin. It is a good idea to run this utility at least once a year, or as often as once a month, to keep your drive in good order.

Tip   You can schedule Disk Cleanup or any other installed programs to run at regular intervals through the **Scheduled Task Wizard**. To start the **Scheduled Task Wizard**, on the **Start** menu, click **Control Panel**, and then click **Performance and Maintenance**. In the Performance and Maintenance window, click the **Scheduled Tasks** icon. In the Scheduled Tasks window, double-click **Add Scheduled Task**.

In this exercise, you will run the Disk Cleanup utility on your computer.

Tip   Depending on the number of files to be compressed and deleted, Disk Cleanup takes approximately one to ten minutes to run.

BE SURE TO log on to Windows before beginning this exercise.

Follow these steps:

1 On the **Start** menu, point to **All Programs**, point to **Accessories**, point to **System Tools**, and then click **Disk Cleanup**.

After calculating the amount of disk space the utility can free up, the **Disk Cleanup** dialog box appears:

Disk space freed by cleaning up each category

Total disk space freed

2 Select the check boxes of all the categories that have files available for deletion.

The total amount of disk space that you will gain is recalculated to reflect your selections.

3 To view a description of the files that will be deleted, click each file type (not the check box).

The description is displayed below the check boxes. If a list of the files that will be deleted is available, a **View Files** button is also displayed.

4 Click **View Files** if it is available.

The selected files are displayed in Windows Explorer.

5 Click the **More Options** tab to display other types of files that can be deleted to free up space on your computer.

The **Clean up** buttons in each area open dialog boxes that lead you through separate file clean up procedures:

Troubleshooting   The files that you can delete through the **More Options** tab might be necessary for the running of your computer, so you might not want to make selections through this tab unless you are desperately looking for ways to free up space.

6   Click the **Disk Cleanup** tab. After you have selected all the files you want to delete, click **OK**.

7   Click **Yes** to confirm that you want to delete the selected groups of files.

As Disk Cleanup completes the selected operations, a progress bar indicates how the cleanup is proceeding. You can cancel the cleanup at any point during the operation. The **Disk Cleanup** dialog box closes when the operation is complete.

Defragmenting Your Hard Disk

There can be times when, although there is nothing specifically wrong with your computer, it is not operating at its peak efficiency. You might think that your computer is simply not as fast as it used to be, and although perceived speed can be a function of your own level of patience, it might also be true that your system has slowed down since it was new. Unlike a sewing machine or a blender, a slow computer probably isn't due to the parts getting old and worn out; it might simply be that your hard disk has become cluttered and *fragmented*.

You can use *Disk Defragmenter* to analyze all the data stored on your hard disk and then consolidate fragmented files and folders into contiguous chunks to create the largest possible areas of available space. Your hard disk drive is organized into one or more *volumes* that can each be *defragmented* separately. Each volume has a drive letter assigned to it.

Troubleshooting You must be logged on to your computer with administrative privileges to run Disk Defragmenter.

In this exercise, you will run the Disk Defragmenter utility on your computer.

Tip Depending on the size of your hard disk, Disk Defragmenter can take up to an hour to run.

BE SURE TO log on to Windows before beginning this exercise.

Follow these steps:

1 On the **Start** menu, point to **All Programs**, point to **Accessories**, point to **System Tools**, and then click **Disk Defragmenter**.

The **Disk Defragmenter** dialog box appears:

Tip Each of your computer's storage disks will be listed in the **Disk Defragmenter** dialog box.

2 Click the **C:** volume to select it for defragmentation, and then click **Analyze**.

Disk Defragmenter analyzes the volume and then recommends whether you should defragment the disk.

3 Click **View Report** to see information the program collected.

4 If defragmentation is recommended and you want to do it at this time, click **Defragment**. Otherwise, click **Close** to close the report window.

5 If you choose to defragment the volume, click **Close** to close the **Disk Defragmenter** dialog box when the defragmentation process is complete.

Helping Yourself

It is fairly common for people to purchase furniture, toys, bikes, or other things that require assembly, and then neglect to read the instruction manual until they actually have a problem. Along the same lines, many people never consult a software program's Help file, because they don't realize how much good information can be found there.

Windows XP takes the concept of the Help file to new heights with the Help and Support Center. As the name implies, the Help and Support Center is the place to go when you're having trouble—you can help yourself, or you can ask other people for help. The help offered is more than just a common Help file: It includes multimedia product tours targeted at different audiences, general and specific articles, a comprehensive glossary, tutorials and demonstrations, and links to most of the tools that you need to keep your computer running smoothly. You can choose from a list of common topics on the main page of the Help and Support Center, search the database by keyword or phrase, or look up specific topics in the index or table of contents. When you're connected to the Internet, you can easily include the *Microsoft Knowledge Base* in your searches as well.

When you search for information, your search results are divided into three areas:

- The **Suggested Topics** listing displays topics that are most likely to be of interest to you, because the search terms you entered match the keywords defined by the topic's author.

- The **Full-text Search Matches** listing displays all the topics in which the individual words of your search terms appear.

- The **Microsoft Knowledge Base** listing displays articles that pertain to your search phrase from Microsoft's online database of product support information. This listing is available only when you are online.

You can search the entire support database, and you can conduct a subsequent search within the results of a previous search, thereby narrowing down the search results to define your problem.

If you can't solve your problem on your own, you can communicate with other Windows XP users and experts through online newsgroups, consult online with Microsoft support personnel, or request remote assistance from a friend or co-worker. Using Remote Assistance, you can allow another person to connect to your computer over the Internet and take control of your computer to figure out what the trouble is.

The Help and Support Center links to Web-based information to ensure that it is always up to date. This means that you don't have access to all the features of the Help and Support Center when you are offline.

There are two ways to access the Help and Support Center:

■ Click **Help and Support** on the **Start** menu.

■ Press the **F1** key. Depending on what area of Windows you are in, this might open the Help and Support Center to a page that is specific to that area. For example, if you press the **F1** key from within Control Panel, the Help and Support Center opens to the Control Panel topic.

> **Tip** Pressing the **F1** key opens the Help file for the currently active Microsoft application. Pressing the **F1** key from within a Microsoft Office Word file opens the Word Help file; pressing the **F1** key from within a Microsoft Office Excel file opens the Excel Help file, and so on. Many software manufacturers have made their context-sensitive help available through the **F1** key, which is why context-sensitive help is often referred to as *F1 Help*.

In this exercise, you will open the Help and Support Center and search for useful information.

BE SURE TO log on to Windows before beginning this exercise.

Follow these steps:

1 On the **Start** menu, click **Help and Support**.

The Help and Support Center window opens:

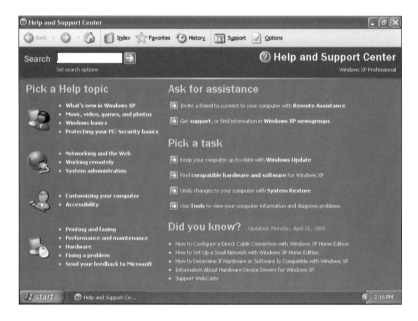

Index

2 Click the **Index** button.

A list of available topics is displayed.

3 Click the **Home** button.

Home

The Help and Support Center appears again.

Start searching

4 In the **Search** box, type getting help, and then click the **Start searching** button.

Tip Search terms are not case-sensitive; typing *getting Help* produces the same results.

The results of your search are shown in the Search Results pane. The total number of "hits" is displayed at the top, and the suggested topics are shown by default.

5 In the **Search Results** title bar, click **Tips** to display a list of useful search tips.

6 When you finish reviewing the search tips, click any topic title in the Search Results pane to display that topic in the right pane.

Locate in Contents

7 Click the **Locate in Contents** button to display the topic in relation to the table of contents.

You can use this feature to locate related information without going through another search.

Back

8 Click the **Back** button to return to the Search Results pane.

9 In the Search Results pane, click the **Full-text Search Matches** bar.

The bar slides up to display the listing.

10 In the Search Results pane, click the **Microsoft Knowledge Base** bar.

Again, the bar slides up to display the listing.

CLOSE the Help and Support Center window when you finish browsing the Help file.

Joining a Windows Newsgroup

Windows *newsgroups* are online forums where Windows XP users and experts from around the world interact to discuss their experiences with Windows XP. These newsgroups are not officially monitored by Microsoft, and Microsoft is not responsible for any of the information available there. You can find discussion threads about many common and uncommon problems. You might find an answer to a question or an interesting discussion that you want to keep up with or join.

Newsgroups are free of charge, and you can join or quit them at any time. You can link to the newsgroups through Microsoft Outlook Express or through a Web-based newsgroup reader. After joining the newsgroup, you can interact with a newsgroup in several different ways:

- You can visit a newsgroup to read messages.

- You can post a new message and wait for a response, either in e-mail or in the newsgroup.

- You can post a reply to a message to the newsgroup; your message then becomes part of the discussion thread and is available to anyone who visits the newsgroup.

- You can send an e-mail message to the person who posted a specific message, or forward the message to someone else through e-mail.

- You can subscribe to a newsgroup and have all its messages sent to you.

- You can subscribe to a specific discussion thread, in which case you will receive an e-mail message notifying you when a new message has been posted to the thread.

A word of warning about newsgroups: Some people see them as a forum for blowing off steam without actually communicating information that is useful or interesting to anyone else. You might find that it takes quite a while to wade through all the available messages before you find information that is pertinent to your situation. On the bright side, although Microsoft does not officially monitor the newsgroups, there do appear to be a fair number of "experts" who post useful information or respond to valid queries.

In this exercise, you will investigate the available Windows XP newsgroups using a Web-based newsgroup reader.

BE SURE TO have an active Internet connection available before beginning this exercise.

Follow these steps:

1 On the **Start** menu, click **Help and Support**.

2 Under **Ask for assistance** in the Help and Support Center, click **Get support, or find information in Windows XP newsgroups**.

3 In the Support pane, click **Go to a Windows Web site forum**.

This Windows Newsgroups page opens:

The world icon overlaid by a red arrow indicates that you are connecting to a non-Microsoft Web site

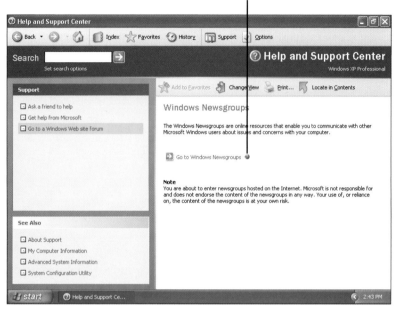

4 Click **Go to Windows Newsgroups**.

The Windows XP Newsgroups Web page opens:

Maximize

5 Click the **Maximize** button to expand the window.

You can read the messages of each newsgroup either in Outlook Express or in your Web browser. If you a newsgroup name or the **Use Web-based reader** link below it, the messages are displayed in your browser. If you click the Open with newsreader link under the newsgroup name, it opens in your default newsreader (such as Outlook Express).

Tip For step-by-step instructions on configuring Outlook Express for a newsgroup, click **Windows XP Newsgroups Setup Instructions**.

6 Select an interesting newsgroup from the list, and click the **Use Web-based reader** link under the title of the newsgroup.

A new Web page opens with all the messages to that newsgroup shown, something like this:

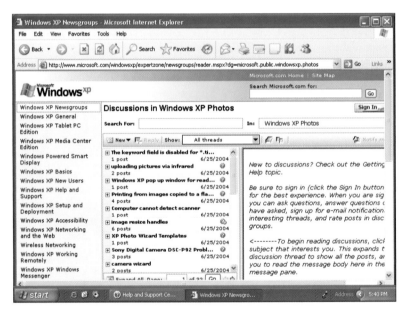

You can click any message to view it in the preview pane at the bottom of the window. You can then post a reply to the message or send an e-mail to the person who posted the message, using the buttons in the preview pane.

CLOSE the Web page, and then close the Help and Support Center.

Contacting Product Support

The product support offered by software and hardware companies varies wildly depending on the type of product, the price you paid, and the company. Microsoft has traditionally offered very good product support, though getting help often involved a long telephone call, with the technician on the other end spending quite a while determining the status of your system and your actual problem.

Microsoft Online Assisted Support

Microsoft Online Assisted Support is the relatively new face of product support at Microsoft. You can use Online Assisted Support to log specific problems with the Microsoft support staff, who then reply to your problem online. This method of handling product support is very efficient, both for you and for Microsoft.

The diagnostic tools included with Windows XP make it easy to send all the information your product support technician needs to diagnose the problem and offer a useful solution. You can either allow your system information to be collected automatically, or you can stipulate which information can be sent to Microsoft. Your Product ID code and operating system version are the only required information. Optional information includes:

- Computer manufacturer and model
- Processor model and speed
- Amount of *random access memory (RAM)*
- General system information
- Information on your system files

If you want, you can review all the information before it is sent. You are not required to send any information other than your Product ID and Windows XP version number, but it can be useful to the technical support people to have a more complete understanding of your computer system, because known issues often affect only certain computer models, sound cards, graphics cards, and so on. You can also send file attachments that aren't specifically requested; for example, you might send a screenshot of an error message that will help to explain the problem.

After you complete and submit an Incident Form, your data is collected, compressed, and sent to Microsoft, and an Incident Number is assigned. You can use this tracking number to follow up on your request for help at a later date. You don't usually need to keep the tracking number, but it does assure you that your problem has become part of the product support database.

Troubleshooting   If for any reason the Incident Form is not successfully submitted, your data is saved on your computer so that you can quickly submit it later.

When you have your Incident Number, you can return to the Online Assisted Support site at a later time to view the results, or you can ask to be notified by e-mail when an answer has been posted.

In this exercise, you will walk through the process of creating an Online Assisted Support Incident report.

BE SURE TO have an active Internet connection and a Passport account available before beginning this exercise.

Follow these steps:

1 On the **Start** menu, click **Help and Support**.

2 On the toolbar, click the **Support** button.

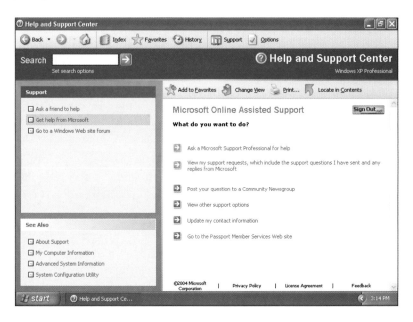

3 In the Support pane, click **Get help from Microsoft**.

Windows XP checks your Internet connection and then connects you to the Microsoft Online Assisted Support Web site, which opens within the Help and Support Center.

4 Click the **Sign In** button, and enter your Passport sign-in name and password when prompted:

Tip If you have set up your computer to sign you in to Passport automatically, you will bypass the sign-in screen.

5 Click **Ask a Microsoft Support Professional for help**.

The first time you request Online Assisted Support, you see the End User License Agreement (EULA):

6 If the EULA is displayed, read it and then click the **I Agree** button.

The next page prompts you to indicate the computer where you are experiencing the problem. If you are reporting a problem from the computer on which it occurs, the Online Assisted Support program can gather information about your computer that will help solve the problem:

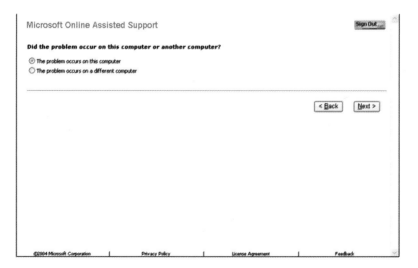

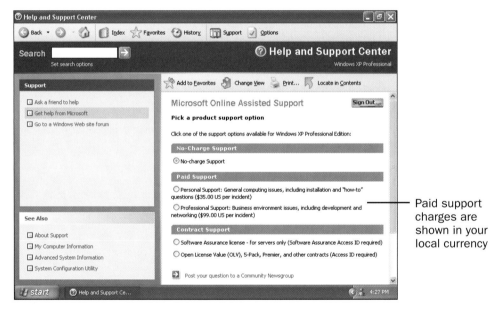

Tip To display the Online Assisted Support site in its own window as shown here, click the **Change View** toolbar button.

7 Barring a major system failure, you will generally be reporting a problem from the computer on which it occurs. Select the **The problem occurs on this computer** option, and then click **Next**.

Online Assisted Support polls your computer and generates a list of the installed programs.

If you select the **The problem occurs on a different computer** option, you are prompted for information about the computer.

8 In the drop-down list, click the version of Windows XP that is installed on your computer, and then click **Next**. Repeat the process in the secondary drop-down list that appears.

You are prompted to choose from the available support options:

Paid support charges are shown in your local currency

9 Select the support option you want, and then click **Next**.

10 If you are prompted to install the Web Response File Transfer Control from Microsoft Corporation, click **Install**.

Tip Your security settings might require your permission for the installation of new controls on your computer.

A new Incident Form opens.

11 If the form window is not already maximized, click the **Maximize** button to expand the window so you can see as much of the form as possible.

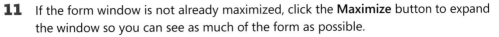

Maximize

The form looks like this:

Microsoft Online Assisted Support

Sign Out

Incident Form - Windows XP Professional EN

Describe the problem

Select the category that best describes the type of problem:

Select One

How often does it happen?

Select One

* What's the problem? Describe the problem in detail. Include any steps or actions required to reproduce the problem. (Required)

Provide information about your computer

With your permission, information can be automatically collected from your computer. The information will only be used to troubleshoot the computer problem.
View Microsoft Online Assisted Support privacy policy

12 Look through the input requested on the form so that you are aware of all the options. If you're actually having a problem at this time, fill out and submit an Incident Form.

CLOSE the Help and Support Center when you finish looking at the site.

Asking for Help from Someone Else

If you've tried to solve a problem on your own and simply have not been successful, Windows XP makes it easy to turn to someone else for help. You have the choice of contacting Microsoft Product Support Services or asking a friend or co-worker to help you.

new for
WindowsXP

Remote
Assistance

You can use *Remote Assistance*, an exciting new feature of Windows XP, to invite another person who is running Windows XP and is connected to your intranet or the Internet to view your computer screen and use Windows Messenger to chat with you about the problem. If you want, you can then give that person permission to work remotely on your computer from his or her own desk.

To initiate a Remote Assistance session, you send an invitation to the other person. You can limit the chance that someone could fraudulently gain access to your computer through the invitation by specifying the duration of the invitation, from 1 minute to 99 days. You can also require that the other person enter a password to access your computer, in which case you would supply the password separately.

In this exercise, you will request and receive Remote Assistance from another person.

BE SURE TO have an active Internet connection, a Passport, and an online buddy who is also running Windows XP available before beginning this exercise.

Follow these steps:

1   On the **Start** menu, point to **All Programs**, and then click **Remote Assistance**.

The Help and Support Center opens to the Remote Assistance page:

2   Click **Invite someone to help you**. If a **Sign In** button appears in the **Windows Messenger** area, click it to sign in and display your online contacts.

Your Remote Assistance options are displayed:

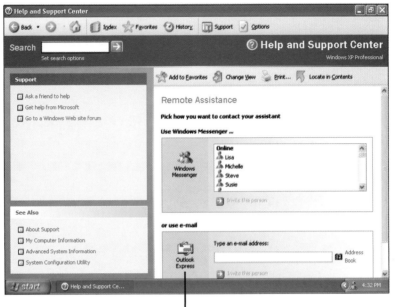

Your default e-mail program icon appears here

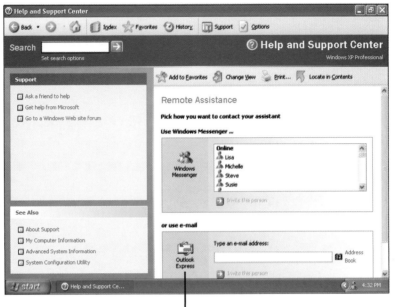

Tip   To display the Remote Assistance program in its own window as shown here, click the **Change View** toolbar button.

3   Click the name of the person who you are going to invite to help you; or type his or her e-mail address in the **Type an e-mail address** box, and then click **Invite this person**. If you used Windows Messenger, skip to step 10.

4   When the remote assistance invitation opens, type an explanatory message in the **Message** box, and then click **Continue**.

You are prompted to specify the duration of your invitation.

5   Accept the default of **01 Hours**.

6   If you want to use a password, enter the password in the **Type password** and **Confirm password** boxes, and then relay that password to your Remote Assistance buddy. If you do not want to use a password, clear the **Require the recipient to use a password** check box.

7   When you are ready to send the invitation, click **Send Invitation**.

Your invitation is initiated through Outlook Express or your default e-mail program. You are notified that a program is attempting to send a message in your name.

8   Click **Send**.

When your invitation has been sent, you will see a confirmation.

9 Click **View invitation status** to view your invitation, which looks something like this:

Sent To	Expiration Time	Status
○ susie@wingtiptoys.com	Tuesday, May 18, 2004 8:08:13 PM	Open
Details	Expire	Resend...	Delete

You can review, expire, resend, or delete invitations from this page at any time.

When your invitation is received and accepted by your Remote Assistance buddy, a Remote Assistance message is displayed on your computer screen.

10 Click **Yes** to allow your buddy to view your screen and chat with you.

This Remote Assistance window opens on your computer:

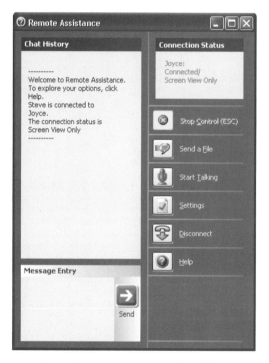

A window also opens on your buddy's computer. At this point, the two of you can chat by typing messages, or, if you both have microphones and speakers, by talking. You can also send files.

Your buddy can see everything you do on your computer, so you can open files or demonstrate the steps that lead up to a problem and then ask for advice.

11 In the chat session, tell your buddy to take control of your computer.

He or she will need to click the **Take Control** button on the Remote Assistance tool-bar. You will then receive a message asking if you would like to share control of your computer.

12 Click **Yes**.

You both now have control of the mouse on your computer. However, you should not both try to move it at the same time.

Stop Control

13 When you decide that you no longer want to share control of your computer, click the **Stop Control** button in the Remote Assistance window.

You now have exclusive control of your mouse.

Disconnect

14 When you finish the Remote Assistance session, click the **Disconnect** button.

CLOSE the Remote Assistance window and the Help and Support Center.

Enabling and Disabling Remote Assistance

The Remote Assistance option is turned on by default. If you are uncomfortable with the idea that other people might be able to access your computer over the Internet, you can turn off the Remote Assistance option on your Windows XP computer.

To disable or enable Remote Assistance:

1 On the **Start** menu, click **Control Panel**.

2 In the Control Panel window, click **Performance and Maintenance**.

3 In the Performance and Maintenance window, click the **System** icon.

The **System Properties** dialog box appears.

4 Click the **Remote** tab, and then click the **Advanced** button.

The **Remote Assistance Settings** dialog box appears.

5 Clear or select the **Allow this computer to be controlled remotely** check box.

6 Click **OK** to close the **Remote Assistance Settings** dialog box, and then click **OK** to close the **System Properties** dialog box and save your changes.

Backing Up and Restoring Files

When *file* and *folder* were terms used to describe things made of paper, it was possible for your important documents to be permanently destroyed by fire, water, coffee, accidental shredding, or a variety of other natural and unnatural disasters. With the advent of electronic files and folders, your data can still be destroyed, but the damage doesn't have to be permanent.

The **Backup or Restore Wizard** creates a copy of the files and folders on your hard disk. If your data is lost or damaged, you can restore it from the backup file. It is advisable to regularly create a backup of any files and folders that are important to you. The frequency of the backup depends on the frequency of changes to the files, because if you lose your data, you will have to re-create anything that has occurred since the last backup. For this reason, many companies back up their important files on a daily basis.

You can select from different backup options, depending on your needs:

- *Normal* backs up all selected files and system settings for a specific folder or drive and marks each file as backed up.

- *Copy* backs up all selected files and system settings for a specific folder or drive, but does not mark the files as having been backed up.

- *Incremental* backs up only the files that have been created or modified since the last normal or incremental backup and marks each file as backed up.

- *Differential* backs up only the files that have been created or modified since the last normal or incremental backup, but it does not mark the files.

- *Daily* backs up only those files that were created or modified today, but it does not mark the files.

The type of backup you perform determines how complex the restoration process is. To restore after several incremental or differential backups, you must restore the last normal backup and all the incremental or differential backups since then.

When you back up your data, you designate a file name and location for the backup file. By default, backup files are saved with a *.bkf* extension, but you can specify any file extension you want. Your backup file can be saved on your hard disk, on a floppy disk, or on any other type of removable media. Considerations when choosing a backup location include the size of the backup file, the types of media you have available, and whether you want to store the file separately from the computer in case of disaster.

In this exercise, you will back up the files contained in a directory that was installed from this book's CD-ROM.

USE the documents in the practice file folder for this topic. These practice files are located in the *My Documents\Microsoft Press\Microsoft Windows XP SBS\Solving\Backup* **folder.**
BE SURE TO have a formatted 3½" floppy disk with 150KB of free space available before beginning this exercise.

Troubleshooting   If your computer does not have a 3½" floppy disk drive, substitute an alternate storage device in the exercise.

Follow these steps:

1   On the **Start** menu, point to **All Programs**, point to **Accessories**, point to **System Tools**, and then click **Backup**.

The **Backup or Restore Wizard** starts.

2   Click **Next** to begin the process of backing up your files.

The Backup or Restore page opens:

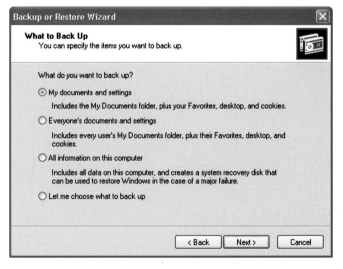

3   Select the **Back up files and settings** option, and then click **Next**.

The What to Back Up page opens:

4   Select the **Let me choose what to back up** option, and then click **Next**.

The Items to Back Up page opens:

5 Browse to *My Documents\Microsoft Press\Microsoft Windows XP SBS\Solving \Backup* by clicking the plus signs to the left of the folders to expand them.

6 Select the check box preceding the practice file folder, and then click **Next**.

Tip If the folder structure is too wide for the pane it appears in, drag the pane's right border to the right to widen the pane.

The Backup Type, Destination, and Name page opens:

7   In the **Choose a place to save your backup** drop-down list, click **3½ Floppy**. Accept the default file name (*Backup*). Insert a formatted floppy disk into the floppy disk drive, and then click **Next**.

8   Review the backup settings, and then click **Finish** to start the backup.

The **Backup Progress** dialog box displays the status of the backup process:

Backup Progress	? X
The backup is complete.	Close
To see detailed information, click Report.	Report...

Drive:	C:
Label:	Backup.bkf created 4/27/2004 at 5:04 PM
Status:	Completed

	Elapsed:	Estimated remaining:
Time:	9 sec.	

	Processed:	Estimated:
Files:	5	5
Bytes:	130,088	130,088

9   When the backup process is complete, click **Close**.

Tip   To restore your files and folders at a later date, repeat steps 1 and 2, select the **Restore files and settings** option, browse to and select the backup file, click **Next**, and then click **Finish**.

10   On the **Start** menu, click **My Computer**, and in the **Devices with Removable Storage** list, double-click **3½ Floppy**.

The Windows Backup File is displayed.

Tip   You can launch the **Backup or Restore Wizard** and select an existing backup file at the same time by double-clicking the backup file in Windows Explorer.

CLOSE Windows Explorer.

Restoring Your Operating System

In the beginning, you had a clean computer with a brand-new operating system. As time goes by, you install new programs, delete programs, change your system settings, and upgrade to new versions of programs. Gradually, things change.

Sometimes you might find yourself wishing you could go back to the way things were, and now you can! You can use **System Restore Wizard** to roll back your system to the condition it was in at a prior point in time. You can roll back to any of these types of checkpoints and restoration points:

- An *initial system checkpoint* is created the first time you start a new computer, or the first time you start your computer after you upgrade it to Windows XP.

- *Automatic update restore points* are created when you install updates that are downloaded through Windows Update.

- *Backup recovery restore points* are created when you use the **Backup or Restore Wizard**.

- You can manually create your own restore points (*manual checkpoints*) at any time from the **System Restore Wizard**.

- *Program name installation restore points* are created when you install a program using an installer such as InstallShield or Windows XP Installer.

- *Restore operation restore points* are created each time you perform a restoration; if you are not satisfied with the results of the restoration, you can roll back to this point.

- *System checkpoints* are scheduled restoration points that your computer creates regularly, even if you have not made any changes to the system.

- *Unsigned device driver restore points* are created when you install a device driver that has not been signed or certified.

System Restore generally saves one to three weeks' worth of restoration checkpoints. The number of restoration checkpoints available at any given time is limited by the amount of space you allocate to the System Restore function. The maximum space you can allocate is approximately 12 percent.

Restoring your computer restores Windows XP and the programs that are installed on your computer to the state they were in at the time of the selected restore checkpoint. Your personal files (including your saved documents, e-mail messages, Address Book, Internet Explorer Favorites, and History list) are not affected. All the changes made by System Restore are completely reversible, so if you don't like the results, you can restore the previous settings and try again.

In this exercise, you will see how to restore your computer to a previous state.

Troubleshooting   System Restore restarts your computer, so be sure to close any open programs before running it.

BE SURE TO *close any open programs before beginning this exercise.*

Follow these steps:

1 On the **Start** menu, point to **All Programs**, point to **Accessories**, point to **System Tools**, and then click **System Restore**.

Tip You can also access System Restore by clicking **Undo changes to your computer with System Restore** in the Help and Support Center, or by clicking **System Restore** in the **See Also** area of the Performance and Maintenance window.

The **System Restore Wizard** starts:

2 Select the **Restore my computer to an earlier time** option, and then click **Next**.

The Select a Restore Point page opens, displaying a calendar. The days on which restoration checkpoints were created are indicated on the calendar by a bold date.

Troubleshooting You can move to different months by clicking the arrows on either side of the month name. These arrows are operational only when restoration checkpoints exist in the previous or next months.

3 Click each of the bold dates to see the checkpoints that were created on that day:

4 On the calendar, click a date that has a restoration checkpoint.

5 In the description pane, click a specific restoration checkpoint.

6 Click **Next**.

System Restore displays information about your selected checkpoint.

Important You have now selected a restore point. Do not continue this exercise unless you want to restore your computer to an earlier state. Although it is possible to undo the restoration, there is always a possibility of loss of data in any action such as this.

7 Click **Next**.

System Restore logs off of Windows XP, restores your files to their condition at the time of the selected checkpoint, and then restarts your computer.

8 If you usually log on to your computer with a user account name and password, you will need to enter them.

Depending on the types of changes that were made since the chosen restoration checkpoint, you might notice a visible difference when the computer restarts.

Key Points

■ Automatic Updates ensure that your computer operating system always has the latest security updates installed.

■ You can clean up and compress the files stored on your computer so that it operates at peak efficiency.

■ If you need help with Windows XP you can consult the local or online Help file or get help from other people through a newsgroup, online assistance, or Remote Assistance.

■ It is a good idea to periodically back up your important files in the event of a system error. If you have a serious computer problem, you can restore your files or even restore your operating system to an earlier state.

Glossary

ActiveX control   An object that supports a customizable, programmatic interface. Examples include text boxes, command buttons, audio players, video players, and stock tickers.

Address Book   A convenient place to store contact information for easy retrieval by programs such as Microsoft Outlook Express. It also features access to Internet directory services, with which users can look up people and businesses on the Internet.

administrative privileges   The highest level of permissions that can be granted to a user account. An administrator can set permissions for other users and create groups and accounts within a domain. Administrative privileges are required to install certain programs.

alias   A name used to identify the recipient of an e-mail message in an e-mail address or on a network. The alias is the portion of the e-mail address that appears before the @ symbol.

attachment   A file, picture, or other external data source sent in conjunction with an e-mail message.

automatic update restore point   A restoration checkpoint in System Restore that is automatically created when users install a downloaded update.

backup recovery restore point   A restoration checkpoint in System Restore that is automatically created when the Backup utility is used.

bandwidth   The data transfer capacity of a digital communications system, such as the Internet or a local area network. Bandwidth is usually expressed in the number of bits that a system is capable of transferring in a second: bits per second (bps). High bandwidth or broadband refers to a network capable of a fast data transfer rate.

bitmap (BMP)   The representation of characters or graphics by individual pixels arranged in rows and columns. For black and white pixels, each pixel is represented by 1 bit of data, whereas for high-definition color pixels, each pixel is represented by 32 bits.

BMP   See *bitmap (BMP)*.

booting   The process of starting or resetting a computer. When first turned on (cold boot) or reset (warm boot), the computer runs the software that loads and starts the computer's operating system, which prepares it for use.

Briefcase   See *Microsoft Briefcase*.

321

broadband connection   A high-speed connection. Broadband connections typically transfer information at a rate of 256 kilobytes per second (KBps) or faster. Broadband includes DSL and cable modem service.

browser   See *Web browser*.

burning   The process of copying data to a CD.

button   A graphic element on a toolbar or in a dialog box that performs a particular function when users click it. The part of a mouse that users press to click something is also called a button.

byte   A unit of data, usually the equivalent of a single character such as a letter or a digit.

cable modem   A device that creates a broadband connection to the Internet by using cable television lines. Access speeds vary greatly, with a maximum speed of 10 megabits per second (Mbps).

caching   The process of storing information in a computer's memory, or storing a Web page on a computer's hard disk, for rapid retrieval at a later time.

capturing   The process of converting analog video or audio to digital data, which can be stored as a file on a computer.

CD key   A unique combination of letters and numbers, usually located on a CD-ROM jewel case, that identifies the product license for the CD version of a product.

CD-R   See *compact disc–recordable (CD-R)*.

CD-RW   See *compact disc–rewritable (CD-RW)*.

chatting   The process of communicating through an instant-messaging program such as Windows Messenger.

Classic   The term used to describe the appearance of the user interface in versions of Windows prior to Windows XP.

clicking   The action of pressing and releasing the primary mouse button.

clip   The audio, video, or still images in Windows Movie Maker. Clips are stored in collections.

command   An instruction to the computer's operating system.

command shell   A software program that provides direct communication between the user and the operating system. The command shell has a non-graphical user interface, and it provides the environment in which the user runs character-based applications and utilities.

command-line tools   The tools that are entered as commands in the Windows XP version of MS-DOS, an older Microsoft operating system.

compact disc–recordable (CD-R)   A type of compact disc on which files can be written.

compact disc–rewritable (CD-RW)   A type of compact disc on which files can be written multiple times.

compression   The encoding of data to reduce file size. Content that has been compressed must be decompressed for use.

Computer Management   A component used to view and control many aspects of a computer configuration. Computer Management combines several administrative utilities into a single unit, providing easy access to a computer's administrative properties and tools.

cookie   A small text file stored on a computer, containing information specific to a particular Web site, such as user name or password.

data storage device   A device on which data is stored, including floppy disks, hard disk drives, CD-ROMs, Zip disks, and so forth.

defragmentation   The process of rewriting parts of a file on a hard disk to increase the speed of access and retrieval. When files are updated, the computer tends to save the updates on the largest contiguous space on the hard disk, which is often on a different sector than the other parts of the file. When files are fragmented, the computer must search the hard disk each time the file is opened to find all of the file's parts, which slows down response time.

desktop   The on-screen work area on which windows, icons, menus, and dialog boxes appear.

device driver   A program that allows a specific device, such as a modem, network adapter, or printer, to communicate with the operating system. Although a device might be installed on a system, Windows cannot use the device until the appropriate driver is installed and configured. If a device is listed in the Hardware Compatibility List (HCL), a driver is usually included with Windows. Device drivers load automatically when a computer is started, and thereafter run invisibly.

DHCP server   A computer running the Microsoft DHCP service, which allows IP addresses to change as needed.

dialog box   A window that contains buttons and various kinds of options through which the user can carry out a particular command or task.

dial-up connection   A network connection that uses the telephone network. This includes modems with a standard phone line, ISDN cards with high-speed ISDN lines, or X.25 networks. A typical user might have one or two dial-up connections, for example, to the Internet and to a corporate network. In a more complex server situation, multiple network modem connections might be used to implement advanced routing.

Digital Subscriber Line (DSL) A type of high-speed Internet connection using standard telephone wires; also referred to as a broadband connection.

digital video disc (DVD) A type of optical disc storage technology. A digital video disc looks like a CD-ROM disc, but it can store greater amounts of data. DVDs are often used to store full-length movies and other multimedia content that requires a large amount of storage space.

direct cable connection A link between two computers created with a single cable, rather than with a modem or other interfacing device.

Disk Cleanup A program that deletes temporary files from the hard disk drive to free up storage space.

Disk Defragmenter A program that locates and consolidates fragmented files and folders on a computer.

display name In MSN Messenger, the alias used for an account.

DLL See *dynamic-link library (DLL)*.

DNS See *domain name*.

docking The process of connecting a laptop or notebook computer to a docking station; or of connecting a floating toolbar to one side of the Windows desktop.

domain A group of computers that are part of a network and share a common directory. A domain is administered as a unit with common rules and procedures. Each domain has a unique name.

domain name The name given by an administrator to a collection of networked computers that share a common directory. In accordance with Domain Name System (DNS) naming structure, domain names consist of a sequence of name labels separated by periods.

double-clicking The process of pressing and releasing the primary mouse button twice in quick succession to give the computer a command.

downloading The process of delivering or receiving information over a network by copying the information to a computer on which it can be played locally. In contrast, when information is streamed, the data is not copied to the receiving computer.

dragging The process of moving an item to another place on the screen by selecting the item and then pressing and holding down the mouse button while moving the mouse.

driver See *printer driver*.

DSL See *Digital Subscriber Line (DSL)*.

DVD See *digital video disc (DVD)*.

dynamic-link library (DLL)   An operating system feature that allows executable routines (serving a specific function or set of functions) to be stored separately as files with *.dll* extensions. These routines are loaded into memory only when needed by the program that calls them.

electronic business cards   See *vCard*.

e-mail   A means of sending messages and data over the Internet. Short for electronic mail.

e-mail address   A series of characters, consisting of an alias and a domain name, that identifies a user so that the user can receive e-mail messages.

e-mail server   See *server*.

emoticon   A symbol created by standard keyboard characters and used to represent an emotion in electronic communications.

End User License Agreement (EULA)   An agreement governing the use of a software product by the user. The EULA can be found in several different locations, depending on the product. The three most common locations are: (1) printed on a separate piece of paper that accompanies the product; (2) printed in the User's Manual, usually inside the front cover or on the first page of the manual; or (3) located online within the software product.

Ethernet   A method of connecting to a computer network that uses cables to transfer information between computers. Ethernet networks can transmit at 10 megabits (10 million bits) per second.

executable file   A program file that can be run. Files that have *.exe* extensions are executable.

expansion slot   A socket inside a computer's case, designed to hold new hardware that the user installs to enhance the computer's capabilities.

extension   See *file name extension*.

external   Outside of a network or organization; not contained inside a computer's case.

EULA   See *End User License Agreement (EULA)*.

file   A discrete, named unit of data or information that can be created, accessed, and modified by a program or a user. Spreadsheets, graphics, and sounds are examples of files. Files are kept in folders.

file name extension   A set of characters added to the end of a file name that identifies the format of a file, the type of content it contains, and the type of program or device it can be used with, for example, *.doc*.

FilterKeys   A keyboard feature that instructs the keyboard to ignore brief or repeated keystrokes. Users can also adjust the keyboard repeat rate, which is the rate at which a key is repeated when it is held down.

firewall   A combination of hardware and software that provides a security system, usually to prevent unauthorized access to an internal network or intranet. A firewall prevents direct communication between network and external computers by routing communication through a proxy server outside the network. The proxy server determines whether it is safe to let a file pass through to the network. A firewall is also called a *security-edge gateway*.

FireWire   See *IEEE 1394*.

folder   A container for programs and files in graphical user interfaces, symbolized on the screen by an icon of a file folder. A folder is a means of organizing programs and documents on a disk and can hold both files and additional folders.

font   A set of characters. Traditionally a font was a particular size and a particular style within a family, such as 10 point italic Verdana. Now the term *font* commonly refers to the entire family.

fragmentation   The scattering of parts of the same file over different areas of the disk. Fragmentation occurs as files on a disk are deleted and new files are added. It slows disk access and degrades the overall performance of disk operations, although usually not severely.

full mode   The default operational state in Windows Media Player in which all its features are displayed. The Player can also appear in skin mode.

GB   See *gigabyte (GB)*.

GIF   See *graphics interchange format (GIF)*.

gigabyte (GB)   1,024 megabytes, though often interpreted as approximately one billion bytes.

graphics interchange format (GIF)   An image compression method that supports color, various resolutions, and data compression, but is limited to a palette of 256 colors, so it is more suitable for illustrations than for photographs.

group   An account that contains other accounts, called members. Permissions and rights granted to a group are also granted to its members.

hacker   A person who attempts to gain access to computers or software programs through illegal means, often with the malicious intent of damaging computer data through the introduction of a virus.

hard disk   A device, also called a *hard disk drive*, that contains one or more inflexible platters coated with a material on which data can be recorded magnetically. The hard disk is contained in a sealed case that protects it. Data can be stored and accessed much more quickly on a hard disk than on a floppy disk.

hardware   The physical components of a computer system, including any peripheral equipment such as printers, modems, and mouse devices.

header   A part of the structure of a Windows Media stream that contains information necessary for a computer to interpret how the packets of data containing the content should be decompressed and rendered.

hibernation   A state in which a computer shuts down after saving everything in memory on the hard disk. When a computer comes out of hibernation, all programs and documents that were open are restored to the desktop.

home page   The Web page loaded each time a user's Web browser is started.

host name   The Domain Name System (DNS) name of a device on a network. These names are used to locate computers on the network. To find another computer, its host name must either appear in the Hosts file or be known by a DNS server. For most Windows computers, the host name and the computer name are the same.

HTML   See *Hypertext Markup Language (HTML)*.

HTTP   See *Hypertext Transfer Protocol (HTTP)*.

Hypertext Markup Language (HTML)   A simple markup language used to create hypertext documents that can be displayed on computers running a variety of programs and operating systems. HTML files are simple ASCII text files with codes embedded (indicated by markup tags) to denote formatting and hypertext links.

Hypertext Transfer Protocol (HTTP)   The protocol used to transfer information on the World Wide Web. An HTTP address—one kind of Uniform Resource Locator (URL)—takes the form *http://www.microsoft.com*.

icon   A small image displayed on the screen to represent an object that can be manipulated by the user. Icons serve as visual mnemonics and are used to control certain computer actions without the user having to remember commands or enter them through the keyboard.

ICS   See *Internet Connection Sharing (ICS)*.

IEEE 1394   A high-speed external bus standard supporting isochronous data transfer rates of up to 800 Mbps.

IMAP   See *Internet Message Access Protocol (IMAP)*.

Internet Message Access Protocol (IMAP)   A method by which e-mail programs can access e-mail messages on a mail server. With IMAP, a user can retrieve e-mail messages from more than one computer.

Indexing Service   A Search Companion feature that maintains an index of all the files on a computer to enable faster searching.

initial system checkpoint A restoration checkpoint in System Restore that is automatically created the first time a user starts a new Windows XP computer, or the first time a user starts a computer after installing Windows XP.

installation checkpoint A restoration checkpoint in System Restore that is automatically created when a user installs a software program.

Integrated Services Digital Network (ISDN) A digital phone line used to provide a high-bandwidth Internet connection. An ISDN line must be installed by the telephone company at both the calling site and the called site.

internal A term meaning within a network or organization; physically contained within a computer's case.

Internet Connection Sharing (ICS) A feature with which users can connect computers on a home or small office network to the Internet using just one connection; intended for use in a network where the ICS host computer directs network communication between computers and the Internet.

Internet directory service An independently operated search engine used to locate people and businesses around the world over the Internet.

Internet Message Access Protocol A method of accessing electronic mail or bulletin board messages that are kept on a mail server.

Internet protocol (IP) address A 32-bit address used to identify a node on an IP network. Each node on the IP network must be assigned a unique IP address, which is made up of the network ID and a unique host ID. This address is typically represented with the decimal value of each 8 bits separated by a period (for example, 192.168.7.27). In Windows XP, users can configure the IP address statically or dynamically through Dynamic Host Configuration Protocol. See also *DHCP server*.

Internet service provider (ISP) A company that provides individuals or companies access to the Internet and the World Wide Web. An ISP provides a telephone number, a user name, a password, and other connection information so users can connect their computers to the ISP's computers. An ISP typically charges a monthly or hourly connection fee.

IP address See *Internet protocol (IP) address*.

ISDN See *Integrated Services Digital Network (ISDN)*.

ISP See *Internet service provider (ISP)*.

Jaz disk drive An external drive that connects to a computer and uses removable Jaz disks to store data.

Joint Photographic Experts Group (JPEG)   An image compression mechanism designed for compressing either full-color or grayscale still images. It works well on photographs, naturalistic artwork, and similar material.

JPEG   See *Joint Photographic Experts Group (JPEG)*.

KB   See *kilobyte (KB)*.

keyboard shortcut   A method of invoking a command by pressing a combination of keys, instead of selecting the command from a menu with the mouse.

Kids Passport   An online service that enables children under 12 to sign in to a variety of Microsoft and commercial Web sites using a single user account name and password. Kids Passports protect the distribution of the user's personal information by specifying what information can be shared with the Web sites and what can be done with that information.

kilobyte (KB)   1,024 bytes of data storage; in reference to data transfer rates, 1,000 bytes.

LAN   See *local area network (LAN)*.

local area network (LAN)   A group of computers and other devices dispersed over a relatively limited area and connected by a communications link that enables any device to interact with any other device on the network.

local computer   The computer that is currently being used. More generally, a computer that can be accessed without using a communications line or a communications device, such as a network adapter or a modem.

local printer   A printer that is directly connected to one of the ports on a computer.

local/locally   A term referring to the computer currently being used.

logging off   The process of disconnecting a computer from a network domain.

logging on   The process of connecting a computer to a network by providing a user name and password that identifies a user to the network.

mailbox   The location In Outlook Express where e-mail folders are stored.

manual checkpoint   A restoration checkpoint in System Restore that users create themselves.

mapping   The process of assigning a local drive letter to a network drive or resource so that it is easily located.

MB   See *megabyte (MB)*.

megabyte (MB)   1,024 kilobytes of data storage; in reference to data transfer rates, 1,000 kilobytes.

menu   A grouping of related commands.

menu bar   The toolbar from which users can access the menus of commands.

Microsoft Briefcase   A program used to store working copies of files and synchronize them with the originals.

Microsoft Knowledge Base   A searchable online database of technical support information and help tools for Microsoft products.

Microsoft Magnifier   A display utility that makes the screen more readable for users who have impaired vision.

Microsoft Narrator   A text-to-speech utility for users who are blind or have impaired vision.

Microsoft Network (MSN)   Microsoft's online service, which includes e-mail, games, software downloads, and many other features.

Microsoft Outlook Express   A program for sending and receiving e-mail messages and participating in newsgroups.

Microsoft Paint   A drawing program with which users can create simple or elaborate drawings. These drawings can be either black and white or color, and can be saved as bitmap files. It can also be used to work with *.jpg* and *.gif* files. Paint pictures can be pasted into another document, or used as a desktop background.

Microsoft Speech Recognition   An internal engine that recognizes spoken words and converts them to written text.

Microsoft Windows Update   A program that regularly scans the computer and communicates with an online Web site to check for available updates for the computer's operating system, software programs, and hardware.

middleware   A type of software that connects two or more otherwise separate applications, which could be software programs or system applications.

modem   A device that allows computer information to be transmitted and received over a telephone line. The transmitting modem translates digital computer data into analog signals that can be carried over a phone line. The receiving modem translates the analog signals back to digital form.

MouseKeys   A keyboard feature with which users press keys on the numeric keypad to move the mouse pointer and to click, double-click, and drag.

MSN   See *Microsoft Network (MSN)*.

MSN Explorer   An integrated suite of Internet programs dedicated exclusively to MSN services and properties. MSN Explorer helps users with varying levels of computer expertise work on the Internet.

MSN Gaming Zone A Web site through which users can play a wide variety of solitaire or multiple-player games.

.NET Passport An online service through which users can sign in to a variety of Microsoft and other commercial Web sites using a single user account name and password.

.NET Passport Wallet An online database in which users can store credit card and other account information, as well as online gift certificates. Users can then transmit that information securely to online vendors.

network A group of computers and other devices, such as printers and scanners, connected by a communications link that enables all the devices to interact with each other. Networks can be small or large, permanently connected through wires or cables, or temporarily connected through phone lines or wireless transmissions. The largest network is the Internet, which is a worldwide group of networks.

network adapter A device that connects a computer to a network. This device is sometimes called an *adapter card* or *network interface card.*

network administrator A person responsible for planning, configuring, and managing the day-to-day operation of the network. A network administrator is also called a *system administrator.*

Network Bridge A tool that automates the processes required to forward information from one type of media to another.

Network Diagnostics A tool that gathers and displays information about a computer's hardware and operating system, Internet connection, and modem and network adapter.

network domain A group of computers that are part of a network and share a common database of files and folders. A domain is administered as a unit with common rules and procedures. Each domain has a unique name.

network printer A printer that is not directly connected to a user's computer, but rather is available through a network.

network time protocol (NTP) A protocol, used by personal firewalls, that prevents time synchronization.

newsgroup A collection of messages posted by individuals to a news server (a computer that can host thousands of newsgroups).

Notepad A basic text editor used to create simple documents or for creating Web pages.

notification area   The area on the taskbar to the right of the taskbar buttons. The notification area displays the date and time and can also contain shortcuts to other programs. Other shortcuts can appear temporarily, providing information about the status of activities.

NTP   See *network time protocol (NTP)*.

OCR   See *optical character recognition (OCR)*.

OEM   See *original equipment manufacturer (OEM)*.

offline   The state of not being connected to a network.

online   The state of being connected to the Internet.

On-Screen Keyboard   A utility that displays a virtual keyboard on the screen with which users with mobility impairments type data by using a pointing device or joystick. On-Screen Keyboard is intended to provide a minimum level of functionality for users with mobility impairments.

optical character recognition (OCR)   A technology that enables devices such as scanners to convert hard-copy or photographic images to data.

original equipment manufacturer (OEM)   The computer systems' manufacturers.

Paint   See *Microsoft Paint*.

parallel port   The input/output connector for a parallel interface device. Printers are generally plugged into a parallel port.

Passport   See *.NET Passport*.

password   A security measure used to restrict access to user accounts, computer systems, and resources. A password is a unique string of characters that must be provided before access is authorized. Windows XP passwords are case-sensitive and can be up to 14 characters in length.

path   A route through a structured collection of stored information, showing where on the storage medium that information is located.

peripheral device   Any external device that connects to a computer.

permission   A rule associated with an object to regulate which users can gain access to the object and in what manner. Permissions are granted or denied by the object's owner.

pixel   The smallest element that display or print hardware and software can manipulate to create letters, numbers, or graphics. Short for picture element.

playlist   A list of links in Windows Media Player to various digital media files on a computer, a network, or the Internet.

Plug and Play   A design philosophy and set of specifications that allow hardware and software to be automatically identified by the computer.

plug-in   A hardware component or software program that adds a specific feature or component to an existing system.

PNG   See *Portable Network Graphics (PNG)*.

POP3   See *Post Office Protocol 3 (POP3)*.

port   A connection or socket used to connect a device—such as a printer, monitor, or modem—to a computer. Information is sent from the computer to the device through a cable.

portable device   A computing device or storage card that is not a desktop computer. Examples of portable devices include Pocket PCs, and storage cards such as Compact Flash cards.

Portable Network Graphics (PNG)   A file format for portable, well-compressed storage of images.

Post Office Protocol 3 (POP3)   A popular protocol used for receiving e-mail messages. This protocol is often used by ISPs. In contrast to IMAP servers, which provide access to multiple server-side folders, POP3 servers allow access to a single Inbox.

printer driver   A piece of software used by computer programs to communicate with printers and plotters. Printer drivers translate the information sent from the computer into commands that the printer understands.

Product Key   A unique combination of letters and numbers that identifies a program's product license.

program icon   See *icon*.

program name installation restore point   A restoration checkpoint in System Restore that is created when a user installs a program.

program shortcut   See *shortcut*.

protocol   A set of rules and conventions for sending information over a network. These rules govern the content, format, timing, sequencing, and error control of messages exchanged among network devices.

Public Profile   A page of information in Passport about the user that the user creates. Users can choose how much of their Profile will be available for other people to see.

Quick Launch toolbar   A customizable toolbar with which users can display the Windows desktop or start a program (for example, Internet Explorer) with a single click. Users can add buttons to start their favorite programs from the Quick Launch location on the taskbar.

RAM See *random access memory (RAM)*.

random access memory (RAM) The memory that can be read from or written to by a computer or other devices. Information stored in RAM is lost when the computer is turned off.

read receipt An electronic receipt in Outlook Express that is sent to the user when the message recipient has displayed the user's message. This is useful when sending time-critical information, or any time confirmation that a message has been received is necessary.

Recycle Bin The place in which Windows stores deleted files. Users can retrieve deleted files, or they can empty the Recycle Bin to create more disk space.

remote access server A Windows-based computer running the Routing and Remote Access service and designed to provide remote access to computers on a network.

Remote Assistance A convenient way for a friend to connect to a local computer from remote computer and help troubleshoot a problem.

Remote Desktop A means of accessing a Windows session that is running on one computer from another computer.

restarting The process of ending a user session, shutting down Windows, and then starting Windows again without turning the computer off.

restore operation restore point A restoration checkpoint in System Restore that is automatically created when a user restores his or her system.

right-clicking The action of pressing and releasing the secondary mouse button.

root The highest or uppermost level in a hierarchically organized set of information. The root is the point from which subsets branch in a logical sequence that moves from a broad or general focus to narrower perspectives.

root directory The top point of a directory tree in a hierarchical disk-based file structure. In the path *C:\WINDOWS\explorer.exe*, *C:* is the root directory.

screen area The width and height of the screen, measured in pixels.

screen saver A moving picture or pattern that appears on the screen when the mouse or keyboard has not been used for a specified period of time.

ScreenTip The small text box that appears when the mouse pointer passes over a button, displaying the name of the command.

scripting The act of writing computer code.

scroll bar A vertical or horizontal bar that users move to change their vertical or horizontal position within a window.

Search Companion   A program that guides users through the process of searching for a file, folder, or resource on a computer, on a network, or on the Internet.

search criteria   The specific information on which a search is based.

security zone   A set of options that secure access on a home machine and local intranet.

server   A computer that provides shared resources to network users.

sharing   The process of making resources, such as folders and printers, available to others.

shared drive   A drive that has been made available for other people on a network to access.

shared folder   A folder that has been made available for other people on a network to access.

shortcut   A link to any item accessible from a computer or on a network, such as a program, file, folder, disk drive, Web page, printer, or another computer. Users can put shortcuts in various areas, such as on the desktop, on the Start menu, or in folders.

shortcut menu   A context-sensitive menu of commands that appears when the item is right-clicked.

ShowSounds   A feature that instructs programs that usually convey information only by sound to also provide all information visually, such as by displaying text captions or informative icons.

shut down   The process of ending a user session and closing Windows so that a computer can safely be turned off.

signature   The text included at the end of an e-mail message to identify the sender.

signing off   The process of disconnecting from a Web site or service.

signing on   The process of connecting to a Web site or service by providing a user name and password as identification.

Simple Mail Transfer Protocol (SMTP)   A member of a suite of protocols that governs the exchange of electronic mail between message transfer agents.

skin   A file that customizes the appearance and functionality of Windows Media Player in skin mode.

skin mode   An operational state of Windows Media Player in which its user interface is customized and displayed as a skin. Some features of the Player are not accessible in skin mode. By default, the Player appears in full mode.

SMTP   See *Simple Mail Transfer Protocol (SMTP)*.

software   See *software programs*.

software applications   See *software programs*.

software piracy   The theft of software through illegal copying of genuine programs or through counterfeiting and distributing imitation software products or unauthorized versions of software products. Piracy can include casual copying of genuine software by individuals or businesses, or widespread illegal duplication of software programs for profit.

software programs   The programs with which users do things on their computer.

SoundSentry   A Windows feature that produces a visual cue, such as a screen flash or a blinking title bar, whenever the computer plays a system sound.

Speech Recognition   See *Microsoft Speech Recognition*.

stand by   The process of maintaining a user session and keeping the computer running on low power with the user's data still in the memory.

Start menu   A central menu linking to important commands, folders, and programs on a computer.

stationery   A template in Outlook Express that can include a background image, unique text font colors, and custom margins.

stationery theme   See *stationery*.

StickyKeys   A keyboard feature with which users can press a modifier key (**H**, **J**, or **G**), or the **I** key, and have it remain active until a non-modifier key is pressed. This is useful for people who have difficulty pressing two keys simultaneously.

synchronizing   The process of reconciling the differences between files stored on one computer and versions of the same files on another computer. Once the differences are determined, both sets of files are updated.

system checkpoint   A restoration checkpoint in System Restore that is automatically created by Windows XP at regular intervals. System checkpoints are created every 24 hours of calendar time, or every 24 hours the computer is turned on. If the computer is turned off for more than 24 hours, a system checkpoint is created the next time it is turned on.

system date   The current date according to the operating system.

system folder   A folder containing files that are specific to the operating system. The contents of a system folder are hidden by default and should not be modified.

system time   The current time according to the operating system.

tagged image file format (TIFF)   A graphics format that can store compressed images with a flexible number of bits per pixel.

tape drive   An internal or external drive that uses tapes to transfer and store data.

taskbar   The bar that contains the Start button and appears by default at the bottom of the desktop. Users can click the taskbar buttons to switch between programs. Users can also hide the taskbar, move it to the sides or top of the desktop, and customize it in other ways.

text-to-speech (TTS)   The ability of an operating system to play back printed text as spoken words.

text-to-speech software   An internal driver, called a TTS engine, that recognizes text and, using a synthesized voice chosen from several pre-generated voices, speaks the written text.

theme   A set of visual elements that applies a unified look for the computer desktop. A theme determines the look of the graphic elements of the desktop, such as the windows, icons, fonts, colors, and the background and screen saver pictures. It can also define sounds associated with events such as opening or closing a program.

thumbnail   A small version of a graphic that is hyperlinked to a larger version.

TIFF   See *tagged image file format (TIFF)*.

time server   A computer that periodically synchronizes the time on all computers within a network. This ensures that the time used by network services and local functions remains accurate.

title bar   The horizontal bar at the top of a window that contains the name of the window. On many windows, the title bar also contains the program icon, the Maximize, Minimize, and Close buttons, and the optional question mark button for context-sensitive Help. To display a menu with commands such as Restore and Move, right-click the title bar.

ToggleKeys   A feature that sets the keyboard to beep when one of the locking keys (**CAPS LOCK**, **NUM LOCK**, or **SCROLL LOCK**) is turned on or off.

toolbar   A row, column, or block of on-screen buttons or icons in a program in a graphical user interface. When clicked, these buttons or icons activate certain functions, or tasks, of the program. Users can often customize toolbars and move them around on the screen.

track   An individual song or other discrete piece of content from a CD.

Trojan horse   A program that masquerades as another common program in an attempt to receive information. An example of a Trojan horse is a program that behaves like a system logon to retrieve user names and password information that the writers of the Trojan horse can later use to break into the system.

TTS   See *text-to-speech (TTS)*.

turn off   The process of shutting down Windows so users can safely turn off the computer power. Many computers turn the power off automatically.

UI   See *user interface (UI)*.

Uniform Resource Locator (URL)   An address specifying the protocol and IP address or domain name of documents or other resources on the World Wide Web.

Universal Serial Bus (USB)   A computer connection port, or interface, for plugging in devices such as a keyboard, mouse, printer, scanner, and telephone equipment. USB ports allow devices to be plugged in and unplugged without turning the system off.

unsigned device driver restore point   A restoration checkpoint in System Response that is automatically created when the user installs an unsigned device driver.

URL   See *Uniform Resource Locator (URL)*.

USB   See *Universal Serial Bus (USB)*.

USB flash drive   A portable flash memory card that plugs into a computer's USB port and stores up to 2 GB of data.

user account   A record that consists of all the information that defines a user to Windows. This includes the user name and password required for the user to log on, the groups in which the user account has membership, and the rights and permissions the user has for using the computer and network, and accessing their resources.

user account name   See *user name*.

user account picture   An individual graphic representing a specific computer user account. User account pictures are available only on computers that are members of a workgroup or are stand-alone, and are not available on computers that are members of a network domain.

user interface (UI)   The portion of a software program with which users interact with the program.

user name   A unique name identifying a user's account to Windows. An account's user name must be unique among the other group names and user names within its own domain or workgroup.

user profile   A file that contains configuration information for a specific user, such as desktop settings, persistent network connections, and application settings. Each user's preferences are saved to a user profile that Windows uses to configure the desktop each time a user logs on.

Utility Manager   A program with which users can check an accessibility program's status and start or stop an accessibility program.

vCard   An electronic business card format for contact information in Outlook Express. The vCard format can be used with a variety of digital devices and operating systems.

virus   A program that infects computer files or other programs by inserting copies of itself into the files, and might execute some harmful or inconvenient action. A program that inserts itself into an e-mail program and sends copies of itself to everyone in the address book is an example of a virus.

Virtual Private Network (VPN)   The extension of a private network. VPN connections provide remote access and routed connections to private networks over the Internet.

visualization   A feature in Windows Media Player that displays audio as moving splashes of color and geometric shapes.

volume   An area of storage on a hard disk. A volume is formatted by using a file system, such as FAT or NTFS, and has a drive letter assigned to it. Users can view the contents of a volume by clicking its icon in Windows Explorer or in My Computer. A single hard disk can have multiple volumes, and volumes can also span multiple disks.

VPN   See *Virtual Private Network (VPN)*.

Web browser   A software application used to locate and display Web pages. The two most popular browsers are Netscape Navigator and Microsoft Internet Explorer.

wildcard   A keyboard character that can be used to represent one or many characters when conducting a query. The question mark (?) represents a single character, and the asterisk (*) represents any number of characters.

window   A portion of the screen where programs and processes can be run. Users can open several windows at the same time. Windows can be closed, resized, moved, minimized to a button on the taskbar, or maximized to take up the whole screen.

Windows Messenger   An instant messaging program with which users can communicate with individual or multiple online contacts.

Windows Update   See *Microsoft Windows Update*.

wizard   A program that guides users through a series of pages on which they select the options they want to use.

WordPad   A program used to create or edit text files that contain formatting or graphics.

working offline/online   See *offline* and *online*.

zip   See *compression*.

Zip disk drive   An external drive that connects to a computer and uses removable Zip disks to store data.

Index

About the Authors

Online Training Solutions, Inc. (OTSI)

OTSI is a traditional and electronic publishing company specializing in the creation, production, and delivery of computer software training materials. OTSI publishes the Quick Course® series of computer and business training products. The principals of OTSI are:

Joan Preppernau has been contributing to the creation of excellent technical training materials for computer professionals for as long as she cares to remember. Joan's wide-ranging experiences in various facets of the industry have contributed to her passion for producing interesting, useful, and understandable training materials. Joan is the primary author of *Microsoft Windows XP Step by Step*, *Microsoft Windows XP Step by Step Deluxe Edition*, *Microsoft FrontPage Version 2002 Step by Step*, *Microsoft Office FrontPage 2003 Step by Step*, and *Microsoft Office Outlook 2003 Step by Step*, published by Microsoft Press, as well as *Quick Course in Microsoft Windows 2000* and *Quick Course in Microsoft Windows XP*, published by Online Training Solutions, Inc.

Joyce Cox has 20 years' experience in writing about and editing technical subjects for non-technical audiences. For 12 of those years she was the principal author for Online Press. She was also the first managing editor of Microsoft Press, an editor for Sybex, and an editor for the University of California. Joyce is the primary author of *Microsoft Office PowerPoint 2003 Step by Step* and *Microsoft Office Word 2003 Step by Step*, published by Microsoft Press, as well as dozens of books in the *Quick Course* computer training series, published by Online Training Solutions, Inc.

The OTSI publishing team for this book includes the following outstanding professionals:

Susie Bayers

Jan Bednarczuk

R.J. Cadranell

Liz Clark

Nancy Depper

Joseph Ford

Minh-Tam S. Le

Jaime Odell

Lisa Van Every

For more information about Online Training Solutions, Inc., visit *www.otsi.com*.

What do you think of this book?
We want to hear from you!

Do you have a few minutes to participate in a brief online survey? Microsoft is interested in hearing your feedback about this publication so that we can continually improve our books and learning resources for you.

To participate in our survey, please visit:

www.microsoft.com/learning/booksurvey

And enter this book's ISBN, 0-7356-2114-4. As a thank-you to survey participants in the United States and Canada, each month we'll randomly select five respondents to win one of five $100 gift certificates from a leading online merchant.* At the conclusion of the survey, you can enter the drawing by providing your e-mail address, which will be used for prize notification *only*.

Thanks in advance for your input. Your opinion counts!

Sincerely,

Microsoft® Learning

Microsoft | Learning

Learn More. Go Further.